CHINA'S GREAT WALL OF DEBT

CHINA'S
GREAT WALL
OF DEBT

**Shadow Banks, Ghost Cities, Massive Loans,
and the End of the Chinese Miracle**

DINNY McMAHON

Houghton Mifflin Harcourt

Boston   New York

2018

hmhco.com

Library of Congress Cataloging-in-Publication Data
Names: McMahon, Dinny, author.
Title: China's great wall of debt : shadow banks, ghost cities, massive loans, and the end of the Chinese miracle / Dinny McMahon.
Description: Boston : Houghton Mifflin Harcourt, 2018. | Includes bibliographical references and index.
Identifiers: LCCN 2017045344 (print) | LCCN 2017054638 (ebook) | ISBN 9781328846020 (ebook) | ISBN 9781328846013 (hardcover)
Subjects: LCSH: Debts, External—China. | China—Economic conditions. | China—Economic policy. Classification: LCC HJ8811 (ebook) | LCC HJ8811 .M36 2018 (print) | DDC 336.3/40951—dc23
LC record available at https://lccn.loc.gov/2017045344

Book design by Chloe Foster

Printed in the United States of America
DOC 10 9 8 7 6 5 4 3 2 1

To my mum and dad, for choosing Chinese

CONTENTS

INTRODUCTION: FEAR AND GREED

IN 1985, HU YAOBANG, the general secretary of the Chinese Communist Party and the second-most important man in China, after Deng Xiaoping, visited Australia. In an action that was somewhat unusual for a world leader, Hu didn't head straight for Canberra, the capital, or any of the major cities. He started his visit by flying into Paraburdoo.

Paraburdoo, or "Para" to the locals, is a small mining town just inside the southern edge of the Pilbara, a sprawling band of red earth that starts at the Indian Ocean and stretches deep into the Australian interior. The town is named for the indigenous word for the white cockatoos that throng the town — or at least the cockatoos would be white were it not for the red dust that coats everything, birds included.

When the rains come at the beginning of each year, they turn Paraburdoo into a riot of color, with Ashburton and Sturt peas sprouting purple and pink along the side of the roads. But for most of the year, Para is a Mars-like red desert punctuated by scrub. It's also one of the hottest places in Australia, and home to swarms of flies — a major concern for the advance team of Chinese officials who visited three weeks ahead of their boss.

What drew Hu to this remote, inaccessible corner of Australia was, in fact, the red dirt. Paraburdoo, and the Pilbara more generally, is one of the richest sources of iron ore anywhere in the world. Soon after consolidating power, in 1978, Deng Xiaoping launched a major program to modernize the Chinese economy after decades of stagnation under Mao Zedong. To do so required resources. Hu had flown into Paraburdoo to visit Mount Channar twenty kilometers down the road, an ore-rich hill that would become the first overseas-resources investment by the Chinese state. Standing atop the future mine site, Hu, speaking halting English, called the hill "a treasure house."

I visited Paraburdoo with my father in 2011. He'd built the mine at Paraburdoo in 1971 to supply a Japanese economy that was in the throes of its postwar economic miracle, but my father hadn't been back in forty years. Superficially the town was much the same. The mine manager's house and its manicured lawn, incongruous amid the red dirt, was still called the Mouse House, named for Mighty Mouse, the nickname Dad picked up for his diminutive stature and his drive to get the first shipment of ore delivered on time. Nearby the golf course was still nine holes of dirt with not a blade of grass to be seen. Even the putting greens were red, made from oiled sand that required careful sweeping before each putt.

What had changed, however, was the workforce. Forty years earlier, to work in Paraburdoo was to live there, which meant putting up with the heat, the distance, and the gender imbalance. But in 2011, that had changed. Instead of being permanent residents, about 20% of the predominantly male workforce were FIFOs, or "fly-in, fly-outs." The company flew the workers in for two weeks of work, then flew them back out to civilization for a couple of weeks off. That change was necessary to find and keep workers.

During Dad's time at Paraburdoo, it was the third mine in the Pilbara. Almost twenty years later, Channar was only the fifth. But by 2011, there were more than thirty mines in the Pilbara, most of which had been built since 2000. To staff that many sites—in addition to the proliferation of mines elsewhere in the country—companies had to find ways to make mining more appealing. That meant employing

FIFOs and paying them among the best wages in Australia. Truck drivers and drill operators in the Pilbara region could earn as much as AUD $200,000 a year. Sydney and Melbourne were all but drained of tradespeople as skilled labor headed to the mines. In sum, these workers were servicing a boom without historical parallel — China's boom.

A couple of decades ago, China was just the world's factory, with little relevance to the rest of the globe beyond its ability to churn out cheap sneakers. Then, large-scale urbanization generated unprecedented demand for resources, breathing life into the Pilbara and creating a bonanza for commodity-exporting nations everywhere. Today, the Chinese economy is graduating to the next stage. A vibrant middle class is emerging, which promises to drive global growth for decades to come as potentially hundreds of millions of consumers develop tastes comparable to their counterparts in rich nations.

Meanwhile, thirty years after the Australian government took a leap of faith by allowing the Chinese Communist Party (CCP) to make one of its first overseas investments, today there is so much Chinese investment flowing abroad that capitals from Canberra to Washington, D.C., to Berlin fret over the security implications. Yet city mayors and state governors in those same countries aggressively court Chinese companies in the hope that their investment will help reinvigorate local communities. And in developing countries, Chinese loans have made possible the construction of infrastructure vital to economic development, such as much-needed ports and roads — as well as less-needed sports stadiums and government offices — that wouldn't get built without China's money.

For decades, the world has depended on the United States and Europe as twin engines of growth, a highly precarious state of affairs if both engines sputter at the same time, as was the case during the global financial crisis. With China forecast to overtake the United States as the world's biggest economy around 2030, China is finally emerging as a third engine. Yet, as the world salivates at the prospect of China's economic ascendancy, it's China's economic weakness that should have us all worried.

I had my first Chinese-language lesson in 1988, when I was nine years old, a few months after China finally signed the deal to develop the Channar mine. It was Dad's idea, but it was my long-suffering mother who was responsible for getting me to go to those lessons after school every Friday afternoon. I repeatedly explained to her, in no uncertain terms, that she was wasting her time and money. Nevertheless, not only did she prevail but somehow I stuck with Chinese through primary school, and then through high school.

In hindsight, the 1990s were still the early days of China's boom. As late as 2003, Japan was still the main destination of Australian iron-ore exports, whereas today more than 80% go to China. Nonetheless, when I was at high school, there was something seemingly inevitable about China's ascent — and something unambiguously good about it, too. I still recall preparing for my high school graduation exams, in 1996, and memorizing sentences that I could draw upon during the final tests: "Learning Chinese will help me find a job"; "China's fast economic development is good for Australia."

After high school, I went to Beijing to study Chinese for a year. Then I went back for another year of study a few years later. When I returned a third time, I stayed. In total, I've spent thirteen years — a good chunk of my adult life — living in China, first as a student and then, for a decade, as a financial journalist. China has changed in ways that my seventeen-year-old self, upon first arriving in China, could never have imagined, but for me one thing has remained constant. I've always found there to be something irresistible about China — the pace of change, the dynamism of the people, their belief in the country's destiny. By merely being present in China, I felt as though I was not only part of history but part of a very specific phase of history: China's race to catch up with the rich world.

During my time there, I saw the economy transform. At least at first, the transformation was unequivocally for the better. But gradually, I watched as an economy that was the envy of the world became increasingly dysfunctional. The problems were seemingly obvious, born from an economic model that had run its course, yet reforms weren't forthcoming. Today, that growth model threatens the very health of both the Chinese and global economies. "In the postwar period, every previous global recession started with a downturn in the United States, but the next one is likely to begin with a shock in China," Ruchir Sharma, the chief global strategist at Morgan Stanley Investment Management and author of *The Rise and Fall of Nations,* wrote in 2016. "China's miracle growth period is over, and it now faces the curse of debt."

A common misconception about the Chinese economy is that it's driven by exports. That was once the case, but it hasn't been that way for more than a decade. When the global financial crisis hit, the ever-increasing volume of exports that had been made possible by household borrowing in the United States and Europe was brought to a shuddering halt, throwing tens of millions of Chinese out of work. To take up the slack, Beijing — much like other major economies around the world — launched a massive economic stimulus, but, unlike in other countries that funded their stimulus primarily with government spending, in China the heavy lifting was done by its banks. As the global economy stalled, China barely registered the crisis, as the financial system lent vast amounts of money toward the construction of new housing, infrastructure, and factories.

Yet the stimulus never really stopped. Instead, debt has become the motor at the core of Chinese growth. In absolute terms, China's debt looks manageable. It's difficult to measure precisely, but at the end of 2016, the total stock of nonfinancial debt in China, relative to the size of the economy, was about 260%, roughly the same as that of the United States (although some estimates put it significantly higher). However, the concern is not the total amount of debt but the speed at which it has accumulated. In 2008, China's debt-to-GDP was only 160%. Experience shows that when a country accumulates too much debt relative to the size of its economy too quickly, a crisis typically follows. In fact, China's debt accumulation could be among the fastest in modern history. According to the People's Bank of China, since 2008, the Chinese economy has added about $12 trillion worth of debt, roughly the size of the entire U.S. banking system in that year. China's banking system has quadrupled in size over the last nine years. Alarms are starting to go off in financial centers around the world.

"This is extraordinary leverage for an advanced, let alone, an emerging economy," Mark Carney, governor of the Bank of England, said late in 2016. He listed the increasing reliance of China's growth "on rapid credit expansion" as the number-one risk to global financial stability.

Driving around China, you can tell that something is not quite right. Many cities are ringed with empty apartment towers. Extravagant new government buildings have more rooms than officials to put in them. Chinese factories produce about half of the world's steel and far more than the country could ever hope to use. Land has been reclaimed from the sea to create factories that have never been built. The country is dotted with factories that were constructed but never used to their full potential. The risk is that the debt that has been wasted on such projects will never be repaid.

Maybe there will come a point during the twenty-first century — which is routinely described as "China's century" — when China will become the world's biggest economy and will achieve the degree of regional, if not global, dominance that is widely assumed to be just around the corner. But before that can happen, China will face a reckoning.

There's no saying with any certainty what that reckoning will look like. It could be a financial crisis, or it could be a lingering economic funk like that experienced by Japan during its Lost Decade. Or maybe growth will fall to 2% or so, respectable for a developed economy but the equivalent of treading water for a developing country like China, which is desperate to catch up. Conceivably the authorities could successfully reform the economy, but at this point reform would be both painful and difficult to pull off, and would result in much slower growth for a time, if not indefinitely. But regardless of what form the reckoning takes, one thing is for certain: the miracle is over. The way Beijing manages what's to come will determine whether it just delays China's ascent or permanently derails it.

Of course, no crisis has been prophesied as repeatedly and for as long as the one that has so far failed to materialize in China. In 2001, columnist Gordon Chang published *The Coming Collapse of China,* a book which argued that China's economy was threatened by a fragile financial system and that the Communist Party would be out of power within a decade. In 2010, Jim Chanos, the U.S. hedge-fund manager best known for having predicted Enron's collapse, described China's economy as being "on a treadmill to hell," and said that its property market looked like "Dubai times 1,000," a reference to the emirate's crisis the previous year. At the beginning of 2014, investor George Soros said in an essay that the Chinese growth model had "run out of steam." He predicted that "the Chinese conundrum . . . will come to a head in the next few years."

"A hard landing is practically unavoidable," Soros said two years later. "I'm not expecting it, I'm observing it."

Yet the Chinese economy has not only remained upright but maintained unrelentingly high rates of growth. For most of the past four decades, it has averaged 10% growth annually, never falling below 6%. The golden days seem to be over, with growth having slowed since 2012, but even in 2016, the economy grew at an incredibly robust 6.7%.

For many, this staunch failure to fail is proof of China's exceptionalism, the result of economic management having been placed in the hands of a technocratic elite that, undistracted by ideology, has been able to make tough decisions in the pursuit of one overriding goal: growth. In the United States, the belief in Chinese exceptionalism typically manifests itself as an expression of America's insecurities. "What if we could just be China for a day?" Thomas Friedman, the *New York Times* columnist, said in 2010 on *Meet the Press*. "We could actually, you know, authorize the right solutions."

In the U.S. media, China routinely is portrayed as being everything that the United States wants to be but worries that it isn't — or that it won't be in the near future; namely, financially sound, technologically dominant, and well governed. At the more benign end of the spectrum is China's portrayal in the 2015 film *The Martian*, where, without China's help, NASA wouldn't be able to rescue Matt Damon from Mars. At the more insecure end is a 2010 U.S. political advertisement that purported to show a classroom scene from Beijing in 2030, in which a Chinese professor explains that the decline of U.S. global preeminence was due to American waste and debt. "So now they work for us," the professor says to laughs from around the lecture hall. According to annual polls taken by Gallup, a majority of Americans, since 2011, have assumed that China was already the world's leading economy, in spite of the Chinese economy's being only 70% of the size of the U.S. economy.

In short, the broad acceptance of Chinese exceptionalism as fact is the source of much of China's power. Former Australian prime minister Tony Abbott succinctly summed it up when, in 2014, German chancellor Angela Merkel asked what drove Australia's policy regarding China. Abbott replied, "Fear and greed."

Australia has benefited economically from China's rise more than almost any other country. The mining boom ended not long after I visited Paraburdoo, but now Australians speak of a farm boom to replace it, as China's middle class buys more and more beef, seafood, wine, honey, and dairy products. Meanwhile, Chinese arrive in ever greater numbers at Australian airports, helping to make education and tourism the country's third- and fifth-biggest export industries, respectively.

But the greed of which Prime Minister Abbott spoke is not about what access to the world's second-largest economy can deliver today. It's about the potential of that economy's becoming number one in a bit more than a decade. Assuming that the United States manages to grow by 2% annually, that will require the Chinese economy to double in size between 2016 and 2026. The sheer scale of its growth presents opportunities that eclipse those of mature markets. But the fear is that, in return for the privilege of enjoying the fruits of China's ascent, there will be a steep price to pay.

China has long used foreign nations' access to its economy as a political tool. When the Oslo-based Norwegian Nobel Committee awarded Chinese political dissident Liu Xiaobo with the 2010 Peace Prize, China punished Norway by heavily curtailing imports of Norwegian salmon. When, in 2016, in spite of Beijing's objections, Seoul agreed to allow the United States to station THAAD — a highly advanced radar system — in South Korea, China responded by curtailing tour groups from traveling to Korea and suspending business at more than half of Korean conglomerate Lotte Group's ninety-nine China stores. And when, late in 2016, the Mongolian government allowed the Dalai Lama to visit, China expressed its displeasure by imposing new fees on Mongolian exports to China.

The fear that Australian prime minister Abbott spoke of is that, in the face of China's efforts to push its territorial claims and to remold the international order to its liking, acquiescence, compromise, and supplication will be the price of admission to the world's single most important source of growth. But both fear and greed are based on a single underlying assumption: that China's uninterrupted ascent — as an economy and as a global power — is inevitable.

Belief in that inevitability, or exceptionalism, is built upon quite an impressive track record. China's technocrats have managed to maintain fast growth for almost four decades, despite the odds. Time and again, China's economic transformation has required vision, skill, and political fortitude. Early reformers did away with communes and the planned economy, which were the basic tenets of communism. A later generation closed down tens of thousands of state firms and tore down trade barriers in order to join the World Trade Organization.

However, the last generation of great reformers retired in the early 2000s. In contrast, the great success of more contemporary leaders — that is, shepherding China through the global financial crisis — was the result of a deliberate decision to eschew reform in the interests of maintaining stability. Since then, the need to overhaul the way in which the economy works has only become more acute as debt and waste have grown to epic proportions. The perennial question is, what will China's leaders do about it? President Xi Jinping is unquestionably aware of the challenges he faces.

"If we don't structurally transform the economy and instead just stimulate it to generate short-term growth, then we're taxing our future," Xi said in a speech published at the beginning of 2016. He said that China had until the end of 2020 to make the transformation. "If we continue to hesitate and wait, we will not only lose this precious window of opportunity, but we will deplete the resources we've built up since the start of the reform era."

Xi has tried to pare back the excesses of the system in efforts that have met stiff resistance from entrenched bureaucrats and have thus far seen only small pockets of success. But he seems uninterested in overhauling the mechanisms that continue to drive the unabated accumulation of debt and waste. Rather, Xi's vision of transformation is one where China grows past its current problems by grafting new nodes of growth onto the existing system. Xi's compromise has been to call for "medium-fast" growth of about 6.5% annually, rather than insisting on the "fast" growth that was previously the norm. The problem is that, even with Xi's experiment to build new industries that can drive future growth, for the economy to continue growing at the pace that China's leadership deems necessary, more and more debt is still needed. Lou Jiwei, China's former finance minister and one of the government's most pro-reform figures, captured the essence of this catch-22 while talking to university students in 2015. "The first problem is to stop the accumulation of leverage," Lou said. "But we also can't allow the economy to lose speed."

The Chinese economy is exceptional, albeit not in the way that we have collectively come to assume it is. Rather than being immune to crises, recessions, and funks, it's unique in that Beijing is willing and able to intervene on a scale that allows it to postpone a reckoning indefinitely, albeit at the cost of storing up greater pain for the future. Chanos and Soros weren't wrong, it's just that China's authorities have an unparalleled capacity to kick the can down the road. But with every kick, the can gets bigger and doesn't go as far. At some point, it will go no farther.

There are many things that this book doesn't attempt to do. This is not a book about elite politics. Anyone looking for insights into the thinking of senior Chinese leaders or the political machinations of factions and cliques will be sorely disappointed. After years spent reporting on

China's economy, I've learned that important change emanates from the bottom up, not the top down.

This is not a book about microeconomic reform, be it piecemeal efforts to clean up bad loans, to close factories, or to make borrowers more accountable. For years now, reforms have typically attempted to superficially clean up excess rather than dig deep and fix the underlying structural problems, and even then, regardless of their good intentions, those efforts are routinely circumvented.

This book is not about the bright spots in the Chinese economy, like entrepreneurs building world-beating tech giants, or Beijing's efforts to develop new markets through its Belt and Road Initiative, which, loosely, is a plan to reinvigorate the economies of the old Silk Road. Although both are fascinating in their own right, neither is likely to have a material impact on the trajectory of China's economy.

And, last, this book doesn't seek or attempt to precisely forecast when things are likely to unravel or what that unraveling might look like (nonetheless, it certainly seems as though the reckoning is fast approaching). Rather, it is about the mechanics of how the Chinese economy works, and why it's ill positioned to save itself. To go about that, I focus on debt: why state firms and local governments have borrowed so much, how the financial system has accommodated them, why the technocratic managers have allowed things to get out of hand, and why the solutions China is pursuing are no solution at all.

One of the most overemployed metaphors used to describe attempts to come to grips with China — though not without good reason — is the old tale of a blind man feeling an elephant. If he grasps the trunk, he may think the beast is a snake; if he takes hold of a leg, then he might believe it's a tree. It's incredibly difficult to get an overall sense of the state of China. There are many reasons for that. It's a geographically large and diverse country with more than a billion people, who speak a language that is extremely difficult for outsiders to learn. That fact is compounded by an opaque political system steeped in a culture of secrecy; a fast-changing economy that operates in ways radically different from our own; unreliable official data and statistics; and a unique and complex set of incentives that influence the economic decisions of individuals, companies, and the myriad branches of the state.

I still feel like the proverbial blind man, and I'm well aware of the imperfection of this book. But when the subprime mortgage crisis hit the United States, people scrambled to make sense of how and why things had gone so wrong when they had seemed so good. As China's economic woes deepen, people will be looking for similar answers, but they will be harder to find. After ten years during which I tried to make sense of the absurdities of an economy that seemed to keep succeeding in spite of itself, this is my attempt to explain why it's now unraveling — and why this fact bodes so poorly for the rest of the world.

CHINA'S GREAT WALL OF DEBT

1

THE BLACK BOX

HUANG KUN'S FACE no longer has the chubbiness evident in older photos of him. He lost forty pounds during the two years he spent confined to a small cell with, at times, as many as thirty-four other men. Huang keeps the psychological trauma of his detention mostly hidden behind a gap-toothed smile and an easygoing demeanor, but when he talks about the time he spent in a Chinese jail, his shoulders slope and his gaze becomes distant. "The detention center is about putting you in inhuman conditions to force you to [sign a confession]," said Huang, a Canadian citizen, whom I met a year after his release. "They have no regard for the law there. The legal system is a joke."

Huang says that the lights in his cell were never turned off, and at night the prisoners were forced to take turns keeping watch over their cellmates to make sure no one killed himself. Daily exercise was an hour spent in an even smaller yard, which was hemmed in by concrete walls. For meals he was fed watery soup made from old vegetables, and stale *mantou*, a Chinese bread roll. The prisoners slept on a wooden pallet the length of the room, which was pushed up against one wall during the day so that the inmates could work, usually making Christmas lights. On one occasion, a fellow inmate refused to work. Huang says the guards tortured him, fixing "a long heavy metal bar . . . between his two legs, and [forcing him] to walk back and forth in the corridor outside of the cells."

Huang was there on charges of criminal defamation. In September 2011, he and Jon Carnes — his boss and the owner of a small hedge fund — published a report about a silver-mining company from Luoyang, a gritty industrial city in Henan Province that was listed on the New York and Toronto Stock Exchanges. In the report, they said that, based on an investigation they had conducted, they didn't believe that the company was producing anywhere near as much silver as it was telling its North American shareholders. The company subsequently sued them in New York for defamation. The judge threw out the charges on the grounds that the men had simply expressed an opinion and defamed no one. But in China, where defamation can be a criminal as well as a civil offense, the men didn't get off so lightly.

Carnes was on holiday in Canada when he got word that he was under investigation. He quickly abandoned the life he'd built in China and never returned. However, Huang couldn't leave, because he didn't have his passport. He'd been planning a trip to India and so had submitted his passport to the Indian embassy in order to get a visa. By the time he got it back, he was on a watch list. Huang was detained at the Beijing airport in December 2011 as he finally tried to leave the country. He was strip-searched and kept awake for three days, after which he was placed under house arrest for six months before being moved into the detention center. After fifteen months in detention, he was found guilty in a trial that was closed to the public and that lasted only one day. He lost again on appeal a few months later. By then, he had only one month left on his two-year sentence. Once it was complete, the police drove him to the airport and told him to buy a ticket. In July 2014, Huang landed at the Vancouver airport, finally home.

When I met Carnes and Huang, they were working from a room on the ground floor of Carnes's two-story home in the Vancouver suburbs. It was more man cave than office. There was a flat-screen TV and faux-leather sofa, plus two coffee machines, a collection of whiskey bottles (in varying states of demise), and a blue recycling bin filled with empty Red Bull boxes. The only hint that the men worked in finance were the five computer monitors along one wall flashing stock prices. There was nothing to suggest that between 2009 and 2011 the men were in the vanguard of a small number of investors–turned–fraud busters who unraveled criminal activity at dozens of Chinese companies that had sold shares in North America.

By their standards, their report on the silver miner — Silvercorp Metals — was one of the mildest the men had ever published. After a three-month investigation of Silvercorp, they felt confident saying they believed something didn't add up, but were wary of accusing anyone of fraud. But on those occasions when they were on surer ground, they never pulled their punches. Before Huang's arrest, the men had accused a total of eight Chinese companies listed on the New York Stock Exchange and NASDAQ of illegal behavior. All eight were eventually delisted from the exchanges they traded on, and the senior managements of four were charged by the U.S. Securities and Exchange Commission. These included the chairman of a coal company who secretly sold the company's mine and pocketed the proceeds without the U.S. investors' knowing; the chairman and the CEO — a married couple — of a wastewater processor who lied about how much the company was earning, then took money from shareholders to buy a house and used the company credit card to go shopping at Chanel and Valentino in Beverly Hills; and the chairman of an oil-field-services company whom the SEC accused of having "misappropriated" at least $40 million of the company's cash.

Carnes, who still speaks with the soft southern twang of his native South Carolina, was in his late thirties when he moved to China in 2006, just as small Chinese companies were listing on U.S. stock exchanges in ever-increasing numbers. Carnes was looking for a few gems he could invest in. Huang, a naturalized Canadian who was born in China, was one of his first employees. They got in early, making good money those first few years as the lure of China's booming economy sent stock prices soaring. But the men could see something that investors back in the United States couldn't.

"Companies would say they were making $10 million and we would work out, no, it was only $1 million," Carnes said. By fraudulently inflating their earnings, these companies could sell shares for much more than they were actually worth, allowing the Chinese owners to fleece American investors, who blindly overpaid. Hardly anyone was doing the sort of vetting that Carnes and Huang were doing—which sometimes was as simple as visiting the factories to make sure companies were actually producing what they claimed—so the lies went undetected. "We were watching the market explode, but we wouldn't buy anything, because we didn't trust the numbers," Carnes told me.

And so, after share prices doubled in 2009, Carnes and Huang decided to short Chinese companies instead. Short selling is a way to make money if share prices fall. Generally speaking, short sellers, or "shorts"—and particularly activist shorts like Carnes and Huang who publicize the reasons why they believe share prices should fall—are reviled by companies and investors and anyone else with an interest in keeping share prices buoyant. However, Carnes and Huang faced more serious risks than opprobrium and scorn. The first time they posted online the results of their research that reflected negatively on a company, the aggrieved firm's vice president tracked Huang down in Chengdu, where he was based. "He said . . . 'To the benefit of both of us, you should take down the post immediately, so that you don't risk losing an arm or a leg,'" Huang recounted. "He didn't seem like a gangster. He had glasses on, and he spoke really mildly."

Still, Huang says the company had a thuggish reputation. He and Carnes took down the post.

From then on, the men published their reports online under the nom de plume of Alfred Little, an elaborate alter ego that Carnes had designed. That ruse kept their identities hidden until the Luoyang police started their investigation. However, although the subterfuge initially kept Carnes and Huang safe, it did little for the contractors they hired to help with their research. On one occasion, a company caught a man hired by Carnes while he was installing a time-lapse camera outside the factory gates, which Carnes hoped would prove that the firm wasn't shipping as much product as it was telling shareholders. The company's chairman threatened to break the man's legs. Another contractor was taken from his home by men from the company he was investigating and held in a hotel for three hours before he managed to escape. On another occasion, a lawyer who was returning home after doing some research at a local-government office was run off the road by men with guns who dragged him into their SUV, pistol-whipped him, and told him to stop the investigation. None of the contractors pressed charges.

Because of all this nastiness, Carnes and Huang made it a policy not to investigate state-owned companies, because there was no telling what the fallout might be if the government got involved to protect its interests. Still, they occasionally came across companies that were, by all appearances, privately owned yet had the sort of backing typically associated with state firms. The lawyer who was pistol-whipped later reported to Huang that the men who assaulted him said they worked for the Ministry of State Security, China's secret police. Another of the companies the men looked into had a police station built right on its factory premises and had been known to give would-be investors a police escort through town.

It's this blurring of state and private interests that finally drove Huang to sue in the Canadian courts for false imprisonment. As far as Huang is concerned, he should never have served a day in detention; he's seeking justice in Canada, where Silvercorp is listed and where he thinks he'll get a fair hearing. What makes his case so unusual is that he's not suing the Chinese state or the city of Luoyang or its police force. Huang is suing Silvercorp, a publicly traded, non-state-owned firm. He alleges that his incarceration was the result not of "independent state action, but rather by Silvercorp exerting its influence over the local" police. Put another way, he is claiming that Chinese authorities acted not in the interest of justice or the law but explicitly to help a private company discredit him and to visit retribution upon him.

The Chinese government no longer controls the economy as it once did. Before Deng Xiaoping set about reforming the economy, in the 1980s, the price of most things was set by the government, whereas today, only energy prices and a few freight rates are state controlled. Whereas once everyone was employed by the government, these days state firms account for less than 15% of the urban workforce. State monopolies have gone from being the norm to affecting only a handful of strategically important industries, like banking, energy, and telecommunications. But though it's clear that many of the traditional mechanisms of state control have seemingly been dismantled, articulating just what's replaced them is far more difficult.

Superficially, China looks as though it's embraced free-market capitalism. Companies make their own business decisions, there is private ownership, and everyone from the tech entrepreneur speaking at Davos to the guy selling food skewers on the street corner is out to make a profit. The country has all the infrastructure you'd expect of a free-market economy: stock markets, mortgage loans, venture-capital funds, auction houses. The cities are filled with skyscrapers, the roads are clogged with prestige cars, and the streets proliferate with Starbucks coffee shops.

But China also bears many of the characteristics of state capitalism. Beijing retains control over state firms that still dominate industries ranging from machine tools to steel. Moreover, Beijing tries to pick winners, throwing subsidies at industries, like robotics and semiconductors, in which it wants China to be a global leader. And it nurtures state-owned champions at home with monopolies and other perks before sending them abroad to buy resources and strategically useful infrastructure.

Still, an economy in which private companies can summon government thugs to do their bidding might best be described as crony capitalism. Certainly corruption appears to still be rampant, despite President Xi Jinping's multiyear anticorruption campaign, and officials and private business continue to have complex — and mutually beneficial — relationships. Yet crony capitalism, state capitalism, and free-market capitalism all fail — both individually and in the aggregate — to sufficiently describe the nature of the Chinese economy. Markets thrive, but the presence of the government is ubiquitous. The interplay between the two is uniquely Chinese.

The Chinese Communist Party's own description of the dynamic goes like this. In 2013, it declared that henceforth the market would play a "decisive" role in the economy (previously it had been limited to only a "basic" role) but that the state would continue to play a "dominant" role. There's no indication that the market has in fact taken a more significant role since that change was announced, but that's not the point. What's significant is that the CCP thought it could promote the role of markets *without* demoting the role of the state. That seems like a profound contradiction. Surely you can't elevate markets from basic to decisive without relegating the state from dominant to, say, just influential or merely consultative. But that assumes that markets and state control are at opposite ends of a sliding scale, such that a step away from one is a step toward the other.

That's not how the Communist Party sees it. China's authorities are willing to dismantle the shackles of explicit state control and to replace them with markets, but they fully retain the right to intervene whenever they don't like what markets are doing. They are willing to trust the economy to the magic of the open market—but only up to the point where they're happy with the outcome. Crucially, the state doesn't need monopolies or price controls or direct ownership in companies—the traditional trappings of state control—to get what it wants. Instead it intervenes in ways that are informal, ad hoc, and in many cases invisible to outsiders.

It was during a casual conversation with a senior official responsible for regulating China's financial system that I first started to understand how Chinese authorities see their relationship with the market. We were sitting opposite each other in his office, separated by a coffee table piled high with recent issues of *The Economist* and the *Financial Times*. It was 2013, and there was mounting disbelief outside China that bad loans in the country's banks could account for only about 1% of their total assets, as was claimed by the official data. Given the pace of lending and the scale of dubious construction projects around the country, that number seemed preposterously low. Are we really expected to believe the numbers? I asked.

"If China were to declare that nonperforming loans were in fact much higher than thought, does anyone really benefit?" he said, without directly addressing the question. His answer caught me off guard. I'd been raised in an economic tradition in which transparency was inherently a good thing. My interlocutor was laboring under no such preconceptions. Such a revision would be extremely costly, he said. To meet international standards, the banks would have to sell shares at fire-sale prices in order to quickly raise more capital. Meanwhile, banks would have to foreclose on loans, seizing land, factories, and whatever assets they could in order to claw back what they were owed. Companies that might otherwise return to financial health if they could only hold on until better times would be forced into bankruptcy.

He called the approach "trading space for time," which was the World War II strategy used by the Chinese Nationalists after they lost Shanghai to the Japanese. Faced with better-equipped and better-trained invaders, the Nationalists withdrew to China's far west, ceding much of the country to Japan. The hope was that the pursuit would exhaust the enemy as they traveled farther from their base and overextended their supply lines, ultimately buying the Nationalist army time to regroup and counterattack.

There was a certain appeal to his reasoning. Why should China endure unnecessary pain if the authorities could just waive the rules for a while? (Of course, the strategy works only if authorities use the time they buy to clean up the mess. Five years after that conversation, the scale of the problems has only worsened.) But waiving the rules meant that banks could avoid raising the capital they needed to cover their bad loans; it meant the market didn't have accurate information with which to value Chinese bank shares; and it meant that the public had a falsely positive view of the health of the economy. The state — or at least a group of officials — took the opinion that the national interest warranted deceiving the market.

THE RESTLESS HAND

Misleading and inaccurate data is a widespread problem in China. In 2010, then–party secretary of Liaoning Province Li Keqiang (he would be promoted to premier two years later) allegedly told the U.S. ambassador that China's GDP data was basically manufactured, confirming widely held suspicions. Internationally there is so little faith in China's GDP figures that they've become a punch line. "I am always amazed at the alacrity with which they report their [GDP] numbers. Kind of like Radar on [the old hit sitcom] *M*A*S*H*, they seem to know their numbers before the quarter is over," Richard Fisher, president of the Federal Reserve Bank of Dallas, said to general laughter from the Fed board in 2009 after he returned from a trip to Beijing.

Nearly all of China's statistics suffer from a credibility deficit. The urban unemployment rate has hovered around 4.1% for more than a decade, abdicating any claim to realistically reflect actual joblessness. The official inflation rate remains reassuringly low even as residents of Beijing and Shanghai complain to anyone willing to listen about the rising cost of living. Premier Li, in conversation with the U.S. ambassador, said that all of China's official statistics are "for reference only." And it's not just statistics that fall victim. The media is kept on a tight leash, constrained by daily lists circulated by the Party that dictate what issues can be reported on, and another list of words not to be used during coverage of certain stories.

Meanwhile, any source of information that contradicts the official version of things — or somehow embarrasses the powers that be — quickly feels the chill wind of state control, as China's private investigations industry found in 2012. Partly as a result of Huang and Carnes's sleuthing, it became clear that the problem of fraudulent U.S.-listed Chinese companies was more than just a case of a few bad apples (the SEC would eventually deregister more than sixty Chinese companies for various violations). Rather than step in to weed out the shysters or to cooperate with the SEC to see that justice was done, Beijing just cut off access to various company documents that had previously been freely available and that the shorts had drawn heavily upon in their investigations. There was no formal directive, just oral instructions to government officials. Then, in April 2012, Beijing cracked down on the investigators whom shorts had been using to do their on-the-ground research into suspect companies. Overnight about one thousand people were detained. An American I knew who worked for an investigations company packed a bag and gave his apartment key to a friend so that if he had to hightail it to the airport, never to return, then at least someone would be able to pack up his belongings.

The upshot is that all this government meddling makes China's economy incredibly opaque, not only to foreigners but to the Chinese as well. But this control of information — be it the massaging of data, faking it outright, turning a blind eye to its misreporting, rationing its publication, or cutting off its availability — is not the root cause of China's opacity. It is merely a symptom. What makes China so opaque — and, indeed, what gives the government such control over information in the first place — is that its rules are fluid.

The bedrock of the free market is a level playing field where the rules apply relatively fairly and equally to everyone, including the government. In other words, markets need the rule of law to be in effect if they're to function properly. But as a one-party state, China has none of the constraints on state power that we take for granted. There are no elections to remove unpopular governments. There's no division of power among the executive, legislative, and judicial branches of government. The Party is in charge of all three, as well as every provincial, city, township, and county government. Moreover, the courts are political, subject to the influence of both the Party and the government, thereby freeing the state from being bound by its own rules. The government can bend the rules, ignore them, or manipulate them as it sees fit. It can deploy the police for explicitly political purposes. Rules are simply a tool of governance, not to be adhered to but rather to be applied — or ignored — in the service of any given agenda.

In a 2008 interview with CNN, Premier Wen Jiabao explained the interplay of markets and government power like this: "We have one important piece of experience of the past 30 years, that is to ensure that both the visible hand and invisible hand are given full play in regulating the market forces," he said.

That sounds reasonable. After all there's no such thing as a perfectly free market. Even in liberal democracies, the government's visible hand is everywhere, imposing rules to regulate safety and health standards, and environmental emissions, and workers' pay, and financial-sector risks. It creates a framework within which the market operates.

But in China the visible hand doesn't simply build a framework. In the interests of achieving the outcomes it wants, it meddles constantly. The presence of the visible hand is so pervasive that the Chinese instead refer to it as *xian bu zhu de shou*: the restless hand.

Its interventions sometimes take the form of a whispered directive, as in 2010 when privately owned cooking-oil producers complied with a direct order from Beijing not to carry out planned price increases. Sometimes it intervenes by changing the rules by which markets operate, such as in its inclination to impose moratoriums on new IPOs whenever it fears that an increase in the number of stocks will depress share prices. Sometimes it tries to mold the attitudes of market participants by controlling the supply of information, as when a private-sector provider of independent data on China's housing prices — data that showed prices rising faster than what official numbers suggested — suddenly ceased publishing in the name of "social stability." And sometimes it operates within a black box, such as in the way it manages the value of the currency despite having set up a mechanism that, to all outward appearances, allows the value of the yuan to be set by market forces.

In effect, the government creates market infrastructure but then fiddles with the rules or applies them inconsistently, ignoring them when necessary and drafting them in ways that allow them to be flexibly interpreted. That has allowed the state to blur the line between public and private. Private companies require the beneficence of the state in order to function, whether it be to secure permits or licenses, to avoid anticorruption scrutiny — warranted or otherwise — to obtain subsidies and tax waivers, or to be treated fairly by the courts. Consequently, authorities are able to co-opt private companies, much to the consternation of governments in liberal democracies that, on principle, welcome private investment regardless of where it comes from.

Internationally, investment by private companies typically undergoes far less scrutiny than investment by state firms does, but China's private companies pose a problem, because they increasingly seem to be acting explicitly in the interest of the Chinese state when they go abroad, by acquiring high-tech firms in sectors that are central to Beijing's industrial policy. That's not simply coincidence. China's authorities have an incredible amount of discretion to impose their will on markets and firms alike, giving them power to manage the economy beyond anything bureaucrats in liberal democracies could ever dream of. However, this power isn't concentrated in the hands of a small group of officials in Beijing. Such discretionary power is shared, to some extent, by every level of government. And it's subject to rampant abuse.

Early in 2015, Wu Hai, the fortysomething CEO of a chain of midtier hotels, wrote an open letter to Premier Li Keqiang. Not knowing how to get the letter to the premier, he posted it online. It went viral. "Government officials are natural born sons, state firms are the children of concubines, and private companies are the offspring of whores," he wrote with great candor. "Although we all share the same father . . . us sons of whores have no choice but to offer our right cheek once our left has been slapped."

The letter was the result of years of frustration over the near-constant abuse his business had suffered at the hands of the bureaucracy. Wu, who at the time of writing the letter had sixty-five hotels and was building another fifty across thirty cities, said that the complexity of China's bureaucracy meant that he had to deal with more than a thousand different officials, ranging from tax collectors to fire-safety inspectors. He complained about all of the inconsistent rules, arbitrary fines, and officials who always had their hand out.

It's probably not much of an exaggeration to say that every private businessperson in China has similar stories. One businessman I know who runs a consultancy in Chongqing complains that the local tax man invites himself over for tea once every quarter. The businessman dutifully slips the tax man an envelope full of cash as the official prepares to leave, the cost of insuring against having a dozen more tax officials camp out in his office for a couple of weeks while doing an audit. At the extreme end of the spectrum, I met another man who told me that his finance company had been expropriated by a local government. He and his partners were called in to city hall, told to put their phones in a box, ushered into a room that was allegedly wired to prevent electronic eavesdropping, and instructed to sell their company at a fraction of its market value to three companies whose names were written on a piece of paper they were handed.

"All the entrepreneurs [whom I heard from afterward] supported me 100% . . . Some said that they cried [when they read the letter]," Wu said a few weeks after posting his letter. The letter eventually got the premier's attention and was republished in the state media. The letter jibed with one of Premier Li's pet peeves. Following is an extract from a speech he gave in 2013:

> One minister told me that he once got a complaint letter, saying that a young man, after he graduated from university in Beijing and returned home, wanted to start his own business in a county town in central China . . . He chose to open a bookstore . . . After borrowing more than 20,000 yuan from his parents and relatives, he spent three or four months getting dozens of papers stamped with official seals, which was necessary

to get the license. Not long after he rented a place, inspectors came. A batch of law enforcement officers went in, and said the shop's window glass was the wrong color, as the reflection would cause "light pollution" in the street, and told him to fix it. The young man replied saying he was out of money. The law enforcement officers then offered to take books instead of money, and went away with dozens of books. Did the books contain any adult or illegal content? No . . . Most of his stock was textbooks . . . Eventually, the graduate could not afford the inspections and chose to close down the store.

"We don't dare speak up because we want to survive," Wu the hotelier said in his viral letter. "If we speak up . . . we could end up in jail, or we could be crushed."

Carnes published the first of a series of reports on Silvercorp in September 2011, after a three-month investigation. Huang had secured a copy of the provincial government's geological report on Silvercorp's largest mine, which estimated that the mine had produced 35% less ore and 75% less silver in 2010 than what the company had reported. To corroborate those figures, the men had a camera installed on the road just outside the mine to count the number of trucks carrying ore to the processing plant. By their calculation, traffic was 34% lower than what it needed to be to align with Silvercorp's figures. They also collected lumps of ore as they fell off the trucks, which, when analyzed, showed silver content of only a fraction of what Silvercorp was reporting.

The research was suggestive, but it was, of course, far from scientific proof that the mine wasn't producing as much as Silvercorp had claimed. Still, it was sufficient, Carnes felt, to argue that Silvercorp should commission a new geological report to clear up just how much silver the mine was actually capable of producing. Carnes called for a new report to be conducted by an independent, internationally recognized firm. The company chairman responded with a letter to shareholders in which he called Alfred Little a group of "nefarious short sellers utilizing the Internet, fictitious names, and distributing false allegations." The company filed defamation charges in New York, and Huang was arrested at the Beijing airport.

Huang says that from his very first interrogation, something felt a little off. Many of the questions being put to him by the police seemed unrelated to violations of Chinese law but rather were "directed towards obtaining information that could be used by Silvercorp in connection with its defamation action in New York," according to Huang's false-imprisonment lawsuit. Moreover, Huang says, his interrogator received a constant stream of questions via text message, as though his line of questioning were being directed by someone outside. Huang suspected it was someone from Silvercorp, so he and Carnes started documenting instances when they could detect the influence of the company upon the actions of the police.

Huang and Carnes claim that information used by Silvercorp in the New York defamation case could have come only from Huang's laptop, which had been confiscated by the police; that during Huang's trial, "the Silvercorp lawyers effectively acted as the prosecutor"; and that during Huang's time under house arrest, Silvercorp was covering police expenses related to the case. Huang says that on one occasion, while he was still under house arrest, he was required to travel with the police to another province. When checking out of the hotel where they stayed, he heard the officer in charge request that hotel staff make out the receipt for his stay to Silvercorp's main Chinese subsidiary, a company called Henan Found Mining Company. (Huang later went back and got copies of the hotel receipts.) On another occasion, he heard the officer call someone to ask to borrow a car. The Canadian newspaper the *Globe and Mail* later confirmed that the car's license plate, which Huang jotted down, belonged to a black Lexus owned by Henan Found.

And then there's the video made by Huang's colleague Michael Wei. The police arrested Wei in December 2011 but let him go after he agreed to testify against Huang. Wei, a Chinese national, later managed to escape the country, whereupon he wrote to the courts rescinding the confession he'd given to police, saying it had been coerced. But prior to his escape, he used a camera hidden in his backpack to secretly record a visit he made to the office of the Luoyang policeman who was in charge of the investigation. At one point during his visit, the policeman stepped out of the room, and Wei took out his phone and started photographing the papers strewn across the policeman's desk: receipts for airfares, road tolls, meals, and taxis made out to Henan Found, and a reimbursement form in the company's name stamped "Paid in Cash."

For Huang, the recording is bittersweet. On the one hand, it's compelling evidence for his case. On the other, as he watched he could barely contain his anger as the policeman in the recording offered insight into the scale of injustice Huang has suffered. "The criminal code does not specifically say which particular law your activities have violated," the policeman says. "However, as long as the state finds your behavior to be harmful to the country . . . they can always charge you with something."

At the time of this writing, Silvercorp was trying to stop Huang's case. The company asked that the case be heard in China, and argued that the Chinese court had already dealt with the matter at Huang's trial, but so far its efforts have been unsuccessful. The case was due to go to court in Canada early in 2018.

The great irony is that Carnes and Huang's report ended up doing very little harm to the company. Silvercorp's share price dropped 20%

immediately after Carnes's first report, but it bounced back a few days later, because, Carnes believes, he merely outlined his concerns and didn't claim fraud.

But it turns out that the British Columbia Securities Commission had concerns similar to those of Carnes and Huang. In November 2011, two months after the men published their first report, the commission's chief mining adviser sent a letter — a letter that was never made public — to Silvercorp's chairman in which he complained that the company's technical reports contained "errors that could individually or collectively result in material overestimation of mineral resources." The company has steadfastly denied any wrongdoing.

Still, the following year, Silvercorp revised down the official estimate of just how much silver ore the mine in question contained. Eventually its share price fell from around nine dollars, where it was when Carnes published the first report, to less than a dollar by the end of 2015. (It was back up to around $2.50 at the time of this writing.)

Carnes and Huang think the authorities went after them because they were defending the interests of their most valuable asset. Silvercorp is the biggest taxpayer in a relatively poor county. And that matters because it entwines the company's interests with those of the authorities. "It is likely that some of the companies you guys [shorted] really had problems. But now that you've messed with Silvercorp, the issue has been elevated," the policeman says on the recording made by Huang's colleague. "So you just have to be punished. There's nothing we can do."

THE OVERACCUMULATION OF POWER

The single biggest problem with China's system of government is that, in the absence of an independent judiciary, free press, political opposition, or civil society that can hold the government accountable, the government needs some way to monitor itself. In theory, the Party is supposed to do it, but the Party isn't an independent arbiter. It's intrinsically intertwined with government. Party members often wear two hats — a Party hat and a government hat — or regularly swap one for the other. The chairman of any given state-owned firm is typically also its party secretary. Loyalty to the Party is supposed to come first, and President Xi routinely exhorts members to take their responsibilities seriously. But therein lies the problem. Rather than use institutional constraints, the system of governmental accountability depends on individuals doing the right thing. Given that more than one hundred thousand Party members have been detained since 2012 as part of Xi's anticorruption campaign, the system clearly hasn't worked. Premier Li put it this way: "The over-accumulation of power and lack of oversight is a hotbed for corruption."

Given that local government and the bureaucracy generally lack adequate external oversight and objective internal supervision, it is truly remarkable that they haven't totally run the economy into the ground but rather have merely skimmed off a slice. In the absence of sufficient oversight, the bureaucracy is kept in line — partially at least — by deeply entrenched political incentives.

Officials at every level of government have a number of quantifiable goals they're expected to achieve each year. Promotion prospects are based on success in meeting or surpassing those goals. A city mayor, for example, might be required to attract a certain amount of investment into his jurisdiction, to ensure that there are no public protests and perhaps to do something to improve the environment, such as close down a certain amount of antiquated steelmaking capacity. But of all the things officials need to achieve, fast economic growth and fast-growing tax revenue trump all others combined. Taxes are particularly important. Without taxes, local governments can't achieve all the other items on the list. Keeping public order, compensating laid-off steelworkers, raising educational standards — all the things that Beijing expects of them require resources.

But China's tax regime is heavily biased against subnational governments. They're responsible for about 80% of all expenditures, including health, education, and pensions, but they receive only half of all taxes. Beijing makes up the shortfall by remitting back at least some of the difference, but it also often pushes new responsibilities down to lower levels of government without providing adequate funding.

So, local authorities use their considerable discretion to come up with creative new ways to spur growth and to expand tax revenues. In large part, that dynamic has hugely contributed to China's economic miracle. Local authorities have been able to experiment to see what works in their jurisdictions and to copy successful examples from elsewhere. But Beijing's reliance on quantifiable targets to keep subnational authorities on the same page has perverse side effects. For one, local authorities favor economic growth that maximizes the amount of tax revenue that accrues to them directly, which means they favor industrial companies (like silver miners) over private hoteliers (something we'll go into more deeply in the next chapter). Moreover, particularly as the economy has slowed, they have used destructive and exploitive measures to achieve their targets, without concern for the consequences.

Local governments routinely pressure local firms to pay their taxes a year in advance, despite the Ministry of Finance in Beijing exhorting them not to. Sometimes they top off their income by hosting forums, exhibitions, and training events and then charging local companies for the privilege of their compulsory attendance. And sometimes authorities impose arbitrary fees and fines.

The fear that the city of Shenyang, the capital of Liaoning Province, was going to use fines to make up for a widely suspected shortfall of funds prompted a strike by shopkeepers in mid-2012, turning the city center into a ghost town for three days. The city had spent extravagantly on infrastructure as part of a face-lift prior to that year's National Games, a kind of domestic Olympics at which China's provinces compete against each other. Rumor spread that tax collectors were levying heavy fines on retailers for a swath of infractions ranging from the sale of counterfeit goods to the lack of authentic certification proving that toothpicks were made from legally harvested trees. In response, shop owners simply boarded up their stores. "I closed my shop for a whole day," said Yu Qingqing, a thirty-six-year-old woman running a toy stall, when I visited the city not long after the strike. "I heard people who violated the rules would be severely punished. But who the heck knows what the rules are."

(The Shenyang government eventually posted a notice online urging people to ignore the rumor. But when Shenyang eventually hosted the games, the bill for the opening ceremony came in at only 10% of what had been originally planned, and the opening was held during the daytime for the first time since 1987 in order to save on the electricity bill.)

For many local governments, such quasi- or extralegal sources of income are essential. But if revenue still isn't enough, they can always fake the data.

WORK-AROUNDS

In 2016, the incoming governor of Liaoning Province (of which Shenyang is capital) revealed that provincial tax revenues for the previous three years had been inflated by 20%. A central-government inspection team that visited the province reported that "the entire . . . province had an epidemic economic data falsification problem," according

to the *People's Daily,* the Communist Party's paper of record. The falsification not only affected taxes but also influenced all indicators of economic growth at every level of government. "[We] had a golden decade, but while the data looked great the economy was struggling," said
Jin Donghai, the deputy major of Fuxin, an industrial city in Liaoning.
"In the end it's become apparent that . . . the statistics were padded."

After being caught faking its GDP figures, Liaoning revised its data,
becoming the first and only Chinese province to slip into recession. It's
unlikely that Liaoning is alone in its fabrications, however. One of the
great mysteries of contemporary China is how every one of the country's provinces, year in and year out, is capable of reporting economic
growth faster than the pace of growth for the nation as a whole. Foreigners frequently rail against the pervasiveness of all this fake data, no
doubt suspicious that they are the intended victims. Yet China's leaders
are just as much victims as we are. Officials go to great lengths to ensure that the data their superiors receive reflects positively on them. As
an old Chinese adage has it, "Numbers make officials, so officials make
up numbers."

This is clearly not in Beijing's interests. It has tried to fix the system
by collecting data directly from local companies rather than relying
on submissions from local authorities, but to only mixed effect. In one
instance, Beijing statisticians discovered that all the company submissions coming from Henglan, a river town in southern China that produces a grab bag of small manufactured goods — adhesive tape, ba-
bies' strollers, decorative light fixtures — were coming from the same
IP address, which they traced to Henglan's Department of Economic
Development.

After launching an investigation, the National Bureau of Statistics
found that of the seventy-three large companies that had allegedly
completed the survey, more than a quarter had stopped production,

moved out of town, or ceased to exist. The NBS calculated that Hen-glan authorities had inflated industrial production data by about 400%. Not only do local governments have the ability to fake data, but few have any compunctions about doing so. As another adage has it, "Villages lie to townships, townships lie to the counties, and so on all the way to the State Council."

In the United States, one of the complaints you routinely hear about China is that it "doesn't play by the rules." The accusation is laden with indignation. Every American boy and girl is brought up to play by the rules as a way to ensure that everyone is treated fairly. Not playing by the rules is a blatant violation of trust and goes against the ethical foundations upon which society operates. In China, however, people have a singularly different relationship with rules. The rules aren't about fairness; they merely serve someone's interests. Moreover, the government routinely ignores the rules; sometimes the rules are so broad that they're applied indiscriminately; and invariably there are so many of them that you never know for sure whether you're playing by them at all.

In China, rules are things to be managed and mitigated — like closing up your store until you can be sure that the tax man is done with his campaign, or paying regular, small bribes to ensure that a local bureaucrat doesn't apply the rules indiscriminately to your business. Local governments — and, for that matter, state-owned firms — are no different in their relationship to the rules imposed upon them. Beijing tries to limit risk in the economy and to ensure sound economic management, but such measures invariably affect the ability of local governments to deliver on their two overarching priorities: generating growth and maximizing income. Consequently, local governments are constantly looking for loopholes. The dynamic is best summed up by the idiom *Shang you zhengce, xia you duice:* "From above there is pol-icy, but from below there are countermeasures." Or, put another way, people can always find a way to get around the rules.

We tend to assume that Beijing's writ is absolute. The reality is that the government implements its rules inconsistently, and everyone else — the public, the business community, and other parts of the govern-ment — looks for ways to get around them. It makes China difficult to understand, and it also makes it incredibly difficult to manage.

China has been able to post such outstanding economic growth in recent years not because of the guiding hand of the central government but in spite of it. Beijing designed rules to keep the economy stable and the financial system safe. Instead, both safety and long-term stability have been sacrificed in the interests of short-term growth. Senior of-ficials routinely roll out new rules and launch new campaigns aimed at fixing this problem or that. But throughout the system, there are deeply embedded, intractable forces pushing harder and more effec-tively in the other direction.

This is crucial to understanding how the Chinese economy has come to be bloated with debt and waste. The Chinese media has taken to referring to debt as being the "original sin" of the country's eco-nomic problems, but that's not quite right. The original sin is a system that gives economic actors incentive to borrow with abandon, with-out reference to the long-term consequence and with the freedom to circumvent the best efforts of higher authorities to impose discipline. That sin is no more vividly on display than among China's state-owned firms.

2

THE ZOMBIE ACCOMMODATION

ERZHONG GROUP'S FACTORY campus is not what you'd expect of China's highly touted military-industrial complex. Old men in faded blue overalls squat while weeding the pavement in the steamy Sichuan heat, fighting a losing battle against the vines and creepers that have already taken over the older factory buildings. Around midday, the place empties out as workers go home for their two-and-a-half-hour lunch break. Bicycles leave first; cars are allowed to follow fifteen minutes later. Retirees living in old, company-allocated apartment buildings that skirt the campus raise vegetables on unused land at the base of the factory walls. And the factory's first generation of managers, now in their nineties, live with their children and grandchildren in a handful of villas shaded by trees growing Chinese kumquats and ball-bearing-sized *huajiao,* the mouth-numbing spice used in Sichuan cooking.

Erzhong — literally "Second Heavy," as in China Second Heavy Machinery Group — started life as an offshoot of the Chinese Red Army. In 1958, workers from China's northeast, the country's industrial heartland and the home of First Heavy, were relocated to Deyang in western Sichuan Province to make large-caliber artillery at what was deemed a safe distance from the Soviet Union in case China's one-time ally decided to invade. Even today, the thick, guttural drawl of the northern transplants and their children sticks out among the lispy pronunciation of the native Sichuanese. But, for all its backwater charm, Erzhong is part of the backbone of China's industrial infrastructure. No longer just a defense contractor, it makes entire steel mills and most of the parts needed to build a nuclear-power plant. It makes crankshafts for cargo ships and the blades for hydroelectric power turbines, pieces of metal so large that diesel locomotives are needed to move them on train tracks between factory workshops.

The company's proudest achievement, however, towers ten stories over the otherwise squat compound. Housed in a gray and red prefabricated hangar with a glass viewing platform on one side is the world's biggest closed-die hydraulic-press forge, a 22,000-ton steel behemoth that China hopes will allow it to technologically leapfrog the United States when it comes to engineering the next generation of military hardware. The machine was built specifically to produce metal components like bulkheads, landing gear, and engine parts for China's air force and commercial passenger planes. Advisers on the project say it could also be used for manufacturing aircraft carriers, armor plating, spacecraft, and high-pressure mining tools. Crucially, it was built to create pieces of metal that are bigger, stronger, and lighter than anything the United States is currently capable of producing.

I caught a glimpse of the forge from underneath a roller door. It was mid-2014, a year after the forge was officially put into operation, and its camouflage-green paint still looked fresh. "China Erzhong" was written in four bold red Chinese characters along its crossbar, behind which five massive pistons sat idle. As I wandered up the driveway, the half-dozen engineers in blue overalls and yellow hard hats who were laughing and goofing off in the entrance went quiet, and one hit a button that lowered the door. After I futilely attempted to engage them in small talk, I was directed to the company's propaganda department, which duly informed me that the forge is a state secret. The roller door stays down for everyone except government officials.

Heavy-press forge technology has been around for a while. It was developed by the Germans during World War II as a way to build their air force from parts made out of magnesium rather than aluminum, which was running in short supply. In its simplest form, forging involves little more than beating a piece of hot metal into shape with a hammer, but magnesium is typically too brittle to beat. Heavy-press forging gets around that by slowly pushing a piece of metal into the desired shape, placing it under so much pressure that it moves like clay and takes the form of the mold, or die, that it's sitting in. More importantly, the pressure changes the metal's internal grain, making it stronger. The bigger the forge, the larger and lighter the components it can produce, making for more efficient aircraft.

At the end of World War II, the Soviets disassembled Germany's 33,000-ton forge and carried it back to Russia. The Americans were left with two 16,500-ton machines. It was soon clear that heavy-press forging would be vital to the jet age, so to close the gap with the Russians, the U.S. government bankrolled the construction of ten heavy forges. Some have since been decommissioned, but the biggest, in Cleveland, Ohio, is still operating. It is capable of exerting 50,000 tons of downward pressure and has produced components for virtually every U.S. military aircraft in operation, from the F-35 Joint Strike Fighter to the sixty-year-old B-52 Bombers. In Russia, the world's second-biggest forge can generate 75,000 tons of pressure and is used by Airbus to mold the A380's landing gear, slender cylinders of titanium that support the weight of the world's largest passenger plane as it hits the ground. Erzhong's forge eclipses the Russian machine. Officially it can exert 80,000 tons of force — enough power to bench-press China's new aircraft carrier with room to spare for a handful of submarines — although during tests it has managed to get up to 100,000 tons. In the words of Shi Changxu, the metallurgical scientist who is credited as being the father of Erzhong's forge, "Others cannot make what we can now make."

In recent years, China's state-owned firms have emerged as a symbol of China's strength and of the West's relative decline. Beijing uses them as tools with which it can make long-term strategic decisions at a time when the West has neither the budgets nor the political bandwidth to similarly invest in the future. Beijing uses state firms to build products that are too risky for the private sector to take on, like large passenger aircraft, which such firms have been working on for years with the goal of one day breaking Boeing's and Airbus's duopoly. State firms are used to buy up natural resources around the globe that are important to China's development. They build infrastructure in developing countries, a core part of Beijing's foreign policy aimed at cultivating friendly nations. Sometimes they are mobilized to defend China's economic interests, as when Aluminum Corporation of China, or Chinalco, spent $13 billion in 2007 buying Rio Tinto shares to stop the Anglo-Australian mining company from merging with BHP Billiton, a merger that could potentially have made it more difficult for China to negotiate prices for iron-ore imports by combining two of its three biggest suppliers.

What is easy to overlook is that all this comes at a cost. The Comac C919, the single-aisle plane that is supposed to challenge Boeing and Airbus, has been a money pit and is years overdue. Buyers were originally supposed to start taking delivery of the plane in 2014. That's been pushed back to 2018, but delivery could be as late as 2020, and the plane could be outdated even before it arrives. Rio Tinto's shares have traded at less than half of what Chinalco paid for them for most of the time since it acquired them. While China's state companies regularly outbid foreign firms to buy overseas mines, they also routinely overpay for the privilege. Many of the countries where China has built infrastructure are now struggling to repay those loans and have grown increasingly wary of Chinese influence. And in western Sichuan, 2 billion yuan was spent on a forge that's hardly been used.

"China now has the biggest forge in the world, but it's not the most advanced," said Yan Yongnian, a former professor of manufacturing automation at Tsinghua University, who was part of the group of advisers put together by Erzhong to consult on the machine's development. He wasn't invited back after his second visit. "I had a difference of opinion with the company," he told me. Yan's issue was that the forge lacked the controls of more modern machines and so wasn't as accurate as it needed to be. Yan blamed the company culture. Rather than innovate, it had modeled the forge on old Russian designs from the 1980s. Since then, forging technology has grown more complex. Forges need to respond quickly and regularly to changes in the metal to ensure that the grain ends up flowing in just the right way. The Cleveland forge recently underwent a $100 million upgrade to ensure that it continues to remain state of the art.

Yan said that politically it was safer for engineers at Erzhong — an organization in which thousands of Party members routinely meet in small groups to discuss Marxist-Leninist-Maoist thought — to use a tried-and-tested old design than to come up with something new. In other words, there's no culture of risk taking. "If you copy something word for word, then it's not your fault if something goes wrong," Yan told me.

Just a year after the forge was fully operational, it was clear that China didn't need the world's largest forge. The United States has been able to get by with forges little more than half the size of Erzhong's since the 1950s, and China is nowhere near producing aircraft the size of Airbus's A380. China's smaller forges — like the more technologically advanced 40,000-ton forge launched in Wuhan a year prior to Erzhong's — are capable of producing anything the Chinese military or industry currently requires. Moreover, what was anticipated as being the forge's main source of business never materialized. During its launch ceremony, the first component the forge manufactured was the landing gear of the C919 passenger plane, but so far the C919 has failed to generate regular work for Erzhong, and perhaps never will. "There's currently an excess of large forges, and there's just not enough work to go around," Zeng Fanchang, an adviser on the project, told me.

THE LEVIATHAN

Most countries have at least a few companies that are owned by the state. France, which is more comfortable with the idea than most free-market economies, has a hand in many of its biggest industrial companies, including two carmakers, three aerospace companies, and the national airline. Even the United States has a few, like the Postal Service and Ginnie Mae, which it keeps around to make it easier for people to buy homes. But China is in a different league. It has more than 150,000 companies that are owned by various strata of government, accounting for about 25% of economic output and one in five urban jobs. At one end of the spectrum, the central government directly owns the commanding heights of the economy, a stable that includes the world's second-biggest aluminum company, the world's fifth-, sixth-, and eleventh-biggest steel companies, and two of the world's biggest shipbuilders. It owns three oil companies, three airlines, and three telecommunications firms, all of which have a virtual oligopoly over their industries.

But at China's lower levels of government, there is little rhyme or reason as to what is state owned. The Chongqing municipal government, for example, owns hundreds of companies, including construction firms, the local water utility, two banks, and a steel company. It also owns eight riverboats that do scenic tours of the Three Gorges, an amusement park with performing dolphins and a bungee tower, and a traditional Chinese-medicine company that grows a type of lily used as a cough suppressant.

However, the one element that this vast group of disparate companies has in common is debt. State firms might account for only a quarter of the economy, but they've borrowed almost 60% of all the corporate debt. China has little mortgage debt relative to the United States, and official government debt is very low, unlike in Greece; but China's companies — and in particular its state-owned companies — have borrowed incredible amounts. According to the consulting firm McKinsey, between 2007 and mid-2014, China's companies — both state and private companies combined — went from owing $3.4 trillion to $12.5 trillion, a faster buildup than in any other country in modern times. The faster debt accumulates, the harder it is to find productive places to invest it, which means that the volume of bad loans rises, and with it the risk of crisis. At the end of 2015, Chinese firms had borrowed debt equivalent to 163% the size of its economy, up from 120% at the end of 2011. That was higher than South Korea (105%), the United States (71%), and Germany (52%), all of which had been fairly steady over the previous four years.

Still, the question commonly posed is, if most of China's corporate debt is government owned, why should anyone worry about it? Certainly, China's state companies don't seem to. Shi Changxu, the father of Erzhong's forge, said that before the state economic-planning agency gave the project the green light, there was much debate over whether there would be enough work to justify building such a large machine. In the end, they decided it didn't matter. Self-sufficiency was more important than efficiency. Erzhong then built the forge, not with government grants but with money borrowed from banks in the knowledge that the forge might not be able to pay for itself. That surely means the debt comes with a government guarantee.

However, only a fraction of the debt racked up by state firms can claim to be strategic. Riverboats and amusement parks benefit just as much from the financial system's willingness to lend to state firms. But even then, why should we worry if loans to state firms don't serve some greater national interest? After all, government-owned companies borrow from government banks, which surely means that the government is ultimately responsible for all of it. You could just merge all those balance sheets into one big government ledger and the debt would disappear.

Except that it's not the government's money; the loans are made from the savings of ordinary people who deposited them in the banks. As more and more companies fail to repay their loans, at some point the government needs to bail out the system so that citizen savers get their money back. When that day comes, the Chinese government has the same options available to it as every other government that's ever been in that position: it can let banks and companies fail (at the expense of jobs and pensions); it can raise taxes and issue government debt to bail them out (whereby the public foots the bill); or it can let inflation eat away at the size of the bad loans (and the value of people's savings). Conceivably it could sell its equity in state-owned firms in which it has trillions of dollars' worth of wealth locked up, but despite talk of such reform for years, it doesn't yet seem to be politically viable. Ultimately, there are real costs that will fall on the public.

The real advantage of China's system of state ownership isn't that the cleanup is easier than in market economies; it's that the cleanup is easier to put off, something that it can do indefinitely but not forever. State firms may be "backed" by the state, but in practice that doesn't mean that the government covers the companies' debts if they can't repay them. Rather it means that the banks are safe from political fallout if the loans go bad. They will just hold bad loans on their books and, with the government's acquiescence, pretend that they're fine — as they've been doing for some years already. In the short term, there's no real fallout. Sure, bank profits erode — after all, a big chunk of their loans aren't paying any interest — but otherwise no one has to take responsibility for mounting bad loans. And most importantly, deadbeat companies are kept alive.

"In the last one or two years, I haven't taken anyone around for a tour. No media, and certainly no investors. They just don't have any interest in the company," Liu Shiwei, a public-relations official for Erzhong, said to me when I visited Erzhong in the summer of 2014. By the time we sat down in his office, overlooking the lunchtime exodus of workers through Erzhong's main gates, Liu had shed any pretense of trying to spin the company's predicament. Erzhong was listed on the Shanghai Stock Exchange, but after years of not making a profit, its removal was just a matter of time — it was finally ejected a year later — and Liu knew his job would soon become obsolete. A child of people who had moved for the company from the northeast, Liu had inherited their accent and had grown up during a time when Erzhong was at the heart of community life. He was clearly nostalgic for Erzhong's good old days, but it was becoming harder to maintain company pride. Bonuses — no small part of total compensation for Erzhong's thirteen thousand employees and the ten thousand retirees it still supported — had dried up along with company profits. "Workers at other companies [in Deyang] are doing better," said Liu. "Shopkeepers treat them better. When they hear the accent of Erzhong folk, they're not as welcoming."

Three months after the forge was launched, Beijing announced that it was going to merge Erzhong into another state firm, China National Machinery Industry Corporation, or Sinomach. Sinomach does a little bit of everything. Of its forty-three subsidiaries, one makes excavators and other construction machinery, which it exports primarily to developing economies. Another makes the components that allow China's spacecraft to dock with the country's space laboratory. And in 2010, Sri Lanka celebrated the construction of a coal-fired power plant by a third Sinomach unit by putting an image of the plant on its hundred-rupee note.

By 2015, Erzhong had borrowed so much with so little payoff for its investments that without Sinomach's intervention it would have collapsed. The company's fortunes had turned for the worse in 2011, when it lost $40 million. Over the next four years, it would cumulatively lose about $2 billion. When I visited, what little work Erzhong had was being done at night so it could take advantage of off-peak electricity prices.

As far as bailouts go, Sinomach did the bare minimum. It paid out investors when Erzhong was on the brink of defaulting on its bonds. It negotiated with the banks that Erzhong had borrowed from to ease the debt burden. It promised to share any innovations its R&D divisions happened to come up with, as well as to introduce Erzhong to other state firms to try to drum up business, and to use its connections overseas to boost Erzhong's exports. But it hasn't given Erzhong a cent. "The way to help a company is by restoring it to health, not by giving it a blood transfusion," said Ren Hongbin, Sinomach chairman. "The more you support a company [with cash], the more impoverished it becomes."

In early 2015, Erzhong's management tried to downsize, asking workers to take voluntary layoffs and early retirement for a monthly stipend of 380 yuan, roughly a quarter of the minimum wage in Sichuan. Its workers took to the streets in protest. "We devoted our youth [to the company], and now workers have to pay the price for bad policy making," read one banner that was marched through town. "Don't ask the workers to shed blood and sweat, and now tears," read another.

"These last few years . . . no one has asked who is responsible for these losses," said an Erzhong worker interviewed on foreign television at the time. "It's really a case of 'heaven is high and the emperor is far away,'" an idiom meaning management could do as it liked without oversight from Beijing. "State assets have been lost, creating a huge hole, but the central government turns a blind eye, and in the end it's the workers who bear the brunt."

RESPECT FOR THE DEAD

Erzhong is a zombie, a company that doesn't generate enough revenue to repay its debt and is being kept alive by the willingness of banks to keep reissuing new loans. The term was originally coined to describe Japanese companies that were being kept alive after Japan's property-market collapse in the early 1990s, but in recent years "zombie" has gained currency among Chinese officials as well.

Chinese pop culture has a zombie tradition that differs a little from the brain-eating undead version that has been the U.S. standard since George A. Romero's *Night of the Living Dead*. China's zombies — or *jiangshi*, "rigid corpses" — trace their lineage at least to the Qing dynasty. They're as much vampire as zombie, craving blood rather than brains. And, in a markedly different take on how rigor mortis affects the dead's perambulatory skills, they get about using a two-footed hop rather than to stagger and slouch their way forward like American zombies. The differences between U.S. and Chinese zombies spill over to include the corporate variety, with the Chinese displaying an unhealthy willingness to accommodate the undead among its firms.

"It's not easy, but we need to find a way to lift their vitality," Premier Li Keqiang said of China's zombies in 2015. "We need to avoid having zombie companies, we need to help them, to let them live and live well."

At the heart of this tolerance is a fear of instability. Social stability has been the overwhelming preoccupation of the CCP for the past decade. Massive amounts of money have been dedicated to improving surveillance, monitoring social media, and beefing up internal security. Local officials are expected to maintain social stability over and above all other responsibilities. Regardless of how successful an official has been at generating growth, one protest above a certain size automatically puts an official's promotion prospects on ice. Social instability, very broadly defined, is the one thing that renders all other achievements moot, providing officials with the motivation to keep companies alive, their workers employed, and their pensions intact.

That said, not all company failures are as destabilizing as others. Factories run by private firms routinely go out of business, with workers often learning that they're out of a job only when they turn up to work to discover the gates locked and the managers have vanished. But private-sector factories are relatively easy to deal with when they shut down. Their employees often tend to be migrant workers, people who are required by law to leave the city and return to their homes in the countryside if they can't find work. State firms, however, are different. Their employees are usually locals who have nowhere to go if they lose their jobs, and are more likely to protest. And state companies are often the linchpin of the local economy, with whole towns being built around them, such as Deyang, where Erzhong is based.

Moreover, private firms tend to be smaller and consequently have a much smaller impact on the local authorities' other preoccupation: taxes. Local government keeps large companies afloat because even as zombies they can still contribute significant tax revenue. Sure, zombies, by definition, aren't making any profit, so there's no corporate tax to be had. But local governments get to keep 25% of the value-added tax that gets collected on the sale of manufactured goods (the rest goes directly to Beijing). So a company that's losing money is still generating taxes for local authorities as long as it's making sales. In other words, a factory might be utilizing only 60% of its capacity, nowhere near enough to break even or repay its loans, but for local officials drawing tax revenue from sales, closing the plant means that it loses a big chunk of fiscal revenue, whereas the cost of keeping the company alive is borne by the financial system.

Local officials will do whatever they can to keep a zombie alive, whether that be finding another firm to merge it with, or forcing employees to take pay cuts or early retirement, or just pressing banks to keep lending money. In 2016, the provincial government of Shanxi, a major coal producer, called on banks to lend at least as much money that year to the coal sector — an industry suffering declining prices and laden with too many mines — as they did the year before, and in particular asked that they not call in loans from the province's seven biggest coal companies.

Meanwhile, the Shandong provincial government posted a notice calling on banks to continue extending loans to companies that just had "liquidity problems," code for firms that weren't earning enough to cover their interest payments. There's no way of saying just how many zombie companies there are in China. In 2016, the International Monetary Fund collated data published by local governments showing there were about 3,500 state-owned zombies across eleven provinces. That seems a little on the low side. Banks report that almost 2% of their assets have turned bad, but some economists suspect that the real number is closer to 15%, as banks choose to keep companies alive rather than demand their money back.

But the burden of state firms on the economy is not limited to zombies. The political incentives that keep zombies alive manifest themselves in a raft of other distortions that give the state sector the patina of health while hiding endemic waste. According to Unirule, a Beijing-based economics think tank set up by one of China's most famous liberal economists, between 2001 and 2009, China's state-owned firms collectively generated profits of 5.8 trillion yuan. But if those companies had paid market rates for items like land, credit, water, and electricity, and hadn't received any cash subsidies or tax rebates and holidays, there would have been no profit at all. With such massive subsidies, profits don't really mean anything. They're not a reflection of success, efficiency, or return on capital. To a certain extent, subsidies are farmed out by Beijing in the quest to support the development of industries like steel and car manufacturing, which it deems strategically important. But for the most part, subsidies are the tools of local governments competing with each other. The end result is waste and debt problems that go far beyond a small horde of zombies.

WE DUG OUT A VOLVO

The local officials in Shiyan, a city in central China's Hubei Province, were proud of their town's air quality. The year I visited, on only a handful of days had the city exceeded the national upper limit on acceptable pollution, or so the officials told me. I wasn't sure how to respond politely. I could barely see the hills that surrounded the city, because of the lingering haze. In fact, I'd heard such clean-air enthusiasm from officials before. I once visited a coal town in central China where the smog burned the back of my throat even as the locals gushed about how much the air had improved. But Shiyan's haze was different. It wasn't the acrid gray mist that plagues many of China's industrial cities. It was yellow and grimy. You could wash it off in the shower at the end of the day. It wasn't industrial pollution; it was demolition dust, and it was the result of relandscaping on a massive scale.

Were it not for the same quirk of history that saw Erzhong move to Deyang, Shiyan would likely never have been anything more than a sleepy mountain village. In 1968, the Second Automobile Works — which later became Dongfeng Motor Corporation, one of China's four biggest state-owned automakers — was set up in Shiyan as a precaution against Soviet invasion. The area is extremely hilly, and the auto industry squeezed itself into the thin corridors of flat land between the slopes, making life complicated for any Russian bomber bent on wiping out central China's truck industry. When I visited in 2013, those same hills were complicating life for city planners, who worried that they were presiding over a dying city.

The problems started in 2003, when Dongfeng moved its headquarters out of Shiyan — which calls itself China's motor city — to Wuhan, the provincial capital, which also claims the same title. General Motors, Honda, and Peugeot-Citroën all produce cars in Wuhan, one of China's biggest cities and a major logistics hub. It sits at the intersection of major rail lines and has a port on the Yangtze, which flows deep into China's heartland. Shiyan, a city of about eight hundred thousand people, has none of those advantages.

In 2006, Dongfeng's joint venture with Nissan Motors left Shiyan for Wuhan as well, but the Shiyan authorities decided that their city's problem wasn't its poor location. According to the Shiyan Bureau of Land and Resources, before moving, Dongfeng had asked for about eighty acres of land, which the city couldn't provide. "After Dongfeng decided to move the headquarters of two of its units, it looked as though the motor city could become an abandoned city," the bureau said in a fax it sent me. Clearly, if only Shiyan had more land — land that could be built on — then the city could avoid this situation happening again. In 2007, the city government settled on a plan to create four hundred square kilometers of new, flat land—more than doubling the city's original footprint—by getting rid of the hills. Almost all this new land is being created so that companies can move in and build factories. "Leveling mountains has become the golden key to resolve the problem of Shiyan's development impasse," said the land bureau.

"It's very difficult for Shiyan to attract investment," said Gong Bailin, a section chief with the National Development and Reform Commission in Shiyan. "We've paid a high price, but there's now large scope for further development."

I was sitting across the table from three officials from the local National Development and Reform Commission (NDRC), China's economic planning agency. It was very unusual to have a chance to talk with the NDRC, and even more so for its representatives to be so forthcoming about the extent of the problems they were facing. They'd recently taken a pummeling from the Chinese press for tearing down the Shiyan hills, and in an effort at crisis control they had taken the rare move of talking to a foreign journalist. Part of their openness came from what they saw as the unequivocal success of their strategy.

AB Volvo had recently decided to team up with Dongfeng, investing 5.6 billion yuan in a new business to build commercial vehicles. The firms that had decided to put the facility in Shiyan. The site of the new venture was about a twenty-minute drive from downtown and was overlooked by a sheer man-made white cliff, the remaining half of a hill that had been flattened to make space.

"By leveling the mountains, what did we dig out? We dug out a Volvo," said Pu Guolin, the head of agricultural zoning at the Shiyan NDRC. He was sitting next to Gong. "If Shiyan hadn't razed the mountains, there is no way Volvo could have come here."

"Shiyan is mountainous and remote, and investors don't want to come." It was Gong's turn again. "Compared with other cities, Shiyan doesn't have any particular advantage, and these days, everywhere in China offers similar preferential policies."

One of those preferential policies is land — free, or at least very cheap, industrial land. Beijing has strict rules against giving land away for less than what it cost, but local governments routinely manage to get around these rules. Shiyan needed land not because companies were itching to expand; in truth, land was needed as part of a package of subsidies that the city felt was necessary if they wanted to compete for investments against every other city around the country.

Local-government competition for investment — and the tax revenue that goes with it — is one of the basic ingredients responsible for China's economic miracle. By giving local governments a large degree of autonomy, the hope was that they'd come up with innovative techniques, suitable to the local environment, to generate growth. However, competition for investment has turned into a zero-sum game; investment that one city gets is tax dollars that another doesn't. And rather than designing solutions based on local conditions, everyone competes by offering the same incentives. As a result, China's urban footprint has a disproportionately high ratio of industrial land. Generally speaking, in most parts of the world, industrial land might take up 10% to 15% of a city's area. In China it's about a quarter, and in some cities it's even higher.

For a city that isn't surrounded by flat farmland that can be converted easily into industrial parks, Shiyan's experience isn't unusual. In Lanzhou, a city in western Gansu Province that's hemmed in by mountains on one side and a river on the other, about seven hundred large hills have been leveled to make way for a new satellite city. Yan'an, the Shaanxi town where China's Communists once took refuge from Nationalist troops by holing up in mountain caves, is also demolishing some of its hills in order to make more space, albeit at a safe distance from those that had a role in Party folklore. And up and down China's coast, cities that have no more space to expand inland have taken to reclaiming land from the sea. Between 2015 and 2020, municipalities have plans to create new land roughly equivalent to the total area of Delaware by dredging up the seafloor and building seawalls. Yet the sad reality is that much of this industrial land sits idle. China is littered with industrial parks that are underutilized or almost entirely empty.

Land is just one part of a menu of subsidies fed to Chinese companies. The problem for local government is that almost every city in China is working from the same playbook. Hence, subsidies aren't enough. Consequently local authorities feel compelled to protect local businesses not just from foreign competition but also from companies based elsewhere in China. Zhang Weiying, another of China's most respected economists, argues that one of the reasons China is so enthusiastic about global free trade is that trade barriers between provinces — and even between counties within provinces — are pervasive and have proved much harder to remove than barriers between nations. "When China waves the flag of free trade on the international stage, it should not forget that the domestic market is more in need of free trade," writes Zhang.

The Office of the U.S. Trade Representative, which is responsible for monitoring whether China complies with its World Trade Organization commitments, complains that one of the difficulties in getting fair treatment for foreign firms is that Beijing "has difficulty enforcing its own industrial policy measures at the local level." Barriers are seldom explicit but emerge from the discretion that local authorities have in enforcing the rules. Provincial food and drug administrations routinely use vague laws about advertising in order to fine pharmaceutical companies from other provinces for "illegal" marketing. Similarly, outsider companies might find themselves facing stiff penalties for failed health inspections, or for product safety or quality failures.

Or the local courts will be encouraged to find in favor of local companies in contract disputes. Or a court decision from elsewhere won't be adequately enforced. Or contractors on local-government projects will be expected to purchase their materials strictly locally.

The combination of subsidies, domestic protectionism, and a willingness to keep zombies alive has resulted in Chinese industry's being capable of producing far more than is actually needed. Specifically, subsidies reduce the cost of building and running factories, so companies borrow to build more of them. Protectionism means that even if there isn't a strong business case for building another factory, at least local sales are assured. And local governments' predilection toward keeping zombies alive means that the Chinese economy is stuck with all these extra factories, which forces prices down and undermines the health of entire industries.

Since 2014, China has produced more than half of all the steel in the world. However, of the 1.1 billion tons of steel Chinese factories were capable of making in 2015, only 70% was actually produced. That year, more than half of China's steel companies posted a loss, and prices were driven so low that steel was cheaper than cabbage, as was the popular observation at the time. That sort of excess has played out again and again across Chinese industry. Consider that China produces thirteen times as much aluminum as the United States, and about half of the global supply. At its peak, China was producing more than 40% of the world's ships. According to state media, twenty-one industries suffer from "serious" overcapacity, a list that includes cement, aluminum, shipbuilding, steel, power generation, solar panels, wind turbines, construction machinery, chemicals, textiles, paper, glass, shipping, oil refining, and Erzhong's sector, heavy engineering.

That sort of excess waste is possible only because the companies themselves are complicit. State firms aren't micromanaged by the government. They have enough autonomy from the government to make management decisions on a day-to-day basis as they see fit, and they are judged according to a list of goals they're expected to achieve each year, just like local-government officials. Profit is, of course, supposed to be one of those metrics, but subsidies mean that China's companies have the veneer of profitability without really needing to be efficient. Moreover, the government authorities they report to don't really care about profit. Dividends typically get plowed back into the companies that generate them. The government might say it cares about good, sound management, but what it really cares about is growth and taxes. And that in turn shapes the incentives for state-company executives. "Capacity, production and market share goals are used as the primary benchmarks to assess the performance of these state-controlled corporations," the European Union Chamber of Commerce in China concluded in a 2016 report on industrial overcapacity. "Size matters in China."

With great discretion to do as they see fit, and with ready access to credit from the banks, managers at state firms find that the easiest way to grow their companies is to simply borrow more and build more. The result is that a massive amount of debt has been accumulated and wasted by building factories that no one needs.

In fairness, a bit of bad luck contributed to Erzhong's fall from grace. After a 2011 tsunami and earthquake triggered a nuclear meltdown at Fukushima, Japan, governments around the globe hit the pause button on the construction of new nuclear-power plants, killing off one of Erzhong's main businesses overnight. But the real source of distress was the company's reckless expansion, specifically a decision to spend 5.2 billion yuan ($825 million) in building an entirely new factory in Jiangsu Province that would duplicate much of what Erzhong already did in Sichuan.

The new facility was supposed to fix Erzhong's single greatest competitive disadvantage. While its Sichuan location is well suited to evading Russian bombers, it's not particularly convenient when it comes to making deliveries to customers. That's partly because Erzhong is so far away from China's industrial heartland, which is clustered along the eastern seaboard and in the northeast. But, distance aside, Erzhong's biggest challenge was just getting its products *out* of Sichuan. The machines and components that Erzhong builds are so big and cumbersome that ordinary roads can't take the weight. From its factory, all of Erzhong's heavy components are trucked along a 250-kilometer stretch of road that has been specially reinforced to handle weights of up to 1,000 tons, on trailers with more than a dozen wheels. The road ends at a port on a tributary of the Yangtze River, which empties into the East China Sea near Shanghai, a fifteen-day voyage away.

The port is little more than a concrete slab with a big orange gantry crane that hoists goods from the dock out over the river and onto barges. It's in direct sight of the Big Buddha, a seventy-meter-tall statue that was carved into a cliff at Leshan 1,300 years ago to try to calm what had been a particularly difficult stretch of water to navigate. Sadly for Erzhong, the Buddha only calms the water; it doesn't ensure that there's enough of it. During autumn and winter, the water level on the river is so low that barges carrying anything more than 500 tons can't transit. In fact, sometimes the water is so low that 100 tons is the limit, so that for a good chunk of the year, Erzhong can't make deliveries. The new factory is closer to Erzhong's traditional customers and is built alongside a river that is sufficiently deep all year round. But by the time it was finished, there was really no need for it. "So we built the new facility, but then the entire industry turned bad . . . There are no contracts," said Liu Shiwei, Erzhong's public-relations official. "There's just not enough market demand, and there's nothing we can do."

When I visited Erzhong's new Jiangsu factory, the roads inside the compound were potholed and filled with water from recent rain. Stray dogs wandered in and out of the wild grass that had grown taller than the handful of workers who were milling about. There was no road connecting the main entrance — a grand sandstone affair — to the rest of the compound. Local truck drivers had graffitied their cell-phone numbers on the wall of the main entrance in order to advertise for work. And the factory's wharf on the river was overrun with weeds. Local salt traders used it to tie up their barges while waiting for new orders from a nearby chemical factory.

Back in Deyang, Erzhong still holds on to relics of its glory days. It has a theater and a sports center with two swimming pools. It has a television station whose broadcasts are available on the factory grounds and to people living in old company housing. Programming is limited to four shows a day and features *Family Album USA,* an English-teaching program from 1991 starring American actors who would later become moderately well recognized for their roles in *The West Wing* and *Desperate Housewives.* It also maintains an in-house newspaper, a four-page broadsheet published regularly by the propaganda department that reports on production achievements and includes such scintillating reads as "Company Secretary Wang Meets Guests from Ningxia." Perhaps most importantly, it tries to keep alive a sense of community even as its fortunes fall apart. At least once a year, grassroots-level Party members — both active employees and retirees — volunteer to give town residents free haircuts, wash their cars, take their blood pressure, repair their watches, or sharpen their kitchen knives. In the month before I visited, about five hundred Party members had turned out to do volunteer work for the community.

Erzhong has had two golden eras. The first was during the early days of the reform era in the 1980s, when the company had a pivotal role in building the industrial infrastructure needed for economic modernization. It was showered with resources and was a particularly privileged place to be employed. "Daughters, grow up quickly so you can marry into Erzhong," went one rhyming couplet from the time. But, like all state firms of the period, Erzhong wasn't just a company but an entire government in miniature. It had a kindergarten and primary school, a hospital, and its own police force and law courts. That ended in the 1990s, when Beijing started to unravel the planned economy. Companies like Erzhong found themselves weaned off state grants and were told to borrow from banks instead in the expectation that the banks would force some market discipline upon them. Instead, state firms used them as piggy banks, taking out loans to fund social services and to keep their businesses afloat. Around the turn of the century, the banks were bailed out, the state assumed responsibility for providing social services, and companies like Erzhong got a clean slate.

As a result, unencumbered of its debt and freed from managing schoolchildren, Erzhong boomed along with the rest of the economy during the early 2000s. It wasn't just that the economy was growing at 10%; it had been growing that fast for the past twenty years. What was different was that the types of companies that Erzhong supplied — China's heavy industry — were booming in a way they hadn't before. China went from being a relative minnow in the world of steel to being the biggest fish. The same went for aluminum. A shipbuilding industry had been built from scratch, so that China was now producing more dead-weight tonnage each year than Japan and South Korea, the previous industry leaders. And more and more power plants were needed just to keep up with all the industrial demand.

In that kind of booming environment, debt hardly mattered. No matter how much you borrowed, you could always grow through your problems. Everyone was expanding, and Erzhong needed to keep up. The year 2007 was the high-water mark for Erzhong. In that year alone, company profits quadrupled. But just as quickly, a few years later the demand for new factories started to peter out, as it became obvious that heavy industry had overextended itself.

So far, for most of the twenty-first century, profit and expansion have gone hand in hand in China. What made that breakneck expansion possible — indeed, what made it rational — was that the economy was growing so quickly. But the factories weren't the primary source of growth; they were merely supplying the projects that made growth possible. Steel, cement, glass, and construction machinery were all needed because China was urbanizing. But just as China has built excess factories, so has its urbanization become excessive. The risk is that an industrial sector that's already in poor financial health stands to suffer further if China's ability to continue building more and more comes to a halt.

3

GHOST CITIES

WHEN ZHANG JINGQIANG became mayor, in 2005, Tieling was the poorest city in Liaoning Province. A graying, former Ming-dynasty garrison town of about 440,000 people in the country's frigid northeast, it was part of China's rust belt, but large-scale industrialization had long ago bypassed the city. Tieling — which means "iron ridge" — had some coal mines and steel furnaces, but its economy was mainly built on the farms that raised corn, soybeans, and peanuts at the city limits.

Zhang wasn't a highflier. A lean but jowly man with a left-to-right comb-over, he'd spent his entire public-service career in Liaoning, and this was to be his last posting before mandatory retirement, at age sixty. But a few years after becoming mayor, Zhang found himself enjoying a rare moment in the national spotlight for the way he'd turned around the fortunes of his backwater town.

"Tieling has become . . . a city that you visit and don't want to leave," Zhang boasted with great pride at the peak of his success, in 2010. Soon after becoming mayor, Zhang rolled out a fifteen-year plan to reinvigorate Tieling, the centerpiece of which called for massive investment in new infrastructure fifteen kilometers southwest of the city. There, he built Tieling a twin: Tieling New City. It could well be one of the most pleasant cities in China. New Tieling was envisioned as a city-sized Chinese garden that incorporated elements of feng shui, an ancient Chinese philosophy that seeks harmony with the environment. An ornamental lake was dug in the city's south, and the excavated soil was used to build a hill at the city's northern limit, topped with a carefully curated rock garden. A winding tree-lined canal was dug from the lake through the future city to a wetland that keeps the new Tieling separated from the old.

The wetland — a kind of marsh, with banks of reeds poking up out of the shallow water — had shrunk over time to make way for agriculture, and what remained was used by the old city as a dumping ground for raw sewage. Under Zhang's direction, the wetland was expanded to its original size, a sewage-treatment plant was built, a nearby river was redirected to flush the ecosystem with fresh water, and flora was planted to naturally filter pollutants. The number of migratory birds using the wetland as a stopping-off point on their annual summer flight to Siberia had declined since the 1970s, but after Zhang's restoration they had started to return.

But, for all that Mayor Zhang may have wanted to believe he had built a city that no one would want to leave, the reality is that no one actually came. "People have been buying units in Tieling, but they don't want to live there," said Hu Jie, the landscape architect who designed Zhang's new city, as we sat in a Starbucks in Beijing. "In ten to twenty years, Tieling could be a good development, but only if you can manage to bring businesses in."

I first visited New Tieling early in 2013. The government had moved its offices from the old city to the new part so that during daylight hours there were bureaucrats milling about. But come dusk, when the commuters finished work and headed home, the city emptied. The lights in countless row after row of apartment buildings remained off. The city itself was lit up like a fun park, with apartment towers illuminated with spotlights and government buildings flashing with colored LEDs, but no one was there to appreciate the spectacle other than bored traffic cops. As we trudged along outside rows of empty shop fronts, the only footprints in the early spring snow were my colleague's and my own.

In most parts of the world, a ghost town is a place where the community simply got up and left. The American West is dotted with them, places that sprang up overnight with the California gold rush and then dwindled just as quickly as the ore ran out and the miners moved on. Russia has thousands of what are known as "dead towns," places that hollowed out with the end of the Soviet Union either because the military left or because state support for industries in far corners of the empire dried up.

In China, however, the idea of a ghost town has been turned on its head. Dotting the Chinese landscape are places that weren't abandoned but rather barely had any population in the first place. And to call them towns doesn't do justice to their scale. A city of villas and apartment buildings that were built to one day accommodate a million people rises from the Inner Mongolian steppe, but it remains largely empty years after a local financial crisis ended the construction boom. A city of a few dozen office towers that bills itself as China's Manhattan sits pretty much empty on the outskirts of Tianjin. An ecocity built on reclaimed land dredged from the sea is a shell looking over the heavily polluted Bay of Bohai, the roofs of the villas built on its outskirts having been blown off by the wind.

There are no hard-and-fast rules that define what makes a ghost city, but their common characteristic is not that they're entirely empty — local planning agencies almost always have a way of getting at least some people to move in — but that the population is a mere fraction of what they were built for. The government doesn't publish numbers on housing vacancy rates, so it's difficult to know just how many there are. The most scientific estimate comes from researchers at Baidu — China's Google — who were able to track usage of the company's search engine to calculate the density of people living in residential areas. That was a vast improvement on the previous methodology, which involved journalists visiting likely candidate cities at dusk to count the number of lights on in apartment windows. In any event, the Baidu researchers determined there were at least fifty ghost cities around the country.

Regardless of how many there are, ghost cities are routinely dismissed by economists as not relevant to China's economic big picture. After all, it is argued, they're the product of unconnected local planning decisions, and despite their proliferation, the national economy hasn't seemed to suffer for it. But to think of them as simply a glitch in the matrix is wrong. They're part of the code, and they represent how the urbanization process has been hijacked by local governments in their blind and endless pursuit of growth.

Few places have handled rapid urbanization as well as China. It's avoided the favelas and shantytowns that plague other developing nations, despite having needed to accommodate the greatest migration in human history. Between 2000 and 2015 alone, more than 270 million people — equivalent to the combined population of Germany, France, the United Kingdom, and Spain — have moved from the countryside to China's cities. The consulting firm McKinsey forecasts that by 2030, China will have an urban population of 1 billion, up from about 730 million in 2013. After having been a rural society and economy for millennia, China is on track to achieve in just fifty years a level of urbanization that took the United States a full century.

The key to China's success lies in the scale and speed at which it's been able to build infrastructure. The sort of growth China has enjoyed for three decades could too easily have been brought to a shuddering halt if the construction of new roads, ports, and power plants hadn't been able to keep up with what the economy needed, as has been the case in India and Brazil. It's hard to imagine that Shanghai, a city without even one subway line twenty years ago, could have absorbed the 10 million people it's added in that time without building the world's longest subway system, one which is almost 60% bigger than New York's. There was a time when China's power grid couldn't keep up with the demands of the economy, so much so that some parts of the country suffered from rolling brownouts. By 2012, the country was opening three new power plants a week. People, freight, and coal once had to compete for space on the country's railroads — with people routinely losing out — but China has since spent hundreds of billions of yuan building a high-speed rail network from scratch, an investment that was once dismissed as an expensive boondoggle but is today celebrated globally as the crown jewel of China's transportation system.

China will unquestionably need even more infrastructure if it's to accommodate all the additional migrants McKinsey anticipates. But just because China needs things that haven't yet been built, that doesn't mean that everything that gets built is truly needed. Even the casual observer driving around China can see that something is wrong. You can see it in the industrial parks that are empty except for a small handful of factories, and in the government buildings that are so large it seems impossible that they will ever fill in with civil servants, and in the airports that only sporadically host an arriving plane, and in the glut of exhibition centers and museums that every town seems compelled to build.

Urbanization — the construction of new housing and infrastructure — has been the driving force behind the Chinese economy for close to two decades. It has created demand for massive volumes of steel, cement, and glass; for the ships that bring iron ore from overseas; for the power plants and coal mines needed by the steel mills; and for the machinery that is needed on construction sites. But this constant and nonstop building has become an addiction for local governments. It's a way of stimulating the local economy and maintaining growth, all loosely justified by the needs of migrants. The World Bank calls urbanization an "enabling parallel [process] in rapid growth"; in other words, urbanization can support growth, but it can't drive it. China has put the cart before the horse, and the result is waste on an epic scale. Tieling's story is one of how ambition and a lack of restraint by local governments, masquerading as planning for the future, have laid the foundation for financial problems that have been replicated throughout China — and how the promise of further migration isn't going to fix them.

In 2010, Mayor Zhang's plan for Tieling must have seemed like a success. For a time, Tieling had the fastest-growing economy of any city in Liaoning, driven by the sheer amount of construction required to build an entirely new city. Tax revenue soared on the back of all the business created for developers, construction companies, and their suppliers. The city won an award from the UN for building affordable housing. And New Tieling had been selected as the only city to be put on display inside China's pavilion at Shanghai's 2010 World Expo, an event that aimed to re-create the prestige of the world fairs of the 1950s and 1960s.

The Expo, themed "Better City, Better Life," was about showcasing ways to improve China's generally soulless, polluted, and blandly similar cities, a phenomenon widely lamented as "one thousand cities, one face." What earned New Tieling national attention was Zhang's radical decision to prioritize livability over utilitarian, cookie-cutter urbanization.

Zhang's concern with the urban environment was part of a deliberate strategy. If people liked living there, so the thinking went, then that would encourage migrants to settle there, particularly the more affluent kind who might be looking for a second apartment for weekend getaways. Only an hour's drive from Shenyang, the polluted provincial capital, Tieling, as Zhang spoke of it, would become "Shenyang's back-yard."

To realize the dream, Zhang drafted Hu, the landscape architect. Hu felt that Chinese cities had lost their distinctiveness. He wanted to make them more uniquely Chinese by incorporating elements of classical art, like mountains and running water. Hu had studied and worked in the United States for fifteen years, but he had returned to Beijing to help with the face-lift that city was undergoing in prepara-tion for the 2008 Olympics. Hu was building a park twice the size of New York's Central Park, a little to the north of the main Olympic fa-cilities. After visiting Beijing in 2007, Zhang grilled Hu on every aspect of his Olympic Forest Park, from the lake shaped like a dragon, to the gray water used to feed the ecosystem. Zhang then asked the expatriate landscaper to apply his vision to Tieling.

That vision hasn't come cheap. Since the first wave of development — which included building a water-treatment plant, a power substa-tion, a central heating plant, and the planting of almost two hundred thousand trees — the spending has been unrelenting. Today, hulking, quasi-brutalist government office buildings made from concrete and glass line one side of the lake, overlooking a town square dotted with giant-sized red lanterns. There are two major high schools and a vo-cational-training center; a tennis center, built for the 2013 National Games — a kind of low-rent, domestic Olympics — hosted by Shen-yang, which outsourced the event; two glass office towers for the local banks, which have their own lake-front location; a tram line that goes from downtown out to a nearby logistics park; and a high-speed rail station that connects the city with the rest of China's northeast.

Initially, the frenetic investment paid off. Tieling outstripped the national economy for years, peaking in 2007, when it grew by 20.8%, which was fast enough for the local economy to double in size within three and a half years, and significantly faster than the 13% growth for

China as a whole. But the growth was built entirely on public works that weren't generating any income.

The city government first acknowledged that something was wrong in 2013, when tax revenue fell by 10%. The following year, tax receipts fell a further 15%. By 2015, the Tieling economy was barely growing at all. The city — or, specifically, city-owned companies — had borrowed heavily and now didn't have the resources to repay what it had borrowed. For local officials, the flip side of what they'd done was starting to sink in. "The government debt burden is heavy," the municipality said in its 2015 state-of-the-city report. "It seriously lacks resources to repay interest and principal, and the repayment burden is immense."

BIG-CITY DREAMS

Most countries don't build their cities from scratch except under special circumstances. Australia built Canberra because Sydney and Melbourne couldn't decide between them which should be the capital. Brasília was built so that Brazil's political representatives could meet in the center of the country. The Myanmar military junta decided that building Naypyidaw was a good idea because it wanted a more defensible capital removed from politically disruptive students and monks. China is currently building its own version, albeit in reverse. Rather than building a new capital, it's trying to deal with overcrowding in Beijing by building an overflow city — Xiongan — where state-owned firms and organizations that don't really need to be in Beijing will be instructed to move. The advantage of building capital cities from scratch — or even a place like Xiongan — is that when they're finished, there is a population of bureaucrats ready to move in. But to build a city without a captive and waiting population — one that's dependent on the choices of thousands of individual families and businesses — is a leap of faith that few countries are willing to take, particularly given the massive financial resources involved.

Over the last decade, building new cities — and adding entire new "districts" to the outskirts of existing cities — has become business as usual in China. A survey of twelve provinces in 2013 by the China Center for Urban Development, an in-house think tank for the central government's National Development and Reform Commission, found that the capital cities of those provinces were each building an average of 4.6 new districts (which are often indistinguishable in size and ambition from new cities) or new cities in their immediate orbit. The sample's 144 prefecture-level cities (China has more than three hundred prefectures, which are the next administrative level down from provinces) were building, on average, 1.5 each. And the center found that many new cities and new districts — a jumble of central business districts, resort strips, ecocities, and administrative zones — were being built to house populations "basically equal" in size to the original cities they were attached to.

It sometimes feels as though the basic laws of economics are suspended inside China. Anywhere else in the world, building cities from scratch simply as a matter of course would seem to defy common sense. Yet China has a surprisingly robust track record of building them and then filling them, assuming you're not in a hurry.

Shanghai was one of the first cities to build a new district, turning a stretch of paddy fields across the river to the east into a central business district with a skyline so dense and futuristic that it's been likened to the city portrayed in *Blade Runner*. But Pudong — literally "East Riverside" — got off to a shaky start. Deng Xiaoping, China's supreme leader, visited in 1991 to give the project his blessing and declared that Pudong's future would lie with financial services at a time when China's financial sector was still finding its feet after decades of Maoism. When U.S. economist Milton Friedman visited seven years later, he described Pudong's largely empty office towers and high-rises as "a statist monument for a dead pharaoh on the level of the pyramids." Prodded and cajoled by the Shanghai government into opening offices there, some foreign businesses rented space in Pudong, installed a phone line and a receptionist, and then continued to operate as usual back across the river. A local aphorism held that it was better to have a bed in the old city than a room in Pudong.

Today, Shanghai's ambition to rank alongside London, Tokyo, and New York as one of the world's great cities would be greatly diminished were it not for Pudong's skyline. The district has a vibrant nightlife and enviably low office-vacancy rates, and residents even say they like living there (although people elsewhere in the city remain skeptical). For all the naysaying, Pudong is now a vibrant city. It is also an exception to the rule.

Pudong was one of China's very first new districts, but in recent years city building in China has spread to plague proportions. Rather than build incrementally, adding infrastructure if and when it becomes necessary, officials across the country have, herdlike, embraced the if-you-build-it-they-will-come model of urban planning. Ubiquitous as you hit the city limits of towns everywhere, new cities and districts come in all shapes and forms. In Luoyang, an industrial town in Henan Province, the new city — a cluster of large government buildings and office towers topped with the logos of state firms — is built around a lake that draws huge crowds of locals in summer for a laser show performed nightly to a recording of *Carmina Burana*. Outside of Lushan, a town in western Sichuan that was hit by an earthquake in 2013, an entirely new tourist district — built loosely in the area's traditional architectural style — has taken form around a huge exhibition center dedicated to showcasing ebony, a type of wood that grows locally. In Qufu, the birthplace of Confucius, a new district caters to resurgent interest in the sage, with exhibition and conference centers and dozens of new apartment towers.

All this construction is a preemptive strike of sorts, a way for cities and towns to accommodate their share of future migrants before they're inundated. But the scale and cost involved are completely out of proportion to the likely scale of migration. According to Qiao Runling, the deputy head of the China Center for Urban Development, in 2013, plans for new cities and new districts were sufficient to house about 3.4 billion people, *more than twice* China's total population. Moreover, China has already passed the peak of migration. While plenty more people are expected to migrate, the *pace* of internal migration has been slowing since mid-2010. Yet local governments' enthusiasm for construction still hasn't cooled at all. The *People's Daily* warned in an opinion column that such mindless expansion comes at a cost:

> [At first] China's new cities and new zones . . . like Shenzhen and Shanghai's Pudong . . . were a node of economic growth . . . However, the new cities and new zones that are now blooming everywhere . . . are moving in the opposite direction . . .
>
> They create massive financial waste, they burden local government with heavy debt, and they make the "development disease" of relying on investment to drive the economy worse and worse.

BETTER LIVING THROUGH URBANIZATION

Historically, China treated urbanization as something to be avoided. Soon after taking control of the country, in 1949, the Communists took the system of household registration that had been around since imperial times and redesigned it such that it tied people to one lo-cation for life. Under what was labeled the *hukou* system, a person, once registered in a certain place, be it village, town, or city, had little scope to move anywhere else. The fear was that, if given the choice, people would migrate from the countryside in great numbers, putting pressure on urban resources and threatening stability. In 1978, on the eve of economic reform, only about 18% of Chinese lived in urban areas.

As China's export machine slipped into gear in the 1990s, migrants moved in ever greater numbers to the cities, attracted by factory jobs and tolerated by officials who recognized that industrialization and ur-banization went hand in hand. Still, the *hukou* system was kept in place as a prophylactic against what China's leaders sometimes referred to as "urban diseases."

"When I was in Rio and São Paulo, I was able to look down and see vast, vast slums. In South Africa, some cities are surrounded by stretches of tin shacks," said President Jiang Zemin in 2001, at a time when about 38% of Chinese were living in cities. "This has created great social problems." In contrast, China made it difficult for migrant work-ers to put down roots in the cities. They had to leave if they couldn't find work, and if they wanted to access public services like health and education, they had to return home. Still, Jiang saw urbanization as a way to help reduce rural poverty by getting people out of agriculture. Industrial jobs pay better than farming, but those jobs cluster in cit-ies. If China was to become more prosperous, then the cities had to accommodate migrants. "Reducing the rural population is something that we can't avoid," he said.

When Li Keqiang became China's premier, early in 2013, more than half the country was living in urban areas. Since Jiang, leaders had often spoken of how China needed to urbanize. Li had gone a step further, building his career around that idea, beginning with the thesis he wrote in 1991 for his economics doctorate, in which he argued that faster urbanization could help support what was then the early stages of China's industrialization. He believed not only that urbanization had to go hand in hand with industrialization and agricultural modernization — the former creates the jobs that pull migrants into cities, and the latter creates migrants by pushing people off farms that no longer need them — but also that it could be an essential part of development, not just something that gets dragged along in its wake. He started to apply his ideas in the late 1990s, when he was promoted to party secretary, first of Henan and then of Liaoning, where he moved in 2004. In 2005, he visited Tieling. "Tieling's population . . . is too small. You need to develop into a big city, build yourself into a regional center, and use the city to develop the surrounding rural areas," he said during his tour. "Expanding the size of the city is an important step in Tieling's development, and the province should support it."

With almost half a million people, in absolute terms the original Tieling wasn't exactly small. However, its reliance on agriculture meant that, relative to the rest of the province, a disproportionately large number of people lived in the surrounding countryside. Tieling's officials took Li's comments to heart. After he left, they set about designing their fifteen-year plan. They presented it to Li the next year.

"The concept is sound, it's innovative, it's unique, and it's in line with the future direction of urban development," the future premier said, signing off. According to the plan, by 2010, the new city would have 60,000 residents. By 2020, that number would increase to 200,000. Mayor Zhang spoke of its one day having a million inhabitants. Within Liaoning, the plan was soon being touted as the Tieling Model. Other towns in the province were exhorted to learn from the approach.

At least at first, seeding the city with people proved relatively easy. But when I first visited Tieling, many of the people living there weren't residents by choice. Among the first residents I saw were two dozen men and women with weathered and deeply grooved faces who were busy shoveling snow from the square in front of the main government buildings. Some wore fluorescent-orange workers' vests as they moved back and forth in orderly lines, clearing the otherwise empty square. They were the land's original inhabitants, farmers who once grew rice where now the city stood. The region's frigid weather meant that rice grew so slowly that they only ever reaped one harvest a year, unlike in the south, where two is the norm; but at least, as farmers, they weren't dependent on anyone. When they moved in as the new city's first residents, there wasn't even a convenience store where they could buy food. Without any way to support themselves, they were put to work by the city, sweeping the streets and clearing snow.

The government also managed to arrange for "instant tenants" by closing down schools in the old city and the surrounding county and reopening them in New Tieling. Relative to the civilian population, there was now a disproportionately large number of students wandering around in their blue-and-white polyester uniforms. One elderly resident described New Tieling as "the city of children." In the countryside, people complained that middle school students now boarding at the new schools were undersupervised, and villagers gossiped about teenage pregnancies and high school dropouts. Meanwhile, rounding out the roster of insta-tenants, government officials were encouraged to move into the new city and were given subsidies to buy apartments near their new offices, which had been relocated from the old city.

Such measures amounted to little more than shuffling around Tieling's existing population. For the new city to be a success, it needed to do more than just siphon people from Old Tieling. It needed migrants, and that required jobs. A logistics park in the suburbs was one of Tieling's great hopes for generating employment; it was supposed to turn Tieling into a trading hub for China's northeast. It's best described as a drive-in wholesale market. The first time I visited the park, its identical orange-colored blocks of three-story buildings, divided by narrow streets and broad avenues, were near empty. "Where are the people? There's no one here," said Bo Yuquan, a Tieling native who had started a flooring store in the park when it first opened. Now, he said he wished he'd opened a store in the old city instead. "I'll be out of business soon. My staff and I are discussing moving to Beijing to find work."

When I went back two years later, the park was just as empty but had doubled in size, with a new section added for soft commodities. I got to talking with Li Peng, a young man who had moved with his wife from Anhui in 2010. They were living above their low-end hardware store with their three-year-old son. Li had originally rented another storefront but had moved as the park's thinly spread businesses started moving closer together so that it was easier for customers to find them. Some wings of the park, like the clothing section, had emptied out altogether. "If anything, business has actually gotten worse over the last few years," Li said.

The city fathers had also hoped to build a financial sector, providing back-end services like data storage to banks and insurance companies that were headquartered in bigger cities. A purpose-built development park was supposed to employ more than fifteen thousand people by the end of 2013. By 2015, it had only two companies, the larger of which employed only twenty people.

Meanwhile, Tieling's most creative employment initiative was to build a Christianity-themed fun park, the brainchild of a Hong Kong property developer and devout Christian, but seemingly an odd choice for a city with no Christian heritage. The park was to be built around dramatizations of Bible stories like Noah's Ark and Moses leaving Egypt. Tieling officials even took fact-finding missions to Israel. International tourists were expected to flock from nearby South Korea, Japan, and Russia. But the approvals needed from the higher levels of government never came through — plans to include a church may have made it too sensitive — and when Mayor Zhang retired, the project lost its spiritual leader. When I last visited, the city was awaiting the completion of its consolation prize, a water park that will include a snorkeling pool and what promoters claimed will be China's first surf machine, a curious choice given that the lakes in the region freeze over for at least four months of the year.

One might think that the failure to create employment and attract migrants anywhere near the scale that the city anticipated would prompt a reassessment of the building plan. Instead, the construction of public works continued. Hu Jie, the landscaper, said that after Mayor Zhang stepped down, in 2011, the incoming mayor asked if Hu had any thoughts on how to help fill the city with people. Hu said that he didn't. But rather than cut his losses, the new mayor doubled down and went looking for more things to build. He made plans to spend a further $1.3 billion on new projects, including an art gallery, gymnasium, and indoor swimming pool.

Today, Hu runs a design institute at Tsinghua University. He has short spiky hair that's graying around the temples, and, unusual for Chinese men of his generation, he smiles in photos, presumably a legacy of his time in the United States, where he designed Legoland in California and redeveloped the Indianapolis waterfront. Hu said that in China, mayoral plans for city expansion are heavily influenced by political considerations. "A mayor has only five years in the role, but it might take twenty years to make this new city work," said Hu. "And when a new mayor comes in, he brings his own agenda and makes his own plans . . . Local governments push these new developments very fast, but the money and people flow in only very slowly," he told me.

Upon becoming premier, in 2012, Li Keqiang initially heralded urbanization as something that could help take up the slack as other parts of the economy slowed, but he soon found himself upbraiding local officials for using urbanization to justify their construction schemes. "People need to be at the core of urbanization," said Li, exasperated. "Urbanization is not about land. It's not about buildings. It's about people."

The mayors of some of China's biggest cities have been routinely derided by local communities for their massive and unrelenting public-works programs. The former mayor of Wuhan was given the nickname Mr. Dig Dig for a building agenda that included a new financial district, two new airports, and 140 kilometers of subway line. Li Chuncheng, former mayor of Chengdu, was popularly known as Li Chaicheng, which means "Li Tears Down the City," for his penchant for demolishing old communities to make way for roads and expensive apartments. And Nanjing's former mayor Ji Jianye was known as Bulldozer Ji, earning public opprobrium for ripping up hundreds of beloved plane trees that lined the city's boulevards in order to make way for the subway.

What makes the building frenzy so intractable is that, first and foremost, it's about money. Bulldozer Ji and Li Tears Down the City are now in jail for corruption, in part for shady dealings with property developers and construction companies. Corruption is endemic throughout China's bureaucracy, but the huge amount of funds that have gone into construction has made the industry particularly ripe for graft. Local-level officials are sometimes caught with dozens of apartments hidden under the names of family and friends, kickbacks that they've received from developers.

Although jailing mayors might make everyone think twice about accepting bribes, it doesn't do much to dilute local governments' desire to build. When Wuhan's Mr. Dig Dig took over from imprisoned Li Tears Down the City in Chengdu, he continued to build just as aggressively as his predecessor. For local officials needing to generate growth and tax revenue, the easiest and most reliable way to do that is through the construction of public works. That gives them reason to build quickly, on a grandiose scale, and in excess of what is actually needed.

Moreover, the political cycle means that the architects of such waste seldom have to take responsibility. City leaders get five years in the role and are often moved onward or upward before then, giving them far too little time to deal with the fallout of misguided investments. They can borrow without having to worry about being responsible for repaying the debt. Officials use new cities to burnish their credentials; "then, when the new city becomes an awful mess . . . the officials [have moved on and] are not liable for their mistakes," said Li Tie, the head of the China Center for Urban Development. "No wonder government officials are so passionate about building new cities."

That leaves their successors to make it work — and sometimes they do. Zhengzhou, the biggest city in Henan Province, started building a new district in the early 2000s as part of a plan to double the city's population — another project that had Li Keqiang's blessing. Zhengzhou, which was best known as a railway hub, spent tens of billions of dollars on the new district, building a dancing fountain, Italian-marble-clad conference hall, and pagoda-shaped skyscraper. In 2013, Lesley Stahl from *60 Minutes* visited the city for a story on China's property bubble. Dressed in a puffer jacket and fluffy black ear warmers, she walked along empty streets, wandered among villagers who were making way for the city's further expansion, and toured a shopping center that still didn't have any tenants three years after construction had finished. "We found what they call a 'ghost city' of new towers with no residents, desolate condos and vacant subdivisions uninhabited for miles, and miles, and miles, and miles of empty apartments," she said in a voiceover.

But by the time it was featured on U.S. television, Zhengzhou's new district was already filling up. The turning point came when Foxconn, the Taiwanese company that manufactures products for Apple, decided to build a factory there. The plant produces almost all of the world's iPhones and employs 350,000 people.

But the truth is, Zhengzhou's success wasn't cheap and it's not easy to replicate. The city provided Foxconn with a $250 million loan; it lowered the amount Foxconn was required to contribute toward social security funding by up to $100 million a year; it built new power generators; it contributed $1.5 billion to the construction of the factory and dormitory housing; it provided subsidies to reduce shipping costs and to reduce the cost of power by 5%; and it eliminated corporate tax and VAT for the first five years, to be followed by tax rates of only half the usual level for the next five years. The payoff has come from other businesses following in Foxconn's wake, most notably other cell-phone makers. By one estimate, one out of every eight smartphones produced globally is now made in Zhengzhou. Workers from Henan Province who had once gone farther afield for jobs now move to the city instead.

Zhengzhou's experience isn't a sign that China's ghost cities are merely a fleeting phenomenon, the result of overly exuberant forward planning. Rather, it's evidence of just how difficult and expensive it is to make a ghost city work. Moreover, any city trying to replicate Zhengzhou's success today will find it far more difficult. Exports once drove urbanization in China's east, with cities sprouting up dedicated to producing umbrellas, zippers, underwear, and dozens of other consumer goods, but since the global financial crisis, Chinese exports haven't generated the growth they once did. With the cost of labor rising in China, many manufacturing firms are now starting to move to cheaper locations overseas. Foxconn, which employs a million people in China, has plans for a massive expansion of operations — in India. And with heavy industry riddled with overcapacity in China, luring state firms to come and build new steel mills or paper plants is not the answer.

Moreover, not only do China's smaller cities face the challenge of creating new jobs to attract people, but many of these cities are already struggling to hold on to their existing population. Based on data from China's 2010 census, Credit Suisse found that of 287 Chinese cities for which numbers were available, about two-thirds, mostly smaller urban centers, had fewer residents than people registered to live there. Given that people are typically registered where they were born, that means people were leaving China's smaller cities and heading for the bigger cities, where there are greater financial opportunities and a more interesting lifestyle.

I revisited New Tieling almost three years after my first trip. I was met at the train station by the same taxi driver who had driven my colleague and me around the first time. Not much had changed, he said, although his wife had a new job. She'd previously worked as a building manager for what had been the most well occupied housing development in the new city, but there were so few people living there that the only thing that kept her busy was the constant complaints from tenants about how badly constructed their apartments were. She'd recently started work at a different management company, but the development she was posted to was even more empty than the last one.

Nonetheless, New Tieling seemed to have more people than I remembered. Most of the city was still empty, but a new shopping center, inexplicably built to resemble a ship, had a mini fun park on the third floor for children under five that was packed with delighted kids. And the shopping strip that had sprung up around where the farmers had been housed seemed longer and busier than before.

But the actual numbers told another story. Tieling was losing people. At the end of 2012, Tieling's combined cities were home to 441,000 people. Two years later, that number was down to 438,000. The city had planned to add 60,000 by 2010, and 200,000 by 2020.

OUR SUBPRIME MORTGAGE CRISIS

The legacy of Tieling's city-building experiment isn't simply empty buildings. Regardless of how many people move in or leave, the sheer scale of investment that went into creating New Tieling is such that local authorities will likely be crippled by this financial burden for years to come. According to the Chinese press, in 2013, after seven years of construction, Tieling had spent 26 billion yuan ($3.8 billion) building its new city.

To put Tieling's difficulties into context, it's useful to compare it to Raleigh, North Carolina. The towns have similar populations. By mid-2015, Tieling owed almost 7 billion yuan, or $1.1 billion, up from nothing eight years earlier. In the same year, Raleigh had about $1.5 billion in debt. But Raleigh is one of the fastest-growing cities in the United States. "When people come here, they don't want to leave," the city planning director said in 2014. People are drawn by new jobs in tech, pharma, and finance, and Raleigh expects to add another 150,000 people between 2015 and 2030, a pace similar to what Tieling prepared for. Raleigh has borrowed to upgrade its water and sewage systems, to widen its roads, and to improve its parks, and it has plans to build a light-rail system. But the main difference is that the size of the Raleigh economy is *ten times* that of Tieling.

Tieling's financial problems are replicated throughout China. "In the last two or three years we have been all over the country investigating, and almost every new district has debt problems," said Li Tie, from the planning authority's urbanization think tank, early in 2015. "And the size[s] of the debts aren't small. They far exceeded anything we had imagined."

Foreigners typically look upon China's urbanization achievements with envy. According to the American Society of Engineers, one out of every nine bridges in the United States is structurally deficient, and water mains sustain 240,000 breaks a year. Many states and municipalities are struggling to pay down the debt they ran up during the good times prior to the global financial crisis back in 2008, and they don't have the funds to stop existing infrastructures from crumbling. Meanwhile, China has built the world's biggest high-speed railway network, and new highways crisscross the nation. The world's top architects flock to China to realize their most creative impulses on government-sponsored opera houses, libraries, and office buildings. Yet the perception that China has managed to do all this without financial constraint is a serious illusion. "Debt repayment pressure on some local-government debt is massive, and is a hidden danger," Liao Xiaojun, the director of the Budgetary Affairs Commission for the National People's Congress's standing committee, wrote in an essay in the *People's Daily* late in 2015. "If we let debt risks continue to accumulate, they will be bound to transmit to the financial world, triggering systemic financial risk."

Even worse, China's cities and towns have amassed a mountain of debt in near-record time. At the end of 2008, China's local governments owed about 5.6 trillion yuan in debt. Eight years later, the amount had tripled to 16.2 trillion, or $2.5 trillion. True, that's less than the $3.1 trillion worth of debt that U.S. states and local governments are responsible for, but the U.S. economy is almost 50% larger than China's, and America's governments have spent two hundred years building up to that level. Many of China's local governments simply don't have the resources to repay what they've borrowed, and many will need to borrow even more in order to support growth with further public works. "Local-government debt is our subprime," said Cheng Siwei, an economist and former vice chairman of the Standing Committee of the National People's Congress. "Banks give loans to local governments that don't meet lending standards, the local governments then have trouble repaying the debt, and the banks either roll them over or end up with bad loans."

Beijing isn't blind to the risks. In fact, it's been acutely aware of them since the 1990s, when it banned local governments from borrowing money. Yet local governments have been getting around that rule for almost twenty years by setting up companies that borrow on their behalf. These local-government financing vehicles (LGFVs) have allowed local governments to deliver growth by borrowing money when they weren't supposed to, and have made possible the construction of projects ranging from high-speed railways to decorative fountains and everything in between.

LGFVs were first used in the late 1990s but really took off in 2008, when Beijing turned a blind eye in the interest of stimulating the economy. By one count, there are more than ten thousand LGFVs across the country, owned by provinces, cities, prefectures, and counties. Many are incredibly opaque and massively indebted.

In 2015, it looked as though Beijing had finally managed to get things under control. It overturned the moratorium on local governments' directly borrowing, allowing some to sell bonds in an effort to introduce some degree of transparency to the whole process. And it imposed hard caps on how much local authorities could borrow, both directly and indirectly.

But by mid-2017, it was clear that local government had continued to balloon, as local authorities came up with new ways to evade the caps and avoid Beijing's oversight. In August of that year, Xi Jinping said that local-government borrowing was one of the financial system's two great vulnerabilities (the other was the debt at state-owned firms).

Zhang Jingqiang left Tieling before things started falling apart, segueing into a successful postmayoral career. After stepping down as required in 2011, he became the vice chairman of the China Association of Small and Medium Enterprises, where he has been a champion of small business, railing about the difficulties that private firms have getting loans. The Tieling Model he championed hasn't fared as well. In Liaoning, there are at least three other ghost cities: Dandong, on the North Korean border, where a Ferris wheel and a basketball stadium sit alongside rows of empty apartment buildings; Yingkou, which lies east of Tieling on the coast, where developers hoped holidaymakers would be attracted to the beach despite the area's unforgivingly long winters; and Shenfu, on the outskirts of Shenyang, where planners first built the town monument — a five-hundred-foot steel circle that has been mercilessly lampooned for its passing resemblance to the transdimensional portal on *Stargate* — before starting on the now-abandoned city center.

Zhang's successors have attempted to make the best of a difficult situation. They've tried to stimulate tourism with an annual lantern festival during Chinese New Year. In 2016, the theme was Chinese literature, with ornate lanterns the size of trucks inspired by *Journey to the West* and *Dream of the Red Chamber* arranged around Tieling's human-made hill. But the festival can do only so much for the economy, and old habits die hard. In 2015, the city announced plans to develop a further 550 hectares of land around the wetland, at a cost of 4–5 billion yuan. This time, however, they wanted private investors to pay for it.

Tieling seems to have avoided default because the loans it has taken out from commercial banks have been transferred to the China Development Bank, one of China's policy banks responsible for acting explicitly at the behest of the government. It's a kind of black box where Tieling's financial troubles can be hidden away from public view. Assuming that Beijing can continue to shuffle around local-government debt in a way that allows bad loans to remain hidden, the biggest risk is not that of a financial meltdown but that at some point, local governments will simply no longer have the financial resources to keep on building. Sure, so much of what they've already built is incredibly wasteful, but it's also a vital component of growth. The risk to the economy is that local governments won't be able to fund new projects.

Tieling managed to grow as long as it did because developers were able to keep selling apartments. Even though Tieling is largely empty, much of the housing that fills the city blocks in between government offices, schools, and the tennis center has nonetheless been bought and paid for. Between 2007 and 2013, almost all the newly constructed housing space in both Old and New Tieling — roughly enough space to accommodate the existing population of Tieling once over — was sold. In effect, the lack of migrants from the countryside didn't matter. People bought housing in Tieling anyway — perhaps as an investment, or as a place to retire, or because they thought they'd move there once the city filled up. But at some point, reality took hold and people soured on the idea of buying a home in an empty city. Yet up until the point they stopped buying, the local government remained solvent, because property developers were willing to keep buying more and more land.

In most of the world, infrastructure typically gets paid for in one of two ways. First, it can pay for itself. A road can charge a toll; an airport receives landing fees; a stadium sells tickets. China does some of that. The country is riddled with toll roads — a particular source of public discontent — but not all public works generate revenue. So, to build things like new offices, city streets, and sewers, local governments in most parts of the world raise taxes. But China's local governments don't have the discretion to raise taxes. Moreover, their existing tax base is already stretched thin. But these governments do have a source of funding independent of taxes over which they have total discretion: land. Land lies at the heart of China's investment-led boom — and it's why the country's economic boom is so fragile.

4

ROBBING PETER

OVER THE COURSE of his sixtysomething years, Liang Shulin had spent relatively little time on his farm. For half his life, he'd been a migrant worker, traveling from his village in Hebei for construction jobs as far away as Guangxi Province, in China's southwest. He'd return home for Spring Festival with a loaf of sweet bread as a treat for the three kids he would see once a year. It was his wife who worked the fields, getting help from the children as soon as they were old enough to be of use. The crops they raised earned very little, but the farm was their nest egg, and it was supposed to be the main source of income when Liang retired. Indeed, he was around sixty when he finally grew too old for backbreaking construction work and settled back in the village where his family had lived for more than a century.

Then, a couple of years later, the government took his land.

Home to about seven hundred people, Liang's village is a jumble of six or seven alleyways lined with redbrick homes, located about 110 kilometers southwest of Beijing. Everything in his village is covered by a thin layer of dust that's blown in from the limestone quarries to the north. The area feels a little lost in time. Out by the quarries, modern cement factories coexist alongside abandoned kilns that are built deep into the hills and look as though they've been there for hundreds of years. In the village, people dry corn in mesh bins bolted to their roofs and front porches.

This is not a rich area. Before the expropriation, each person in the village had 1.3 mu (0.2 acres) of land to farm — not much larger than an average suburban lot in the United States — which Liang says could earn a bit more than 1,000 yuan (about $160) a year. His years working away from home had been necessary to put all three of his children through university. The earnings from a field of peanuts — which the family grew, alongside corn, sweet potatoes, and, later, walnuts — didn't cover a third of one child's annual tuition.

The local authorities first came for Liang's land in 2007, taking a small slice of his family's 7 mu to build a primary school. Liang didn't object. Indeed, he felt as though it was his duty to contribute to something that was so clearly in the public interest. But two years later, the local government came back for the rest of his land. This time, the officials couldn't tell Liang and his neighbors exactly what they needed the land for. It was going to be used for a "new city" that would start at the limits of the old city, only five minutes' drive away. The details would be worked out later.

"They just shoved a piece of paper into our hands . . . 'The new city plans already have state approval, and the plan is legal,'" Liang said, paraphrasing the document announcing that his land was being taken. In exchange, Liang and the rest of his village were offered a one-time payment of 50,000 yuan per mu, with no residual income support or subsidies afterward. Compensation for Liang's 7 mu wasn't even enough to buy one of the 80-square-meter units that were eventually built on his land. Still, most of Liang's neighbors immediately acquiesced and even welcomed the compensation as a windfall, using their payout money to buy the Hyundai and Great Wall sedans that now clog the village's narrow streets.

But Liang protested the expropriations and never accepted the money. He holds that the government didn't go through the proper procedures and that the land was seized illegally. "Land is the lifeblood of China's masses," he wrote in a letter appealing for help from higher levels of government. "Now we have lost our land and any security in our existence."

Land expropriations have been the single greatest source of popular unrest in China this century. Entire villages have rioted against their land being taken by the government. Others have barricaded their land to stop it from being developed. Villagers have even set themselves alight to protest land seizures, and some have died in acts of arson committed by those trying to force them to move. Developers have teamed up with thugs to intimidate farmers into submission. Farmers have woken to find that their land had been salted and would no longer grow anything. And families that have refused to vacate their homes have sometimes seen construction commence anyway, their houses left perching perilously on narrow plinths of rock after the excavators started digging the foundations of the new development around them.

China's farmers have a tenuous claim over the land they cultivate. All rural land belongs to the village collective. Farmers get to use it under thirty-year leases that are designed to prevent avaricious village chieftains from arbitrarily redistributing land in favor of their own family and friends. However, leases offer no protection against governmental officials the next level up, who have the authority to acquire village land and rezone it. Local governments are supposed to do so only if it's in the public interest, but the law doesn't define that term, and consequently the public interest has been interpreted so broadly as to encompass ornamental lakes, golf courses, and amusement parks.

The authority to redistribute land is the linchpin of the local governments' development model. It allows them to seize the land needed for public-works projects that stimulate growth, to create the industrial parks they give away as subsidies to attract investment, and to borrow from banks that are willing to accept land as collateral. But most importantly, the governments need the land in order to sell it, thereby generating the funds that make everything else possible.

The People's Republic has never shied away from taking the people's land. Millions of its citizens have been moved to make way for gargantuan infrastructure projects like the Three Gorges Dam — the world's largest hydroelectric power plant — and the South–North Water Diversion project — three canals built to divert water from the Yangtze River to the water-scarce northern provinces. Selling land, however, represents a major ideological detour.

For all the compromises the Party has made in reconciling itself with the trappings of capitalism, such as setting up stock markets and allowing entrepreneurs to become Party members, it remains deeply uneasy about private ownership of land. All land in China is owned by some state organ, and technically none of it is for sale. However, in 1988, the Party changed the constitution so that the right to use the land (but not to own it) could be bought and sold under long-term leases. Today, developers get to lease land zoned for residential use from the state for seventy years, and commercial land for fifty years. (Generally speaking, no one expects land to revert to the government at the end of a lease, and for simplicity's sake I refer to "leases" as "sales" throughout this book.) At its heart, this system allows China's Communists to hold on to the traditional principle that all land is collectively owned by the people. But the constitutional change was a clever compromise that allowed the government to turn land into cash when, less than a decade into the reform period that followed the ascent of Deng Xiaoping as supreme leader, the Party found that it didn't have the funds it needed to march the economy into modernity.

"During the early days of reform, the problem in attracting foreigners to open factories and businesses was that our infrastructure was not good enough," Zhao Ziyang, China's former premier and Deng's chief lieutenant, wrote in his memoirs. "We had no funds to build roads for cities or to bring in water and electricity." Zhao, a liberal reformer who was removed from his post after the Tiananmen massacre in 1989, said a Hong Kong property developer introduced him to the idea of land finance when Zhao mentioned that he just couldn't find the funds for urban development. "He asked me, 'If you have land, how can you not have money?'" Zhao wrote. "I thought this was a strange comment. Having land was one issue; a lack of funds was another. What did the one have to do with the other?"

The concept may have been new to the CCP, but land has been used as a source of finance for centuries. The model of land finance adopted by China most closely resembles that used by Baron Haussmann, who, in the mid-nineteenth century, transformed Paris into the City of Light. Haussmann started by exercising eminent domain over the slums in the heart of Paris, which he tore down, replacing warrens of narrow alleys with what have become the city's trademark boulevards. But, in addition to taking the land needed to lay roads, Haussmann also expropriated the land to either side. Once the roads were built and water and gas mains and sewers installed, the land that lined the boulevards leaped in value and was sold to developers at prices well above what the city paid to the original residents. The money from land sales helped fund new town-hall buildings, parks, railway stations, and a viaduct that brought in fresh water from far outside the city.

In China, local authorities have similarly sold urban land, tearing down old apartments and government buildings to make way for progress. But to accommodate expanding cities, they've also seized a huge amount of agricultural land, which, once it's been rezoned for housing or retail and connected to utilities, is then routinely sold for ten times what they paid out to farmers in compensation.

Estimates of just how many Chinese have had their land taken or their houses demolished range as high as 65 million over a decade, roughly equivalent to the entire population of the United Kingdom.

But for all the pain this has caused, land expropriations have been an absolute boon for local governments. From 2009 to 2015, the seven years following the global financial crisis, China's governments collected 22.01 trillion yuan just from selling land. That's comparable to selling all the land in Manhattan two and a half times over. Nationally, land sales in China account for roughly a third of all fiscal revenue. That would be the equivalent of the U.S. Congress selling enough land each year to cover the military budget and most of the spending on Social Security.

This land money has made it possible for China to transform its infrastructure from something that was retarding growth in Zhao's time to something that is the envy of the world. Foreigners often look upon this transformation as a sign of the superiority of China's economic system, when in fact it was made possible solely by the one-time privatization of a state asset. Land has allowed the construction of projects that would have been impossible if the financial burden had fallen upon the Chinese taxpayers. But it's a privilege that has been abused by local governments that treat land finance as though it's free money. They've built whatever they wanted — subways, airports, new cities and districts — without reference to any underlying need, and without financial consequence. And even worse, they've become addicted to it. In 2014 alone, local governments raised thirty-one times more money from land sales than they did in 2001. For cities hemmed in by mountains or the ocean, the greatest fear was that they'd run out of land to sell. Consequently, when there's been no more land to take from villagers, the government has now created more by leveling hills and reclaiming it from the sea.

"If the land markets cool, land prices drop and the volume of land sales fall, not only will the funding of some projects experience difficulties, but it will likely produce financial crises," Ba Shusong, one of China's most influential economists, wrote in the *People's Daily* late in 2013. For local authorities to assume they could go on selling land indefinitely was sheer folly, particularly as the land available for sale moved farther and farther away from city centers. New cities and new districts are an attempt to get around this problem. Moving schools and government buildings out to a new city frees up valuable land in the center of the old city that can be resold for far more than what newly expropriated land on the city's periphery can fetch.

Land sales have been on a roller coaster in recent years, with sales revenue falling 22% in 2015 and then rising almost 20% in 2016. As yet, there haven't been any major financial crises as Ba predicted. No one has defaulted, and no one is likely to — bad loans can always be hidden away in the state financial system. But fallout on the economy will be harder to avoid.

Land sales helped stimulate the economy by funding an increase in public works in the wake of the global financial crisis. But stimulus is supposed to be a temporary measure. Once an economy returns to normal, you stop stimulating. But China's stimulus never stopped. Massive land sales and correspondingly large public works have become pretty much business as usual. Hence, as the economy slows, a fall in land sales will compound the slowdown. What was once a stimulus threatens to become a diuretic.

Of course, all will be well if land sales remain sufficiently robust. That seems increasingly unlikely, however. At the heart of the problem is the thing that made land finance such a success in the first place: housing.

THE PEASANTS' RICE BOWL

Construction began on a portion of Liang's land roughly a year after it was taken. A cement company had acquired part of it on the grounds that it needed to build accommodation for workers at its plant, which was located out by the quarries. Excavators arrived accompanied by between thirty and forty police; the police were insurance to prevent a minor insurrection or pitchfork rebellion from breaking out. (In a later dispute, neighboring villagers would use their cars to build a cordon around their fields to prevent construction equipment from commencing work.) Liang says he tried to force his way onto his land to stop the machines but was restrained by the police. His son — the village's doctor and a Communist Party member — tried as well but was bundled into a police van and locked up for ten days. He was warned he'd be sent to a labor camp if he tried something like that again. Construction went ahead. Meanwhile, the bulk of Liang's land remained empty — the cement company had acquired only a small slice — and it would stay that way for another three years. "It's fairly obvious that they were waiting for the price to rise even higher before they sold the land," Liang said of the local authorities. "It's a serious waste of state resources, and yet it doesn't constitute a crime."

The land remained idle for so long that Liang started farming it again. When it was eventually sold, to a property developer, the new owner tried to assert his rights by dumping rubble on the land in order to make it unusable for agriculture. Liang cleared it and planted walnut trees. At the end of 2012, the developer sent forklifts to rip out the trees. Liang then returned to plant new saplings. His eldest daughter was temporarily suspended from her job as a high school teacher in the city as punishment for her father's intransigence, and was told she would be reassigned to a remote school in the countryside if she didn't get him to fall in line. Her father didn't budge, but she was eventually reinstated anyway. Finally, almost four years after Liang had his land taken, the developer began construction.

On March 23, 2013, workmen began digging the foundations of what would become a complex of sixteen 18-story apartment towers.

When Liang's son saw them, he jumped on his electric bike and raced out to the fields to try to salvage what he could of the walnut saplings. But whereas last time the construction workers had been accompanied by police and local officials, this time the developer hired his own security. According to Liang, there were about a hundred thugs cordoning off the plot.

As Liang's son approached the field, he heard a voice shout, "Someone's coming. Get him!" He turned his bike around and tried to get back to the village, but was quickly chased down. He was knocked off his bike and beaten with steel pipes. His parents, seeing what was happening, came out to help. They were beaten as well. All three ended up in the hospital. Liang had a seven-inch gash in his head and a broken bone in his hand. His son had similar injuries, albeit a slightly smaller head wound. Liang's wife, also in her sixties, sustained a fracture in one of her lower vertebrae.

The police didn't make any arrests following the attack. The Liangs' hospital bills were paid for, although they weren't told by whom. While they were in the hospital, their neighbors in the village, who had grown increasingly restless as it became apparent that the cash they'd been given wasn't enough to support them for more than a few years, were warned that they could expect the same treatment if they too made trouble. Liang says that village leaders were given 10,000 yuan each to fall in line. The opposition simmered down.

The housing development built on Liang's land is now complete. It's largely indistinguishable from the thousands of similar complexes dotted across China. The towers line up in two neat rows, one behind the other, each facing in the same direction, out toward the main gate. However, one thing that struck me when I visited was that there seemed to be a disproportionately large amount of space between the towers. I thought that maybe I was just being overly sensitive to Liang's loss, until the young saleswoman who emerged from the air-conditioned showroom to give me a tour touted the extra space as a selling point. It wasn't worth my checking out a nearby development, she said, because the towers there were clustered too closely. It was much better to enjoy all this space. I couldn't help imagining it filled with walnut trees.

With no more land left to defend, Liang has tried to go over the heads of the local authorities by petitioning the central government in Beijing, a tradition going back to imperial times. With the local judiciary closely entwined with local authorities, petition offices and not the courts are often the only venue that holds out at least a little hope for ordinary people that their grievances will get a fair hearing. Millions of people petition every year, but in truth, it's often an exercise in futility. "The petition office in Beijing doesn't care," Liang said after his third visit. "As far as they're concerned, the issue is already resolved."

I met Liang a couple of years after the developers started construction. His salt-and-pepper hair was short and spiky, and he spoke passionately about his rights and what his family was entitled to under the law. His face was tanned and creased, but he walked straight-backed, with an almost patrician air. I asked how he rated the chances of getting his land back. "Probably not very high," he said with a resigned sigh. But Liang was no longer agitating for the return of his farm. With so much concrete having been poured over it, that was impossible. He now wanted economic rights over the land. He wanted to be able to earn rent from the developer, or at least to receive something that represented the market value of what was taken from him. What has fueled his rage over the years is the injustice of having his land taken so that others could grow rich.

"The local government took our land and then gave it to a property developer to reap huge profits," he wrote to the authorities. "This project has been paid for by throwing away the peasants' rice bowl."

• • •

The Chinese economy is built around housing construction. Between 2011 and 2013, China laid more cement than the United States did during the entire twentieth century. That's difficult to conceptualize until you travel through China by train. The defining feature of the landscape, regardless of where you are, is high-rise apartment towers. Endless row after row race past, starting well outside the limits of any given city — often somewhat out of place among the fields and tractors — before gaining density as the train heads toward town. Allowing for differences in color and the occasional architectural flourish, there's a certain sameness to all the apartments. They cluster in gated communities, each with about a dozen towers of between sixteen and twenty stories high. This effect is particularly striking in the northern provinces, where the apartment towers all face south to maximize sunlight during the short winter days.

What has allowed China to build so much, especially relative to the size of the economy, is that it's playing catch-up. After all, China's commercial-housing market is relatively young. During the days of China's planned economy, people living in cities were allocated housing by their state employer. Accommodation was typically cramped and utilitarian. Families often had to share kitchens and bathrooms with their neighbors. State firms had neither the resources nor the motivation to build additional housing on a sufficient scale.

To redress the problem, the central government experimented with liberalizing the housing market throughout the 1990s by letting people buy commercially built apartments. But the turning point came in 1998, when the authorities decreed that state companies could no longer provide housing to their employees for free. People were encouraged to buy their homes from their state employers, which sold them at heavily discounted prices. By acquiring housing at well below market prices, newly minted homeowners were then able to sell their apartments for more than what they had paid, giving them the financial resources to upgrade their homes and unleashing years of pent-up demand for better accommodation. China's housing market was born.

For about twenty years, that market has boomed. Rising incomes have allowed people to upgrade their homes again and again. Young men, expected to have bought a home before marrying, are a steady stream of buyers who otherwise would have been renters. Starved for options in the mainstream financial system, people have plowed their life savings into bricks and mortar. And the millions of migrants flowing into the cities have meant that, despite a decades-long construction frenzy, there's always a need for more housing.

In Beijing, my wife and I lived in a six-floor walk-up built during the 1980s by the Ministry of Foreign Affairs for its staff, many of whom worked in the nearby embassies. By the time we moved in, it was in the heart of Beijing's bar district and was surrounded by upmarket shopping. A two-minute walk in one direction led to a Bentley dealership; two minutes in the other was an Alexander McQueen boutique. But across the road was a slum. Nestled between a high school and a newly built office building, it was little more than fifty meters long and fifty meters deep — a postage stamp by the standards of Beijing's city blocks. It was made up of one-story redbrick homes separated by dirt pathways that were so narrow that if you spread your arms, you could touch the walls on either side. Power came in from a jerry-rigged tangle of overhead wires. The dwellings were typically two rooms: a multipurpose bedroom–dining–living room, and a white-tiled kitchen. Some had windows that were covered with paper for privacy; others had wire for security.

It was like a slice of quasi–village life in the center of the city. People washed their vegetables in pans on the stoops of their dwellings, but otherwise they looked like anyone else in Beijing, the young men and women wearing the same fashions and toting the same smartphones. But the land was simply too valuable to have migrants living on it, and the government eventually moved everyone out, chaining up the communal toilet block to deter people from coming back. It wasn't a sufficient deterrent. After a year, the shanties still hadn't been demolished, and there were signs — an electric light shining through a papered window, and a new bicycle outside a locked door — that people had moved back in.

China's major cities are a magnet for rural migrants, some of whom live in places like this or rent rooms in villages on cities' fringes. Others live in tents on construction sites. As many as one million people live underground in Beijing in basements, air-raid shelters, and storage spaces. And many people live in dormitories, like the one my landlord was running next door to our apartment. The dorm and our place had originally been one dwelling, but he'd split it in two and rented the other half — which was about sixty square meters — to a Japanese company that was using it to house upwards of ten female staff. To placate the other residents of the compound, many of whom had lived there since the 1980s and were ill at ease with the constantly changing roster of faces moving in and out of the apartment, our landlord eventually capped the number of tenants at eight.

ARRESTED DEVELOPMENT

With so much latent demand for decent housing, developing property has become a license to print money for the Chinese. According to researchers from the University of Pennsylvania and Peking University, in the decade between 2003 and 2013, China's biggest, most affluent cities — first-tier cities like Beijing and Shanghai — experienced annual real-price growth of 13.1%; second-tier cities—which include most provincial capitals — grew by 10.5%; and the third tier by 7.9%. In comparison, in the lead-up to the subprime mortgage crisis, U.S.

housing prices grew 7.1% on average annually in the four years prior to the market's peak, in 2006.

Consequently, real estate has been a magnet for anyone with money to invest. By 2010, so many state firms had become involved in developing real estate that the central government issued an edict telling them to divest their property arms and to focus more on their core businesses. The directive was roundly ignored. The money from real estate was too easy. Housing prices only ever went up. There were occasions when sales declined, but they were merely temporary, and the overall lesson that developers took away was that it always paid to keep building.

In recent years, however, the picture has grown more complicated. It's misleading to talk of a single Chinese property market. China has not one housing market but two. While hundreds of thousands of migrants live underground in places like Beijing for want of anything better, China's smaller cities have not drawn anywhere near enough migrants to justify the scale and growth of construction they've experienced. Developers have built so much new housing in small cities that it will likely take years to sell it all, and, assuming it does sell, to then fill it with people. Around 2013, billboards, bus-shelter advertisements, and flyers stuck under windshield wipers started appearing throughout the hinterland, offering promotions that, while leaving the sticker price unchanged (thereby allowing officials to say prices hadn't fallen), effectively discounted new apartments by up to 50%. In one ghost city I visited, a newly built housing complex was giving away free cars and a session with a wedding photographer to anyone who bought an apartment. Another was offering a buy-one-get-one-free deal on new apartments, and free street-level shop space for anyone who bought a villa. I've seen offers of free European furniture and brand-name appliances with a new condo; promises of 20% of the value of an apartment to be returned to the buyer in cash to pay for renovations; three rooms for the price of two; and a free plot of land for growing vegetables to new apartment buyers. (The last one appeared on a flyer in my bicycle basket, advertising an apartment complex 400 kilometers away, in Shandong Province. The marketing department may have misjudged its target demographic.)

In some places, demand has since bounced back, in part because prices in major cities have risen so high that people have gone looking to park their savings in more affordable, smaller cities. But when demand picks up, construction of new housing invariably starts racing ahead again.

All of this has had a major effect on the economy. It's no coincidence that the economy has been slowing since 2012. Real estate — which includes shopping malls and office towers as well as apartments, both of which are suffering their own gluts — is the bedrock of the Chinese economy, accounting for about 20% of GDP in 2013, a level similar to that of both Spain and Ireland when they were hit by the Eurozone crisis, and triple the level of the United States prior to the subprime-mortgage crisis.

But real estate's contribution to the economy is actually far greater than these levels suggest. Housing construction is essential to buoying dozens of industries that are already mired in overcapacity, like steel, cement, and glass. Moreover, construction provides employment for 16% of the urban population. And with banks making about 30% of their loans to the property sector, the health of the financial system requires buoyant property prices. Given that two-thirds of all housing sales are in China's smaller cities (loosely, those occupying the third tier and lower), a glut means that developers build less housing and buy less land. Local governments are worse off, because they no longer have the resources to stimulate the local economy with public works, or to repay their debts. As a result, with less construction going on, local governments earn less tax revenue with which to provide public services. In short, real estate bolsters growth during the good times but exacerbates the slowdown during the bad.

Housing has been the engine of China's growth for two decades, but it is also the weakness at the heart of the economy. With demand for new housing no longer sufficient to grow the economy as quickly as it once did, Beijing has attempted to take up some of the slack by increasing spending on infrastructure projects like high-speed rail and new airports. They're not necessarily wise investments — as of 2017, China was planning to build seventy-four new airports by 2020 despite dozens of existing airports showing losses for years — but at least they generate demand for steel and concrete.

Still, there's no substitute for reviving the housing market. The authorities need to find a way to fill all the empty housing with people so that developers are willing to commence work on even more new housing projects.

One mooted solution is to route migrants toward China's smaller cities by offering them entitlements. In the *hukou* system, subsidized health care is available to migrants only back in their villages, as is free schooling for their children. Whereas in other developing economies an entire family — children, parents, and grandparents — might migrate to the city, in China more than sixty million children have been left behind by their parents so that they can get an education. Migrants who get too old to work don't hang around in the city but head home to their village, where they're entitled to pensions and health care. Still, it seems unlikely that entitlements by themselves will be enough to change migration flows. "Rural people make their own decisions," said Xiao Jincheng, a researcher on land issues for a think tank under the National Development and Reform Commission. "They go wherever the jobs are, wherever the wages are higher, no matter how far it is from home . . . They are extremely rational."

The only approach to stimulating construction that consistently works is credit. When Beijing wants to boost housing sales, it makes getting a mortgage easier. Still, by making home loans more accessible, the central government is playing with fire. In 2016, it managed to resuscitate the housing market by lowering the interest rate on mortgages. Sales shot up nationwide. Construction picked up. Local governments earned more from land sales. But housing prices soared by 33% in Beijing and by similar levels in other first- and second-tier cities. While China has a surplus of housing in small cities, in the biggest cities it is dealing with an affordability crisis. Pumping credit into the housing market stimulates housing construction and land sales, but it comes at the expense of ordinary people.

Stories of housing stress permeate Chinese society. Terms like "mortgage slave" (someone who spends more than 40% of income on loan repayments), "ant tribe" (university graduates who live in cramped but cheap communities on the peripheries of the cities), and *diaosi* (which translates as "male pubic hair" and is used, with some derision, to refer to a young man with no prospects, average looks, no connections — and no apartment) have moved their way from the Internet into mainstream conversation, and they directly link people's inability to buy housing with how they see themselves.

The lack of affordable housing is exacerbated by a curious surfeit of apartments that have been bought yet remain vacant, particularly in cities where housing demand is most acute. A 2014 survey estimated that, the previous year, about 20% of the urban housing stock was empty. No doubt some of that stock was in ghost cities where no one wants to live, and some was empty because it's being renovated. But very often people deliberately choose to leave their investment properties empty, assuming that housing prices will rise sufficiently quickly so as to dwarf any rental income they could otherwise be earning. Next door to where I lived in Beijing, down the alley from the slum, was a new housing development for upper-middle-class residents. Yet for three years, I hardly saw a light go on at night in any of the windows. I knew a foreigner who moved in who found herself genuinely creeped out by how empty it was. In major cities, it's not an unusual phenomenon. The youngest daughter of Liang, the farmer, lives in Beijing (where she rents) but owns an apartment in Shijiazhuang, an industrial city in Hebei, which she leaves empty. She says she'd be happy to rent it out to a local white-collar worker, but she doesn't trust migrants to take care of it properly. For the sake of simplicity, it's easier to leave the apartment empty and enjoy the capital gains.

High housing prices in places like Beijing and other big cities are being underwritten by a massive amount of unsatisfied demand for decent housing, but that doesn't mean those prices are a rational expression of demand. Millions of Chinese have been priced out of the housing markets in the cities in which they live, and the situation is only getting worse.

BLOWING BUBBLES

These days, Liang mostly sits at home brooding and watching television, hoping he can learn something about land rights and the legal system that will help his cause. He occasionally gets a few hours of work as a watchman, and his wife — who still hasn't fully recovered from the beating — rents a small plot where she grows just enough to eat, and pays the owners in vegetables. For a little extra money, Liang and his wife, like many others in the village, rent a spare room to a family of migrant workers — a man and woman who have moved from Anhui with their baby to find construction work in the new city.

The new development built on Liang's land has been fully sold out, but, surprisingly, the apartment tower built by the cement company is empty and increasingly dilapidated. When I visited, seven years after construction started, a number of windows on the ground floor were broken. As it turns out, the apartments weren't built for employees after all. Rather, upon their completion, the company tried to sell them to the public, a much more lucrative way of making money than selling cement. The local scuttlebutt was that the company hadn't been able to secure the right permits to sell the housing commercially, and so the building sat idle.

A few minutes' walk away, Liang's village has the bombed-out feel of a boomtown that ran out of money. Most of the houses have a newly built second level, but there's no glass in the window frames and the interiors are unfinished. Where houses once had vegetable gardens outside, they now have annexes and sunrooms. A few years after receiving compensation for their land, the villagers found that the money wasn't going to be enough to see out their days. They responded to their predicament with a frenzy of their own construction, using the last of their payout money to build extensions to their homes. They hope that when the government needs more land, it will come for the land upon which the village sits, at which point the compensation will be relative to the size of their homes. Most people don't need the extra space. Families aren't growing. As in most villages in China, the young people long ago moved to the cities in search of better jobs.

There seems to be a good chance that Liang's neighbors will get their wish. When I visited, a nearby village had been tapped for demolition, and a half dozen six-story apartments with blue pitched roofs and orange walls had been built in a nearby paddock to relocate the residents. In 2015, the local municipal government sold 34% more land than it had the previous year. Moreover, land sales were equivalent to about 60% of what it collected in taxes, well above the national average.

Demand from developers for new land continues unabated; in fact, it has been relentless. What's driving demand is the plan made in Beijing—a two-hour drive away—to turn the capital into a mega-city that will subsume peripheral towns like Liang's. No one really knows what that will mean in practice, but the prospect sent housing prices soaring. Liang's youngest daughter, who lives in Beijing, ended up buying an apartment near her parents' village a year after swearing she wouldn't. Prices were irrationally high, she had said. But as the prices headed even higher, she changed her mind, grabbing what she could for fear that if she didn't, prices would move beyond her reach and she would never be able to move home. In Beijing, people pay more than twenty times their annual income for a home, compared with two and a half times in the United States. In Liang's city, prices were driven up to fifteen times the average local income. The city wasn't going through a population spurt. Ironically, the migrants who had arrived to build the new city couldn't afford the housing they were working on. The city was undergoing a gigantic speculative bubble.

The perennial question is whether the same can be said of all of China's major cities. The threat of a housing bubble is that once it pops, all the economic problems that go along with fewer land sales and less housing construction will be compounded by a financial crisis like the one that devastated the United States in 2007. Yet China seems to have inoculated itself against that event. Before 2007, almost anyone could get a home loan in the United States, and a typical down payment was only about 2% of the value of the mortgage. When interest rates started rising and home prices started falling, many people owned so little equity in their homes that they just walked away from them rather than repay loans that were now greater than the value of their property. In contrast, the minimum down payment for first-time homebuyers in China is typically no lower than 20%, and people buying an investment property can expect to put down as much as 70%. Because of these substantial down payments, Chinese homebuyers have so much of their savings sunk into their apartments from day one that the possibility of their defaulting en masse seems highly unlikely.

That doesn't mean a sudden fall in property prices isn't dangerous. Almost 60% of bank loans are backed by property as collateral, such that a fall in prices would have a massive contractionary effect on the ability of the financial sector to lend. It's just that, to the extent there's a bubble to worry about, it's not a housing bubble. It's a *land* bubble.

When someone buys a home in China, what that person is really buying is the land. The quality of Chinese housing is so poor that McKinsey estimates that the average newly constructed building has a life span of about twenty years, half that in Europe. That makes an apartment — as distinct from the land it sits on — less like an investment, which retains its value over time, and more like a car, which starts losing value the moment you drive it off the lot. Chinese contractors routinely skimp on materials by diluting cement or using substandard drywall. Speed is prioritized over quality, and workmanship suffers in a culture that regularly equates "close enough" with "good enough." Apartment buildings generally start to look old only a few years after completion. Hence, the value of housing as an investment is not four walls and a ceiling; it's the land they're perched on. Consequently it's land that drives housing prices.

Land prices in China increased fivefold between 2004 and 2015. Before 2008, land values accounted for, on average, 37% of Beijing housing prices. After 2010, that had risen to 60%. Households have been able to pay for rising prices because of rising wages. Even home prices that were higher than twenty times those of local annual incomes — as in Beijing and Shanghai — weren't so bad when China's economy was growing annually at 10%. People could realistically expect to double their incomes in less than a decade, transforming onerous mortgages into something far more manageable after just a few years. But as wages stagnate with the slowing economy, people will be less able to take sharp increases in housing prices in their stride.

Yet land prices have reached absurd levels. In mid-2016, developers were paying more for land in some of China's biggest cities than what the prevailing market prices would allow them to earn on the apartments they planned to build. Using an old Chinese idiom, the local media described the phenomenon as paying more for the flour than the bread. Developers were speculating that in lieu of wages increasing, China's increasingly overstretched households would be willing to borrow more and more in order to purchase ever more expensive housing — and that the central government would enable the borrowing in order to maintain and boost economic growth.

What makes the land market a bubble is that prices are no longer determined by the supply of land relative to the demand for housing. Rather, they're set by the supply of money relative to the demand for somewhere to invest it. Developers have borrowed a massive amount of money in recent years, and many of them are already showing signs of financial distress. But what keeps them afloat — and allows them to pay higher prices for land — is their ability to continue borrowing, particularly from shadow-banking sources. They've taken advantage of a great wave of money sloshing around the Chinese economy that, with the economy slowing, has struggled to find places to go. The risk is that when those people and institutions putting up the money start losing faith in property, there will be subsequent demands for higher interest rates or lending stops altogether, pushing developers into default, sending land prices tumbling, and spreading distress throughout the financial system.

"The biggest problem currently facing the country is how to reduce reliance on real estate," said Yin Zhongqing, deputy director of the Finance and Economics Committee of the National People's Congress, in mid-2017. "The real estate industry's excessive prosperity has not only kidnapped local governments but also kidnapped financial institutions — restraining and even harming the development of the real economy, inflating asset bubbles and accumulating debt risk."

But so far, the government hasn't found a way to change that. The money that property developers need has always been forthcoming, the result of a financial system that has expanded massively over the last decade. That's allowed land prices to stay buoyant, enabled state firms to remain solvent, and given local governments the wherewithal to keep building. But this unprecedented credit expansion isn't the product of some grand design. While Beijing is undoubtedly happy to enjoy the growth it's delivered, the financial system has slipped the leash of government control, behaving in ways that are neither in the national interest nor in line with Beijing's wishes. More importantly, it has evolved in a way that now threatens the very sustainability of China's economic miracle.

5

THE ISLAND OF MISFIT TOYS

CHINA'S FINANCIAL SYSTEM is a little like the Island of Misfit Toys in *Rudolph the Red-Nosed Reindeer,* the 1964 animated Christmas classic. From a distance everything looks familiar, but up close it becomes clear that things aren't built the way you might expect.

For example, China's money-market funds are managed not by storied investors like Vanguard and Fidelity but by China's equivalent of Amazon and Google. Insurance companies generate most of their premiums not from selling insurance but from selling investments that mature after only a year, insure nothing, and promise a fixed return a little higher than bank deposits. In the United States, trust companies help rich families preserve their wealth from one generation to the next, but in China trusts have become the second-biggest class of financial institution after the banks, facilitating loans to everyone from property developers to local governments. And whereas in the United States most households own shares in publicly traded companies, whether in a 401(k) or a mutual fund, in China families are most likely to hold short-term, fixed-income investments called wealth-management products, which are sold by banks as a no-risk, higher-return alternative to deposits.

The curious shape of China's financial institutions is not the result of some grand design hatched in Beijing. Rather, it's the result of unprecedented tolerance by the Chinese authorities of financial innovation and experimentation. Consequently, members of the public now enjoy immense choice when it comes to how they invest their savings. But at the same time, Beijing's tolerance has unleashed a perpetual-motion machine of debt creation over which it has seemingly lost all control.

Were it not for the stack of white surgical masks and an air purifier on his desk — prophylactics against the Beijing air — Liu Yannan's office could have stood in for that of any twentysomething start-up CEO anywhere in the world. Figurines of Captain America and Iron Man sat on the top shelf behind his swivel chair. A pair of gray sweatpants were folded neatly in the corner next to a basketball, and a long, thin aluminum case — the type that typically stores poker chips — had been pushed haphazardly under the coffee table. Outside, on the other side of the glass wall that separated Liu from the open-plan office, were rows of similarly young employees hard at work or milling around, chatting, or taking a break to shoot zombies and race motorcycles on the arcade-style games down the corridor.

Liu had launched Yooli, a peer-to-peer lending platform (P2P), three years earlier, in April 2012. P2P uses the Internet to link people who need a loan directly with people willing to lend them money. Rather than go to a bank, a small firm can borrow what it needs from dozens or even hundreds of ordinary people, who can each contribute as much or as little as they like. Liu didn't invent the concept. P2P companies were already gaining traction in the United Kingdom and the United States by the time he came across P2P while searching the Internet for start-up ideas. Having worked for an investment bank after university, and then a private-equity fund, a finance start-up seemed like a good fit. At the age of twenty-six, Liu started Yooli in Beijing with two friends, in an office the size of a one-bedroom apartment. Within a year, they had to move after the staff swelled to thirty. Less than two years later, the company moved again in order to accommodate more than two thousand employees.

Liu had an intensity you would expect from a young CEO. From behind his black-rimmed glasses, he spoke in rapid-fire Mandarin, peppering his conversations with English words like "shadow banking" and "financial stability" delivered in the middle-class British accent he acquired while finishing high school and then attending university in the United Kingdom. He spoke passionately about how he saw Yooli as a way he could contribute to the development of China's private sector, although he clearly missed his days playing pickup basketball games back in Warwick. But unlike a typical start-up entrepreneur, Liu wasn't simply disrupting a traditional industry. He was an uninvited challenger to a state monopoly in an area where the government had little tolerance for private enterprise. That brought certain risks that Silicon Valley generally doesn't have to deal with.

When I visited Yooli — a phoneticization of the company's Chinese name, which means "have profit" — it didn't look like a hotbed of revolution. On a wall by the entrance was a sign that read, "We ♥ Yooli," surrounded by the brightly colored handprints of employees. Inclusive motivational slogans were prominently displayed throughout the halls: "Open your heart"; "We are the best"; and, somewhat incongruously, "Don't stop, never give up, hold your head high and reach the top," a lyric from a song by the 1990s British pop group S Club 7, which was a hit well before most Yooliers — which is how they refer to themselves — hit their tweens.

For all of Yooli's outwardly projected optimism, for the first few years, Liu worried that the government would declare P2P illegal and shut his business down. He joked that in the early days, while he was waiting for the government to make up its mind about P2P, his position was so precarious that he worried the authorities might execute him for economic crimes. Despite his chuckles, the thought had clearly crossed his mind.

The month Liu started his business, Wu Ying, one of China's most successful businesswomen, had her death sentence overturned by the People's Supreme Court following widespread public support for a reprieve. Wu, who had built a nail salon into a diversified conglomerate and at one time was ranked the sixty-eighth-richest person in the country, had been sentenced to death for financial fraud after she was unable to repay 380 million yuan she had borrowed from a handful of individuals. However, she had originally been detained on charges of "illegally taking deposits from the public," otherwise known as illegal fund-raising. In China, borrowing from family and friends is fine, but once you start promising strangers a fixed rate of return and soliciting funds publicly, you potentially face up to fifteen years in jail.

Despite Wu Ying's troubles, illegal financing (which is best understood as unregulated lending) is ubiquitous throughout China. The government generally tolerates it as long as it doesn't disturb the public order by losing people's money. It was that, rather than the act of soliciting funds, which seems to have been Wu's mistake, although her high profile didn't help. (There was a time when a significant number of entrepreneurs who made China's rich list subsequently ended up in jail.) Mostly, unregulated lending carries on uninterrupted, sometimes in plain sight. In one town I visited, a local business magazine carried a monthly two-page insert outlining the rates and conditions being offered by underground banks. In another, "investment companies" lined the streets, offering high-interest loans. Elsewhere I've seen flyers glued to the gates of abandoned factories with a number and a name to call if in need of credit. Such loans usually charge high interest rates — 2.5% per month is not unusual — but there's nonetheless a ready clientele. As Liu put it, "In China, there's just no other way for [private] companies to raise money."

The irony is that China has no shortage of commercial banks, ranging from the 800 or so small rural banks, to about 140 city banks, to 40 foreign banks (which are so small that, combined, they account for only about 2% of total banking-system loans), to 11 banks with national charters, to the 5 major banks, which account for almost half of all loans. China's banking system was designed not to serve the interests of the private sector but to provide credit — cheaply and in large amounts — to state-owned companies. To that end, it traditionally enjoyed an effective monopoly over national savings. The stock and bond markets were too small to absorb more than a small portion of China's savings, and strict capital controls meant people couldn't move their savings overseas into more-developed capital markets. That meant most people invested in housing or put their savings in the state-owned banking system.

For most of this century, Beijing exploited that privilege by keeping deposit rates below the pace of inflation. That, in turn, allowed banks to charge less for loans than would otherwise have been possible, thereby stimulating economic growth by making it cheaper for state firms to borrow. Projects that wouldn't have made sense at higher, market-based interest rates became viable when rates were suppressed. It was effectively a subsidy to any company that could get a loan, and a tax on ordinary people whose savings declined in relative value just by sitting in the bank.

Banks were never particularly popular with the public. In the early 2000s, people would routinely queue for more than an hour at bank branches before being served by staff that swung between militantly unhelpful and catatonic. Although things gradually improved from that low base, by the time I left Beijing, in 2015, my local ICBC branch still felt as though it was working from an operating model that had been developed a hundred years earlier. Bank tellers wore removable cotton sleeves, cinched at either end with elastic, to protect their blazers. Transactions required multiple paper chits to be stamped with red ink. And while there always seemed to be plenty of staff, at any given time a third of them seemed to be on a tea break.

By the time Liu started Yooli, it wasn't just the public that was fed up with the banks. "Let me be frank. Our banks earn profit too easily," said Premier Wen Jiabao in the month Liu launched his firm and Wu Ying was granted a reprieve. "Why? Because a small number of large banks have a monopoly." Only a couple of years earlier, that profitability had been a source of national pride. In the five years between the end of 2007 and 2012, a time when the very existence of some of the biggest banks in the United States and Europe were in question, annual profit at China's banks more than tripled. ICBC was valued more highly than any other bank in the world, and China Construction Bank wasn't far behind. That success wasn't the product of superior management but a quirk of regulation. At the end of the 1990s, China's banking system had been technically insolvent, having been used to prop up the bloated and inefficient state economy. As a result, about 40% of its loans had turned bad, with no hope of being repaid. To recapitalize the banks, Beijing made it easier for them to make a profit. It set an upper limit on the maximum deposit rate banks could offer, and a floor under the minimum lending rate. In other words, Beijing mandated that the banks earn a fixed, minimum margin on every loan they made. The more they lent, the more profit they earned. And when the banks massively expanded lending during the global financial crisis, their profits expanded accordingly. "Banking in China has become like a highway toll system," said Yao Jingyuan, the former chief economist and spokesman of China's National Bureau of Statistics, in late 2013. "With this kind of operational model, banks will continue making money even if all the bank presidents go home to sleep and you replaced them by putting a small dog in their seats."

Even as the banks generated incredible profits and growth, they were failing to meet the needs of the economy. There was a time when it hardly mattered that banks didn't lend to the private sector. When China emerged from decades of economic stagnation under Mao into Deng's reform era, there was no private sector to speak of. Private companies proliferated throughout the 1980s and 1990s, but they were still too small for banks to worry about. Even in the early 2000s, the banks could largely ignore the private sector without the economy's feeling significant ill effects. Moreover, the banks had good reason to avoid lending to private companies. Since the banks were recapitalized, bankers had been under extreme pressure from their political masters to avoid bad loans. Lending to private companies wasn't conducive to meeting that goal.

There is an adage in China that your typical private businessperson keeps three sets of books: one for the banker, one for the tax authorities, and an accurate one for him- or herself (and occasionally a fourth for a spouse). That makes it impossible for a bank to sufficiently trust a borrower. State firms aren't necessarily more trustworthy, but at least lending to them comes with political cover if the loans go bad. Lending to state companies takes the risk out of banking — not the risk that borrowers won't repay, but the risk that the banks will get blamed if they don't. But state firms are significantly more wasteful and less innovative than their private-sector counterparts. For China to unleash the latent potential of its private sector, credit needed to be more fairly distributed. In an earlier era, Liu and the other P2P operators that sprang up at the same time would almost certainly have been shut down. Instead, Liu launched Yooli at a time of unprecedented tolerance for experimentation outside of the formal, state-run financial system. "The regulators are becoming more open to P2P," Liu told me. "They don't want to be seen as anti-innovation."

When he first launched Yooli, finding small, private credit-starved companies to lend money to was relatively easy. But finding people willing to lend money over his Internet platform was more difficult. No one in China knew what P2P was. Liu had to sell people on the very concept. To fund the first batch of loans, he had friends arrange for him to speak to their work colleagues during their lunch hour, where he gave tutorials on how P2P worked. That way, he signed up his first few dozen lenders. However, soon enough he had the opposite problem. By February 2014, so many people were flocking to his website to lend that he didn't have enough vetted borrowers to accommodate them. "For a couple of months, every time we posted a loan, it sold out in seconds," said Liu. "I had to write an apology letter to lenders, because we didn't have enough loans posted on the portal."

By the end of 2014, two million people had accumulatively lent about 6 billion yuan through Yooli's platform. What made it such a success was that the returns it managed to deliver — which were typically between 8% and 15% — were among the best an ordinary person could find anywhere. But part of the frenzy was also the novelty. A few years earlier, the public had been starved for options. P2P emerged as a small part of a vast wave of financial democratization. As recently as 2009, people kept most of their savings in the bank. Today, an entire ecosystem of financial instruments has evolved and been embraced by all strata of society.

At the heart of that ecosystem are wealth-management products (WMPs). WMPs have been around since 2004, but it wasn't until 2010 that banks hit upon the type of product people really wanted: safe investments that mature every three months or so and deliver annual returns of about 4% or 5% (compared with about 3% on one-year deposits). At the end of 2009, just before they started to take off, there were 1.9 trillion yuan's worth of outstanding WMPs. At the end of 2016, that number had risen twelvefold, to more than 29 trillion yuan, equivalent to 20% of bank deposits.

WMPs are everywhere. You can walk into any branch of any bank anywhere in the country and buy them. When I was living in China, I used to receive a constant stream of text messages from banks advertising them. Yooli's Liu said that about half of the people who lent money through his website found him after searching for wealth-management products online. Money raised from WMPs has been invested in tea, diamonds, wine, shares traded on stock exchanges, commodities, foreign currency — anything banks think will deliver a return. But for the most part, WMPs are a blend of three things: corporate bonds, loans to banks (which banks then use to make their own loans), and corporate loans. The combination mixes risk and return. Loans to banks are extremely safe but have low interest rates; loans to companies are more risky but pay more. Put them together and you get a pretty safe investment with a decent return. Most of the fund-management industry — whether trusts, insurance companies, securities firms, money-market funds, or P2P portals — deploy their resources in similar ways. They're a source of credit that has emerged as an alternative to traditional bank loans. Together they constitute a shadow-banking system.

WHAT WE DO IN THE SHADOWS

Broadly speaking, shadow banking includes any nonbank credit that isn't subject to the same careful, thoughtful regulation that governments give to ordinary bank lending. For our purposes, the best way to think of it is as any lending that doesn't take the form of a traditional bank loan. At the more conventional end of things, shadow banking includes corporate bonds; at the more innovative end, it includes P2P; and, somewhat counterintuitively, the banks themselves are often involved in some way. It's commonly argued that shadow banking in China is not a cause for alarm, because, relative to the United States, it's fairly small. At its peak, the U.S. shadow-banking system had about

$20 trillion of liabilities and was almost twice the size of the $11 trillion banking system. In mid-2016, the situation in China was the inverse. According to Moody's, the credit-rating agency, China had about $8 trillion in shadow-banking assets, half the volume of outstanding bank loans. However, in China the risk lies not in the size of shadow banking relative to traditional banking, but rather in the pace at which it has grown. In 2008, the future pillars of China's shadow banking barely existed. At the end of 2014, the amount of credit that had been generated by the shadow-banking system was about 40% the size of China's GDP. By mid-2016, that had doubled, to about 80%.

It's almost inconceivable that any economy could productively deploy such a massive increase in debt in such a short period of time. In China, however, a large part of the economy has long been starved of credit. If all that shadow-banking credit flowed into the private sector, then maybe it could be efficiently used. Certainly it's now easier for private companies to get a loan than it once was. In fact, banks are lending far more to private firms, particularly small banks that are desperate to grow but find that state firms have a preference for borrowing from big banks. But private companies continue to complain that one of their biggest problems is being able to borrow. Even Yooli's Liu, who had started out by lending to private companies, began having reservations about the wisdom of his approach after only a few years. "Lending to small firms is too dangerous," he told me at the end of 2015. "At a time [when] the economy is slowing and you're still adding leverage to companies, that's a dangerous thing to do." He subsequently refocused his business toward lending to consumers.

Although the emergence of shadow banking in China has been a revolution in the way credit is generated, little has changed in the way it's allocated. In fact, shadow banking has grossly exacerbated the problems of local-government debt, industrial overcapacity, and housing oversupply. Part of the reason is that Beijing's newfound tolerance of innovation has been exploited by the banks. They have used shadow banking as a way to do more — much more — of the same, just without the oversight of regulators. At various times since 2010, Beijing has instructed the banks to ease back on lending to local governments, property developers, and heavy industry. To the extent that the banks have complied, shadow banking has taken up the slack — and then some.

It's easy to assume that because the banks are almost all state owned — some by Beijing, others by the provinces, cities, and counties, and still others by other state firms — they are servants of the state. The reality is more complicated. When Beijing instructed the banks to massively ramp up lending in 2009 to stimulate the economy in the face of the global financial crisis, the banks immediately responded by doubling the volume of loans they made relative to the previous year. But banks also have their own agenda. To the extent that it can be boiled down to one word, it's this: size. I once sat through a dinner with drunken bankers from a small, affluent city in Zhejiang Province who were hosting a more senior colleague visiting from Shanghai. When the locals let slip that three other banks had lent more in their district than their bank had, the Shanghai colleague exhorted them to lend more so that their bank would rise up the rankings: "Of course you don't want to lend more, but what choice do you have?"

Successful bankers build bigger banks. Only the biggest banks get to list shares, or get permission to set up branches nationally, or have the resources to expand overseas or into other financial services. Bigger banks have more wealth to distribute to employees. In times of trouble, small banks get taken over by bigger banks. Bigger means more political influence and more resources. China's smaller banks all aspire to be big. That filters through to the lowest branches, where employees' behavior is shaped by a long list of targets they're expected to meet, governing loan growth, deposit growth, and income growth. When lending growth is constrained by government restrictions, the best way to grow is to find ways around the rules. That's what Beijing's tolerance of financial innovation has allowed the banks to do.

China's shadow-banking system came into existence soon after its counterpart in the United States had blown up in the subprime mortgage crisis. At the end of 2009, after a year of stimulus lending, China's banks were told to rein in credit growth. China differs from most developed economies in that the government's main tool for regulating the economy is not interest rates but the supply of credit. Interest rates don't work in China as they work elsewhere, where central banks stimulate economic activity by lowering rates and fight inflation by raising them. In China, interest rates are kept low as a subsidy for state firms. If everyone who wanted to borrow at such cheap rates was able to, inflation would run amok. Moreover, because state firms don't face the same pressure to repay loans as private companies in market economies do, higher rates don't dampen their appetite for credit. So in order to prevent inflation, the government rations credit by telling banks just how much they're allowed to lend.

However, at the end of 2009, it wasn't so easy just to turn off the taps. Many of the projects begun during the stimulus year — things like new roads, factories, and housing developments — had only just started and needed to borrow more if they were ever to be finished, and banks were under pressure from local governments and state firms to keep lending. The banks' solution was to cooperate with trust companies.

China's trusts had only recently been rehabilitated after spending almost a decade in regulatory purgatory. During the 1990s, they helped fuel an economic boom by borrowing from overseas to invest in property and construction. In 1992, there were about a thousand trusts, but when the property market ran into trouble, so did they. By the end of the century, the trusts were responsible for so much bad debt that the government closed most of them down. By 2007, only around fifty were still standing, most of which were owned by state companies or local governments. That year, the banking regulator decided to repurpose them as asset managers for China's wealthy.

What makes trusts so special is that they can perform a simple type of securitization (although, unlike normal securitization, the securities aren't tradable). The trusts' solution to the banks' dilemma was to securitize the banks' surplus loans for a year or two, that is, they divided the loans into pieces, which they sold to investors — wealthy individuals and companies with spare cash. After the securities matured, the loans reverted to the banks. Consequently, the loans temporarily disappeared off the banks' books, and, more importantly, from the central bank's loan data. Meanwhile, the economy continued to boom as though the stimulus were still in effect, much to the confusion of anyone outside the banking sector. The banking regulator eventually managed to shut down the practice, but it took roughly a year and at least one false start.

Since 2009, the China Banking Regulatory Commission has been in a constant game of whack-a-mole with the banks. No sooner does it clamp down on one aspect of shadow banking than the banks come up with another way to get around the various quotas and other restrictions aimed at containing credit growth. Shadow banking has weakened Beijing's control of the economy by allowing banks to lend far in excess of what regulators deem prudent. The banks have deliberately designed shadow banking to be as opaque as possible, because they have no interest in Beijing's being able to work out just how much new credit they've created. To that end, they've created a Rube Goldberg machine of credit generation. By the end of 2015, Moody's estimated that the People's Bank of China was undercounting shadow banking by 16 trillion yuan, roughly a quarter of the size of China's GDP.

Although the specific mechanics of shadow banking keep changing, there are two basic dynamics that remain constant. The first is that shadow banking allows banks to perform a type of financial alchemy whereby a loan can be turned into an "investment asset," enabling it to be removed from the "loans" column of the balance sheet and hidden among more benign assets, like bonds. With the loans safely squirreled away from the watchful gaze of regulators, banks have the freedom to skirt loan limits, capital requirements, and bad-loan provisions (that last one being insurance that banks are supposed to hold against every loan in case the borrower is unable to repay it). Today, banks use trusts, securities companies, and fund-management companies to hide loans beneath complicated, layered investments — the financial equivalent of Russian nesting dolls. The practice has grown so widespread that many of China's smaller banks hold more shadow-banking assets than loans, sometimes by a margin of three to one. By early 2016, the shadow-banking assets held by Industrial Bank, one of China's second-tier banks, were greater in size than the entire banking system of the Philippines.

The second dynamic is that the banks don't make the loans themselves, but instead charge a fee for facilitating them. They take money raised from wealth-management products and lend it to their corporate clients. In theory, it's a risk-free business. The fine print of the WMP agreements states clearly that whoever buys a WMP — whether it be an elderly grandmother or a big, state-owned enterprise — bears all the risk if a loan goes bad. In practice, banks market WMPs as though they are as safe as deposits, and people buy them in the expectation that even if something goes wrong, they'll get their money back. It's a great source of revenue for banks, with little cost — unless, of course, bad loans start rising.

Clearly the complexity of shadow banking has made it difficult for authorities to bring it under control, but complicating matters is that the authorities are also of two minds about reining it in. The conflict was best summed up in 2012 by Xiao Gang, then-chairman of the Bank of China, who, in a column published in the state press, described wealth-management products as being "fundamentally a Ponzi scheme." Yet a few paragraphs later, he wrote, "Admittedly, shadow banking has its advantages. It helps businesses that need credit but who are unable to access it from traditional bank loans. Meanwhile, shadow banking continues to provide funds that allow certain half-finished projects to remain in construction, which spur the GDP growth rate." The following year, Xiao became chairman of the China Securities Regulatory Commission, the agency responsible for overseeing the stock market. Rather than act on his concerns, he allowed securities companies and fund-management companies to provide many of the same shadow-banking services that had hitherto been the sole domain of the trusts, thereby presiding over a massive expansion of shadow banking just as trust companies were having their wings clipped by the banking regulator.

And so, credit keeps rapidly expanding every year, driven by a shadow-banking system that openly flouts the government, while the government is either unwilling or unable to bring it to heel. Surely there must come a point when it's no longer prudent to keep lending, when financial institutions and ordinary people take stock of the risks and rein in the amount of credit they're willing to extend. However, the history of economic booms is that those moments generally come too late. During most booms, people are not only blind to the risks but they devise explanations for why risks don't even exist. People assumed the subprime mortgage crisis couldn't happen, because the United States had never experienced a nationwide decline in housing prices. During the dot-com boom, the delusion was that the new economy had done away with the business cycle. Before the Asian financial crisis, it was assumed that Asian values had created a new, more sustainable type of economic growth. In China, people's faith in the security of their investments isn't based on some pseudoscientific theory that somehow things are different this time; their confidence is rooted in the knowledge that someone will bail them out should the need arise. That deep-rooted sense of entitlement is most viscerally on display when bailouts fail to materialize.

NEVER TOO SMALL TO BAIL

Protests over failed investments in China are increasingly common. As you travel around the country, you regularly see small groups of people outside city halls or the offices of local financial regulators, waving banners demanding the return of *xue han qian* — money earned from their "blood and sweat." Generally speaking, the protesters have invested in some investment scheme you generally wouldn't expect the government to get involved in, like that sold by Fanya Metals Exchange.

When Fanya collapsed, in July 2015, the failure of a bailout to materialize resulted in hundreds of people who had invested money with the exchange protesting in Kunming (where the exchange was based) and outside financial regulators' offices in Shanghai and Beijing. Some took their complaint overseas, by protesting in Hong Kong and becoming active on Twitter — jumping the Great Firewall that blocks foreign social media in China — to try to drum up support in foreign media. Others kidnapped the defunct exchange's chairman and delivered him to the police.

Fanya was a market for trading rare earth metals, which are vital to modern industry — indium, for example, is used in LEDs, and cobalt in lithium batteries — but which are needed in fairly small quantities. The exchange attracted tens of thousands of mom-and-pop investors, not to trade rare earth resources but to buy an investment product that promised annual returns of 13.68%. (To anyone who didn't read the fine print, it would have looked much like a bank's wealth-management product.) The money was nominally lent to companies that were doing actual trading on the exchange. Promotional material said there was "zero risk." When the exchange collapsed, investors were owed 36 billion yuan.

Fanya investors held the government accountable and demanded that it pay them what they'd lost. Fanya was not state owned, but investors claimed that state organs had led them to believe that it had state backing. The exchange ran advertising on state television and in local state newspapers. The Kunming government had licensed it to operate. And major state-owned commercial banks sold Fanya's investments alongside their own wealth-management products.

In market economies, the public would undoubtedly feel sympathy for those investors who had lost their savings. The public would not, however, expect that their tax dollars be used to pay investors what they had lost. High returns are supposed to be compensation for high risk. Something promising almost 14% interest with no risk is clearly a scam. But in China, the basic principle of caveat emptor — buyer beware — doesn't exist. It doesn't matter if an institution isn't state owned. The fact that the government permits it to exist and allows ordinary people to hand over their savings to it means that the state has taken tacit responsibility for its viability — or at least that's how investors see it. What investors in Fanya demanded was the sort of guarantee that the public assumes applies to all mainstream financial institutions.

When a bond defaults in China, a white knight typically appears to ensure that bondholders get everything they're owed. Similarly, trust companies regularly bail out investors in trust products, even though trusts have no formal responsibility to do so. When a wealth-management product goes bad, investors typically don't even hear about it. The bank that issued it quietly absorbs the loss. Even Liu from Yooli felt it was necessary to insure lenders against default, by getting third-party financial institutions to guarantee every loan that sought funding on his platform. People assume that their investments are safe. Financial institutions typically cover any losses in order to preserve the public's trust in their products. If the underlying problem of the U.S. financial system is that some banks are too big to fail, in China it's that the public believes that no investment is too small to be bailed out.

Still, that doesn't explain why banks and shadow banks continue lending more and more, particularly when they're on the hook for any investments sold to the public that go bad. The reason they continue to lend is that they believe that their loans are safe. It's sometimes said that China's banks are little more than glorified pawnshops. They lend based not on what a company needs but according to the value of its assets. Almost 60% of all loans in the banking system are made against collateral, usually property. Similarly, trust companies typically demand anywhere between two and three times the value of a loan in collateral, and other shadow-banking institutions make similar demands. Hence, if a company can't repay the money it borrowed, the financial institutions can claim the collateral, sell it, and recoup their losses.

For those companies which don't have collateral, banks have been willing to accept third-party guarantees, that is, if the borrower can't repay the loan, then some other company promises to repay in its stead. Sometimes it's just a case of a parent company providing a guarantee to repay a subsidiary's loans. Sometimes local-government-owned state firms guarantee local private companies to stimulate local growth. And sometimes unrelated private companies guarantee each other, an arrangement that has opened up bank credit to a swath of small private firms.

But the safety net the financial system has constructed for itself relies heavily on the government's standing by two implicit guarantees: that it will continue to ensure fast economic growth, and that housing prices will remain buoyant. As long as housing prices are rising, financial institutions can continue lending with the knowledge that their collateral is gold plated. Moreover, as long as growth remains strong, there's little need for collateral or third-party guarantees in the first place. But as growth slows, problems with the safety net are starting to show.

So far, Beijing has managed to avoid anything more than temporary dips in housing prices. But collateral is of value only if you can claim it and then sell it. It's almost impossible for banks to claim collateral from state firms that can't repay their loans. Instead, financial institutions have to bear the bad loans. Moreover, rather than protecting the banks, guarantees are spreading financial distress, turning what would otherwise have been isolated defaults into localized crises as the complex networks of interlocking mutual guarantees fall like dominoes. So far, such crises have remained local, but the potential for guarantee networks to spread contagion more widely lurks as an ever-present threat.

Meanwhile, slower growth is starting to expose a multitude of sins. When an economy is expanding in size by 10% every year, middling managers become successful businesspeople, and hustlers turn into feted entrepreneurs. Loans that can't be repaid at a slower pace of economic expansion aren't a problem when the economy is booming. Companies can always just grow through their mistakes. Slower growth exposes the waste, mismanagement, hubris, and fraud that remained hidden during the good times.

Of course, maybe none of this matters. Even without fast growth, and even if property prices fall, everyone assumes that Beijing will ultimately step in to bail out the financial system if need be. However, the massive volume of bank lending, compounded by the complexity and size of shadow banking, increasingly casts that assumption into doubt. Beijing's ability not only to maintain fast growth and support housing prices but also to manage a successful system-wide bailout is looking increasingly fragile — much like the financial system itself.

6

THE GREAT BALL OF MONEY

"IF THE BUBBLES DON'T linger too long or fade too quickly, then it's real."

Liu Jianfeng was teaching me the finer points of spotting fake Moutai, China's premier brand of *baijiu*. He'd taken a cylindrical bottle of the white, high-alcohol-content spirit off the shelf, given it a good shake, and was now shining a light up through the bottom of the translucent glass. There were indeed plenty of bubbles, but I couldn't tell if they were doing what they were supposed to. Liu assured me that they had faded with sufficient moderation.

This was late in 2011, and Liu, the wine-and-spirits expert at Beijing Googut Auction, had himself only recently learned how to distinguish real from counterfeit *baijiu*. In fact, until only recently, Googut had no need for a wine-and-spirits expert. The previous year, an important client of the auction house had asked, as a favor, that Googut dispose of his spirits collection. It was an unusual request. By 2011, China had become the biggest auction market in the world after the sale of art and antiques had increased by 500% in three years, catapulting it ahead of the United States. But no one was auctioning vintage *baijiu*. "[The Googut CEO] looked around and said, 'Jianfeng, you like drinking *baijiu*, you can do it,'" Liu said with a chuckle. "Up until then, drinking had been a hobby."

Baijiu is an acquired taste. It looks like vodka but smells, to the un-

converted, like turpentine. Foreigners, in particular, find it unforgiv-
ing. American television journalist Dan Rather, visiting China with
President Nixon, once described it as "liquid razor blades." (In advance
of the trip, an aide to Henry Kissinger advised that President Nixon
should "under no, repeat, no circumstances" drink *baijiu* during the
customary banquet toasts.) However, the drink does mellow over time.
Unlike wine, *baijiu* has no special vintages; it's made from wheat and
sorghum, which aren't affected by the weather as grapes are. The older
the *baijiu,* the better it tastes. But traditionally, crates of *baijiu* weren't
typically set aside in cellars to mature. China didn't have a culture of
connoisseurs or collectors who stored and traded vintage bottles. A
bottle of aged *baijiu* was something you enjoyed only if a friend just
happened to have one.

Consequently, Liu didn't really know what to expect from his auction, a relatively small affair at which decades-old bottles of Moutai
were sold alongside China's less well loved *baijiu* brands. As the auction developed, the bids turned out to be far beyond anything he had
anticipated. Liu set the starting price for a 1959 bottle of Moutai — its
red-and-white label still instantly recognizable despite years of neglect
— at 120,000 yuan. It sold for eight times that amount.

I met Liu a year later as he was preparing to host China's first-ever
auction dedicated solely to vintage Moutai. No other Chinese brand
of liquor comes close to Moutai in popularity or pedigree. It was Mao
Zedong's favorite drink, and it occupies a central place in Communist Party folklore; the Red Army, while on the Long March, passed
through the mountain town in the country's southwest, from which the
drink takes its name. Realizing their sudden value, Liu spent months
finding old bottles — some were gathering dust in the back corner of
company storerooms, others had been forgotten under people's beds,
and still others were found sitting in the now-deteriorating cardboard

boxes they were originally shipped in — and weeding out counterfeits. (Moutai is so popular that people have been making counterfeit issues of the stuff for decades.)

Two weeks before the auction, the Googut CEO told me that he expected that a 1982 bottle of Moutai would sell for between 10,000 yuan and 20,000 yuan. He chose 1982 as the benchmark because China's moneyed classes had settled on the 1982 vintage of Château Lafite, a French Bordeaux, as their wine of choice, and he felt that Moutai should aspire to the same status. At the time, bottles of 1982 Lafite were selling for about 60,000 yuan — and, in a reflection of its popularity, it was estimated that 70% of the Lafite in circulation in China was actually fake. (I had the pleasure of being served Lafite only once. While visiting a branch of one of China's Big Four banks in an inland coal town, my host announced that he had secured a bottle of Lafite for lunch, and before I was halfway through my remonstrations that such an expensive bottle of wine shouldn't be wasted on a foreign correspondent, the cork was out of the bottle and my interlocutor was pouring. Somehow it didn't live up to my expectations.)

The comparison of Moutai to Lafite was purely a marketing gimmick. Lafite of 1982 is a special vintage that is regarded as being vastly superior to older, more mature wines, whereas for Moutai, 1982 is a year of no particular significance. Moreover, the production dates on old Moutai bottles are so badly marked — with a blue stamp not dissimilar to that on a milk carton — that determining a bottle's year of production can sometimes be a guessing game. (At the auction, the Moutai was typically sold in batches grouped together by decade.) Still, despite being a gimmick, the comparison proved to be remarkably prescient.

The auction was held in a Beijing hotel ballroom, tricked out for the occasion in faux-wood paneling in a loose approximation of an old-world European auction house. The event had something of a carnival feel to it, with as many sightseers as buyers. The buyers were easy to spot — flashily dressed entrepreneurs with man-bags and expensive loafers. I sat next to an elderly couple who, after a lifetime of receiving *baijiu* as gifts, had accumulated quite a collection, and they were there to get a sense of what their collection might be worth. Starting around 7:30 p.m., the auction didn't finish until the small hours of the following morning, dragged out by starting prices that, as soon became obvious, were far too low. The auction-house CEO was way off on his predictions. The average price for a 1980s bottle — the benchmark for judging the evening's success — came in at about 30,000 yuan, 50% higher than his original upper estimate.

I next saw Liu Jianfeng three years later. After arranging the first *baijiu* auction with only one assistant, he now had two hundred people working for him, including a team that had taken over responsibility for weeding out counterfeits. Googut's spirits business had been spun off into its own company, and Liu was now talking about launching an IPO. But perhaps the biggest change was the auction itself. The atmosphere at the 2014 event was radically different from my previous experience. Curiosity and amateurism had given way to the reserved polish of the professional investing class. Along one wall, absent buyers called in their bids to a phone bank. Meanwhile, no one present in the room seemed to be bidding on their own behalf. The floor was filled with young men and women dressed in crisp white shirts and pressed black suits who dashed in and out of the room to take urgent phone calls. Liu had turned a cultural icon into a financial asset and created a market where there had been none. That market had sent Moutai prices soaring beyond Googut's original ambitions. That year, the average 1980s bottle sold at auction for a little less than 70,000 yuan, more than twice the price of three years earlier (a new bottle fresh from the factory cost only 2,000 yuan). By then, Lafite's prices had tumbled. Ironically, the 1982 vintage was trading for less than half that of Moutai.

The proclivities of China's wealthy have proved to be both boon and bane to niche-asset markets the world over. In Vancouver, the influx of Chinese money has fueled a real estate bubble that has made housing unaffordable for many city residents. Chinese demand for jade has created a multi-billion-dollar mining industry in Myanmar that has given rise to fraud and corruption and has helped fund armed conflict in China's southern neighbor. In Nepal, Chinese demand for a parasitic fungus that grows out of dead caterpillars — known colloquially as Himalayan Viagra for its origin and purported effects — has made the fungus more expensive than gold, creating what has been dubbed the "Himalayan gold rush." But it has also generated theft and violence as the laborers who flock to the Nepalese plateaus compete over dwindling stocks. And in Europe, Chinese soccer clubs paid twice as much as their counterparts in the English Premier League to hire top-level players during the 2016 trading period, inflating the market price of these international players by paying record amounts in transfer fees. The *People's Daily* warned that the clubs' spending "far exceeded the economic value brought to the [Chinese] league," calling it a bubble.

It's easy to look at such spending as the inevitable result of China's newfound wealth, and to attribute the willingness to overpay to the irrational exuberance of the country's nouveaux riches. No doubt there's an element of that, but there's a more important and more serious factor at play as well. Since 2008, the world's biggest developed economies have run the printing presses overtime in a controversial attempt to shore up their financial systems and to stimulate growth by creating new money. But while debate has raged back and forth about whether the monetary expansion pursued by the U.S. Federal Reserve, the European Central Bank, and the Bank of Japan has been necessary or foolhardy, one fact is routinely overlooked: the amount of new money that China has created over the same period has dwarfed all three of the major industrial economies *combined*. Between 2007 and 2015, China was responsible for 63% of all new money created globally. The reason China's monetary expansion isn't lumped in with that of the developed economies is that most of China's money wasn't created by its central bank. Rather, it was created in what passes for the usual or customary way in modern economies. That is, commercial banks create new money every time they make a loan, not just in China but in all economies. That's how a nation's money supply usually expands. When a bank makes a loan, the borrower invariably uses the money to make some sort of payment, maybe to buy a house or a car or to pay university-tuition fees. Whoever receives the payment then typically puts the money into the bank, creating new deposits. At that point, the banking system can use the deposit to make a new loan, which, as a consequence, creates a new deposit. Whereas originally there was only one deposit, now there are two — in effect, the banks have created money. The upshot is that the more banks lend, the more deposits are created and, by extension, the more money is brought into existence.

That's not necessarily a bad thing. A fast-growing economy needs more money to facilitate all the additional economic transactions occurring. But in China, there's a major flaw in all of this: the money supply has expanded on a scale out of all proportion to the growth of economic activity. Whereas before the global financial crisis there were 1.5 yuan's worth of deposits and cash circulating for every yuan of GDP, by 2015 that had risen to 2 yuan. In other words, the Chinese banks have kept making loans, but those loans don't generate as much economic growth as they used to, resulting in a lot of money that has no productive purpose.

Complicating matters is that, in addition to all of the money created by commercial banks, in recent years the People's Bank of China has quietly flipped the switch on the printing presses and pumped trillions of yuan directly into its financial system. That's in part been to offset money that started flowing out of the country in 2016. But the extra money is also necessary in order for banks and other financial institutions to hold and to hide increasing volumes of bad loans. Every loan, whether made by a bank or by some shadow financial institution, is made possible by someone's savings. People hand over their savings with the full expectation that they will eventually get their money back, plus interest. But when loans go bad, that doesn't happen. So in order to ensure that financial institutions have sufficient funds to pay savers — or whoever else has lent them money — what they're owed, the central bank prints money, which it then lends cheaply to the banks. That certainly doesn't make the bad loans go away, but it does allow the financial system to remain solvent, by ensuring that it has the money to pay its debts as they come due. There may have been a time when the central bank regarded such intervention as a way to buy time, which it could use to clean up the system. But what was once a Band-Aid solution has long since become a crutch that's indispensable to the stability of the financial system.

However, the price of that stability is instability elsewhere in the economy. The creation of so much unproductive money should devalue the currency. Consequently the yuan has been under pressure to depreciate and, in 2016, caused the central bank to spend roughly $1 trillion from the foreign-exchange reserves in an attempt to slow the currency's decline. Potentially it could also create serious inflation, but China has so far managed to avoid that, partly because, rather than all that new money being spent on groceries and consumer goods, much of it is saved. That, however, creates another problem. Those savings have to be invested somewhere, and people are no longer content to just leave it in the bank.

• • •

The result is asset bubbles throughout the economy. According to Liu, within a few years of his first auction, there were suddenly one hundred auction houses throughout China — "at least one or two in every city" — selling vintage *baijiu*. In response to the competition, Liu looked into diversifying, and for a time considered listing ten thousand bottles of old Fenjiu — a type of *baijiu* from Shanxi Province — on an electronic exchange in a way that would allow people to trade them like shares. He got the idea after witnessing the price of old coins trading on an exchange in southern China increase more than ten times over.

Such fringe markets have proliferated in China since the 2009 stimulus, which was launched in response to the global financial crisis, first supercharged the money supply. Hundreds of electronic exchanges have appeared across the landscape, creating forums for people to trade almost anything imaginable, from the ingredients of traditional Chinese medicine to vats of prebottled *baijiu*. Some trade niche commodities, like the Fanya Metals Exchange. For a time, an exchange in Tianjin sold art securities — people could buy shares in a couple of Chinese landscape paintings — that went up in value by more than 1,000% in just a couple of months before the authorities took an interest and the bubble popped.

But while the flood of money has breathed life into new markets, it has also wreaked havoc in more-established markets. It pumped up the stock market by 150% in less than a year before the bubble popped in mid-2015, wiping out — on paper at least — about $3 trillion worth of wealth. It has played a role in inflating land prices in China's major cities to nosebleed heights, and did the same to bond prices in 2016 and early 2017, the opposite of what bonds should be doing in a slowing economy with rising bad loans. Even the commodities-futures market has been radically distorted by the rush of speculative cash. On one day early in 2016, the volume of rebar-steel futures traded was so disproportionate to any conceivable demand that it was enough to build the Eiffel Tower 178,000 times over. On another day, the number of cotton contracts that changed hands represented enough cotton to make one pair of jeans for every man, woman, and child on the planet. The foreign press has dubbed this mass of itinerant cash "the great ball of money." Its dangers aren't lost on China's senior leaders.

"We need to thoroughly give up on the notion that we can grow the economy through monetary expansion." So reads an interview published on the front page of the *People's Daily* in mid-2016, with an anonymous source, identified only as being an "authoritative person" widely thought to be Xi Jinping's chief economic adviser. The column called for reform before something went seriously wrong. "For every part of the financial system there exists the risk of financial contagion."

That China could really suffer financial contagion — whereby a shock in one corner of the financial system turns into a full-blown crisis — is not the sort of alarmism the Chinese Communist Party typically advertises on the front page of its daily broadsheet. The column may have been an attempt to shock the bureaucracy out of its complacency. China has never had a financial crisis under Party rule, and it's widely assumed by many inside and outside China that one is highly unlikely, if not impossible. Yet the sheer volume of money that's been created is not the only sign that something's gone seriously wrong with the country's financial system.

The Pearl of the North will be a striking monument when complete. The 565-meter-tall skyscraper at the heart of Shenyang will be topped with a sphere that will glow gold at night and, in a nod to the city's industrial heritage, is meant to evoke molten steel. During daylight, the external ribbing that runs vertically down the length of the tower is supposed to look like the strings of a *guzheng*, a Chinese instrument similar to a zither. When it's finished, in 2018, it will be 27 meters taller than One World Trade Center, the tallest building in the United States.

But perhaps the most notable thing about the Pearl is that it will be only the fifth-tallest skyscraper in China, eclipsed by a triangular tower topped with a glass dome in Wuhan; a tower designed to look like a twisting dragon in Shanghai; a tower with the largest stainless-steel facade in the world in Shenzhen; and a tower in Tianjin that, somewhat inexplicably, is designed to resemble a bejeweled walking stick. Two years later, the Pearl will drop to sixth place if China's tallest building — a 729-meter spire in Suzhou — is completed on schedule. The value of such supertall skyscrapers is invariably couched in terms that have little to do with the provision of adding new office space. "This iconic building marks a solid step in Shenyang's progress toward becoming an international city," the Pearl's developer says on its website. Not leaving anything to chance, the developer had a feng shui master come inspect the site before construction began, to ensure that the location and orientation were sufficiently auspicious. However, if history is anything to go by, the Pearl is more like a very large, bad omen than a harbinger of prosperity.

Throughout history, construction of the tallest skyscraper in the world has been synonymous with the imminent onset of economic crises, an association that goes back to an 1873 financial crisis, when the completion of the 142-foot-tall Equitable Life Building in New York — the tallest building of its day — coincided with the five-year Long Depression, best recalled for wiping out dozens of U.S. railway companies. Since then, every major crisis has had its monument: New York's Empire State and Chrysler Buildings were well under way when the Great Depression hit, in 1929. The Petronas Towers in Kuala Lumpur were finished in 1997, just as the Asian financial crisis ravaged East Asia. And the Burj Khalifa — which currently stands as the world's tallest building — was a work in progress when, in 2009, Dubai's government was forced to turn to a neighboring emirate for a bailout.

China isn't building the world's tallest building. That honor goes to

Saudi Arabia. But, according to the American bank analyst who discovered the correlation between the building of tall buildings and economic troubles, the construction of the world's single tallest building is not the sole indicator of hard times ahead. In fact, the construction of multiple skyscrapers *all at once* is an even better predictor. At the time of this writing, China was building twenty-five skyscrapers taller than the Empire State Building. And of the one hundred tallest buildings under construction anywhere in the world, fifty-five were in China. China is in the midst of an epic, nationwide skyscraper-construction boom that's being replicated in miniature in some cities. Shenyang is building five towers of about 300 meters or taller, and when I last visited, in 2014, a local architect told me that there were plans for an additional thirteen on the drawing board. (Shenyang seems to have already experienced its reckoning. In 2016, Liaoning Province, of which Shenyang is the capital, slid into recession.)

Moreover, China's skyscrapers are appearing in unusual places. Traditionally the world's tallest buildings have been found in business centers like New York, Chicago, Hong Kong, and Dubai, but today they're going up in the capitals of some of China's poorest provinces, like Hefei (which is building the world's nineteenth-tallest building) and Nanning (which is building the sixteenth-tallest). Even Shenyang, which has neither the financial sector nor the white-shoe law firms that usually flock to prestige office buildings, isn't the sort of city that typically builds supertall skyscrapers.

It's difficult to say with great certainty why skyscraper construction works so well as an early-warning system for economic crises. The Long Depression, Great Depression, Asian financial crisis, and Dubai's debt crisis have very little in common, except that they all followed long booms. Like the proverbial canary in the coal mine, skyscrapers seem to signal the presence of two potentially toxic elements in the economic ecosystem that, at the tail end of a boom, are typically in ample supply, namely, hubris and an excess of money. Money, because skyscrapers are incredibly expensive to build; and hubris, because the decision to massively increase a city's supply of top-grade office space — the type that only the most successful investment banks and hedge funds and law firms can afford to rent — a few years into the future is a very large bet that the good times will only keep getting better. In brief, skyscrapers don't cause financial crises, but they reflect the willingness of the financial system to lend large amounts of money for blatantly speculative ventures that, wrapped in the overconfidence of the times, appear to be not only rational but genuinely sound investments. It's when that dynamic — the entwining of credit with speculation — takes hold of other parts of the economy that things start to sour.

Liu Jianfeng's appearance is not what you'd expect of someone who spends his day selling überexpensive vintage alcohol to the nouveaux riches. The fifty-year-old has graying hair and the bad teeth common to his generation. A tall man with gangly limbs, he wears clothes that never quite seem to fit, and I've never seen him without a grin, as though he still can't believe that, after years of bouncing around jobs — at one time doing feasibility studies for chemical plants, and later helping relocate people whose homes were being flooded by construction of the Three Gorges Dam — he has somehow landed the job of his dreams.

When I caught up with Liu in 2014, his operation was no longer just an auction house. He was managing a huge warehouse filled with high-end bottles of *baijiu* for sale to special clients like luxury hotels, and cheaper bottles for sale online, part of an effort to bring *baijiu* connoisseurship to the masses. "With a population of 1.3 billion people, there are still a lot of people who have yet to understand the market," he said. "The market will definitely get better and better. It's just taking its first step."

Liu's warehouse was a four-story building in southeast Beijing that used to belong to a Japanese company that made components for microscopes. There were two German shepherds boxed up by the gate that were let free at night to guard the building's perimeter. With shiny, bright-green concrete floors and exposed air-conditioning pipes running along the high ceiling, the warehouse felt a little like the backstage area of a convention center. Well before getting to the entrance, I could smell the liquor — not the barreled oak of a whiskey cellar but the raw tang of pure alcohol. Liu and I put our phones in a wooden box outside the door. Taking a call inside the warehouse seemed like an order of magnitude more dangerous than pumping gas while using a cell phone.

Inside, the bottles were kept on long trellises six shelves high, each tagged with its age and origin. Liu kept his most precious finds behind a wire-mesh fence at the far end: old Moutai bottles from the 1950s, brands that have since disappeared, and a ceramic jar of Fenjiu that dated from before the Communists took control of China. A sharp-eyed employee of a Chinese state firm had spotted the purple-glazed jar, stamped "for export only," in an antique store while on assignment in South America and snapped it up for pocket change. In total, the warehouse stored more than one hundred thousand bottles, but Liu was worried about his auction business. "It's getting more difficult to find old bottles," he told me. "Old *baijiu* is being drunk, there is more competition, and a lot has already been auctioned."

But Liu wasn't sitting around waiting for the good times to end. To find new fodder for auction, every few months he and a handful of colleagues traveled to the provinces, spending a week to visit as many towns and cities as they could. Advertising in the local media in advance, they would hire a hotel ballroom and then wait for locals to bring in old bottles of *baijiu* for authentication, in a manner not unlike *Antiques Roadshow*, the PBS television program.

Not all bottles are fit to sell. Some are counterfeit, and some are in such a poor state that no investor would likely be willing to buy them. But once Liu finds bottles that fit the bill, acquiring them for auction has its own problems. Liu found that people are reluctant to hand over their Moutai bottles to some stranger who promises to auction them at some point in the future, and so they demand cash up front. The problem is, Liu's operation doesn't have that sort of cash on hand, and no bank has ever been willing to give him a loan. "Banks typically lend to state firms that will never collapse. It's a lot harder for us private companies," he said. "But banks will issue wealth-management products for us."

Since 2010, banks have raised 400 million yuan for Liu by selling WMPs. Liu uses the funds to pay the Moutai owners a down payment for their bottles. After the bottles are sold, the people who bought the WMPs eventually receive what they're owed — typically 10% on top of what they invested in the WMP — and the bottle owners get the remainder. Crucially, however, the system is premised on the expectation that Moutai appreciates in value. Liu didn't see that as a problem. "Originally banks were suspicious of the value of old Moutai, but not anymore," said Liu, explaining that banks increasingly have approached him about providing finance. "There's no risk."

We need "to prevent wealth management funds going into empty investments rather than the real economy." So wrote Shang Fulin, the one-time head of China's banking regulatory agency. As reasonable as that sounds, what Shang was asking is near impossible. Many of the companies at the core of China's real economy — the manufacturing and industrial companies that China's economic miracle was built upon — have no need to borrow. Many industries are simply plagued by overcapacity. Others are squeezed by foreign competition. Rising labor, land, and energy costs are all taking a serious toll. Profits have been so thin for so long that, for many business owners, it's just not worth investing in their own companies anymore.

That's not to say there's no need for credit at all. Infrastructure and housing projects still borrow, as do households who want to buy a home. Many companies need loans to upgrade or to automate their factories, and industries like robotics and semiconductors are taking on debt as part of Beijing's plans to develop high-tech sectors. But all that said, the real economy has no need for credit anywhere on the scale being proffered by the financial system. In fact, many Chinese businesses have such poor prospects that they have moved into more speculative pursuits.

"Almost all big manufacturing companies have, to a certain extent, gotten involved in real estate," wrote Xiang Songzuo, former chief economist at the Agricultural Bank of China, in 2013. "For many companies sales are stagnant, business is difficult, and the ability to earn a profit has sharply declined, so more and more manufacturing companies have started to subsidize their losses by getting involved in real estate or with financial investments."

The Chinese call it *tuo shi xiang xu*: "casting off the real for the empty." Equally, it can be thought of as the financialization of the economy, whereby returns on financial investments — whether real estate or some financial instrument — outstrip those in the real economy, leading industrial and manufacturing firms to direct funds into the financial system rather than back into their businesses.

In practice, this activity takes many forms. Some companies have set up their own property-development arms, like Erzhong, the heavily indebted state-owned machinery maker, which built a complex of middle-income high-rise apartments on the outskirts of Chengdu, about a three-hour drive from its Deyang factory. Others speculate on housing by purchasing newly built apartments. Some firms make loans to other companies, particularly if they're able to borrow cheaply themselves. Others invest their savings in WMPs and trust products. And, anecdotally at least, many entrepreneurs with no prior experience in financial services have set up their own finance companies: for example, there's the steel trader who founded a P2P platform and is now offering 20% annualized returns to people willing to make short-term loans; the Shenzhen property developer who set up a company that disposes of bad loans made by banks in Tibet; the trouser manufacturer who applied for a banking license; and the mining company that had been losing money for years but then bought a car-leasing company in a bid to reinvent itself.

There has also been an explosion in the number of fringe financial companies — the sort that can be set up with few regulatory hurdles — in recent years. At the end of 2015, China had more than 7,100 leasing companies, 2,600 more than the year before and an eleven-fold increase from when the economy first started slowing, in 2012. There were 4,500 P2P platforms at the end of 2016, up from only 200 when the economy started slowing four years earlier.

Meanwhile, the outstanding volume of wealth-management products increased by 56% in 2015 and by about 20% in 2016. "Today everyone is playing in finance — state firms, private firms, everyone," said former Sinopec chairman Fu Chengyu in mid-2017. He said that China's economy had already "become empty," in a play on the idiom. "Those without a financial license all want to apply. With a license, you can immediately get rich. The real economy can't compete."

Ironically, as the economy slows, so should demand for financial services. But in China, they continue to expand, not because the real economy demands credit but because there is so much money that demands somewhere to invest.

"With the fast expansion of the money supply, vast volumes of funds have cycled back into the financial system, vast amounts of liquidity have never entered the real economy . . . and 'casting off the real for the empty' has grown more intense," said Yin Zhongqing, deputy director of the Finance and Economics Committee of the National People's Congress, in mid-2017. Yin noted that financial services currently represent almost 9% of China's gross domestic product, exceeding that of the United States. (In 2015, finance and insurance represented 7.2% of the U.S. economy.)

So where does all the credit go? Most obviously it's gone toward inflating asset prices. It inflates land values by giving developers the financial wherewithal to pay higher and higher prices. It's pushed up housing prices as banks have lent more to homebuyers to compensate for there being fewer good opportunities for the banks in the industrial economy. And credit inflated the 2015 stock bubble after as much as $1.2 trillion worth of shares were bought with money borrowed from a combination of state lenders, trust companies, and wealth-management products. But the higher prices go, the less stable they become.

Five years after I first met Liu, I finally relented and let him open a bottle of aged *baijiu,* a 2000 bottle of Zhu Ye Qing ("bamboo-leaf-green" liquor), which he assured me that "even women like," implying that a foreigner shouldn't find it too objectionable. A new bottle from the liquor store cost 58 yuan. According to Liu's prospectus, a sixteen-year-old bottle was worth 1,188 yuan. Sticker shock aside, the Zhu Ye Qing was a pleasant surprise. The yellow-tinged liquid was warm and mellow. Liu described it as spicy and fragrant, but that was more than my novice palate could discern. We barely made a dent in the bottle over lunch, and Liu insisted over my protestations that I take it home with me. My driver was incredibly grateful for the gift.

Liu was still enthusiastic about the prospects of vintage *baijiu*, but he was spending more time on his democratization efforts at the low end of the market. An anticorruption campaign launched by President Xi Jinping had lasted far longer than expected, dampening people's willingness to be seen drinking ten-thousand-dollar bottles of *baijiu*. At least that was Liu's explanation. In fact, the entire auction industry was having trouble. Winning bidders were reneging on their bids when it came time to settle the bill. Private entrepreneurs, a big part of the market, were finding their finances increasingly stretched by the slowing economy. Liu still thought a bottle of 1980s Moutai would auction for 70,000 yuan, but he wasn't confident enough to put that notion to the test. He hasn't hosted a vintage Moutai auction since 2014.

In addition to speculative assets, the credit created by an ever-expanding financial system has also continued to flow toward the usual suspects — infrastructure, housing, and heavy industry — not only facilitating new investment but also allowing companies that can't repay their debts to remain solvent. As long as there is plenty of money — and plenty of different financial institutions lending it — local governments, and developers in particular, can simply exchange their old loans for new loans.

The developer of the Pearl of the North — a company that builds offices, shopping malls, and housing across the country — is not unusual in funding itself using trusts, securities companies, and wealth-management products. It owns a stake in an online leasing company, which it uses to raise funds from the general public for development projects. And it owns 20% of one of China's fastest-growing insurance companies, which invests money raised from life-insurance premiums in the developer's projects. (It launched a hostile takeover of another developer using funds raised through WMPs.) All these sources of credit give it the freedom to borrow from one lender to pay off another.

This system — where companies swap new debt for old, and financial institutions lend to speculative investments — works as long as there is sufficient cash. So far, the People's Bank of China has proved extremely accommodating to ensure that there is. But what if, suddenly, there weren't? Financial crises aren't caused by bad loans. Much like a conventional bank run, crises occur when people, en masse, no longer believe that their money is safe, and so they rush to pull it out of wherever it's invested. The reason they lose faith might be that they're worried that a bank has too many bad loans, but it's the act of withdrawing the funds that undermines the viability of a bank, or the entire financial system.

In its simplest form, such a loss of faith manifests itself as a bank run, as in the Jimmy Stewart movie *It's a Wonderful Life,* where the sight of people queuing up outside a bank branch leads others to do the same, draining the bank of its cash reserves until it can no longer satisfy depositors' demands for their money back. But China has grown quite adept at dealing with conventional runs. In 2014, two rural banks in Jiangsu Province experienced a bank run that lasted for three days after a number of local underground financiers and unregulated loan shops collapsed, making people jittery about whether the local banks were exposed to the same problems. The People's Bank of China rushed money to the branches. The bricks of freshly delivered cash were stacked up behind the tellers in order to calm nerves.

The modern, more dangerous version of the bank run happens when the trust between banks themselves breaks down and they decline to continue lending to each other. That's what caused Lehman Brothers to collapse in 2008 and plunged the U.S. financial system into crisis. A quirk of the U.S. shadow-banking system is that banks had grown reliant on borrowing from each other and from other financial institutions — like hedge funds — in order to fund their lending activities. Complicating matters is that banks made loans to each other for very short periods of time, typically overnight.

Lehman was dependent on always being able to replace maturing loans with new loans. When its peers lost faith in it and stopped lending, it didn't have the funds to repay its loans. But because of the complex, interconnected lending arrangements between banks, defaults by one had a domino effect on trust throughout the entire system, causing everyone to stop lending to each other. Credit contracted, not only between banks but also from banks to the rest of the economy, bringing global trade to a standstill, pushing U.S. companies to the brink of bankruptcy, and causing the U.S. economy to start shrinking.

China's financial system is increasingly looking like that of the United States prior to the Lehman Brothers bankruptcy. Banks are dependent on each other and on WMPs for funding—which they use to make shadow-banking loans—such that if there were a Lehman-like loss of faith in the system, vast amounts of credit extended through shadow banking would immediately contract. Yet the likelihood of that happening in China is far lower than in the United States.

China's financial system is fundamentally different from those in free-market economies. Although it may appear to be far more stable, that stability is not the result of superior design. Quite the opposite: China's banks are riddled with bad loans, the opacity of shadow banking makes it difficult to regulate, there are regular revelations of large-scale (albeit low-level) fraud, and a morass of complicated lending arrangements linking banks and shadow-banking institutions could easily turn an isolated problem into a system-wide contagion.

Anywhere else, the trust that underpins the financial system—the trust between the public and banks, and among the banks themselves—would have eroded long ago. But in China, financial stability is based not on the relative health and good management of the banks but on the widely held belief that the government will always intervene whenever necessary to ensure the stability of the system, a belief based on Beijing repeatedly doing just that. In most economies, government intervention is typically limited to changing interest rates and printing money. Beijing, however, is far more expansive in its use of state power.

When the stock market collapsed in 2015, Beijing stepped in, deploying all the various powers at its disposal to stop the rout. It mobilized a group of large state-owned firms — what became known as "the national team" — to buy up huge volumes of shares, and they set themselves up as buyers of last resort. Ultimately, they spent about 1.5 trillion yuan to stop share prices from falling any further. Fund managers were pressured to only buy stock and not sell. Television and radio stations were instructed to soft-pedal their coverage and to avoid using harsh words like "slump" or "collapse." People were arrested for "spreading rumors" relating to the stock market. When *Caijing,* one of China's premier financial magazines, reported that the national team was planning on winding up its intervention, the journalist who wrote the story was arrested and, while still in custody, made a televised apology. "I shouldn't have released a report with a major negative impact on the market at such a sensitive time," he said. "I shouldn't do that just to catch attention which has caused the country and its investors such a big loss."

Therein lies China's strength. No one questions Beijing's commitment to maintaining stability. Beijing's willingness to use all the tools at its disposal — whether telling state firms to buy shares, or molding public opinion — has traditionally made the prospect of China's experiencing a financial crisis seem fanciful. But this is also China's Achilles' heel. With financial institutions safe in the knowledge that Beijing is providing a safety net, the system has grown bigger, more complex, and riskier. Moreover, and more disturbing, sometimes Beijing does lose control.

A TREE CAN'T GROW TO THE SKY

Late in 2014, from out of the blue, I got an e-mail from Pakistan suggesting that I contact Masood Textile Mills. Earlier that year, a Chinese textiles and apparel manufacturer, Shandong Ruyi Science and Technology Group, had signed a deal to buy control of Masood for $62 million. But after nine months, the Chinese firm reneged on the deal.

Ruyi is no fly-by-night operation. It is one of the best-respected, most technologically advanced textile manufacturers in China. You'll scarcely find one person in the football-field-sized hangar where it produces yarn. The staff drive around in electric golf carts, using iPads to monitor a factory that is almost entirely automated. In the building next door, workers produce suits for Armani and Canali. The company has spent hundreds of millions of dollars buying clothing brands in Japan and Europe, and farms producing cotton and wool in Australia.

When I visited Ruyi's headquarters, in Shandong Province, just south of Shanghai, company officials intimated that the difficulties of doing business in Pakistan had played a role in the decision to back out of the deal. (President Xi Jinping had to postpone a trip to Pakistan originally planned for September that year because of huge antigovernment protests in Islamabad.) But when I spoke with Masood's CEO, Shahid Nazir, he said that the explanation Ruyi had given him was very different. According to Nazir, Ruyi personnel said that despite having received government approval for the deal, the company just couldn't get a bank loan. "Shandong banks were having some serious issues on defaults," Nazir said Ruyi officials told him. "Because of the general situation in Shandong . . . lots of companies in the province were feeling the squeeze."

Shandong is a powerhouse. It's China's third-biggest provincial economy, after Guangdong and Jiangsu, and, with around one hundred million people, it is one of the biggest provinces by population. Yet from July through September — the three months before Ruyi reneged on its deal — the "general situation" in the province was that credit was contracting. Contractions have occurred before in poor peripheral economies, like that of Tibet, but not at China's core. Debt drives growth. No provincial government would willingly turn off the taps. What seems to have happened is that an unforeseen event caused the banks to panic.

Starting around April 2014, authorities began investigating fraud at Shandong's biggest port in the scenic coastal city of Qingdao. What had started on the other side of the country as an investigation into a corrupt official and his cronies led Party disciplinarians to stockpiles of metal — copper and aluminum in particular — which had been stored in Qingdao port warehouses. Those stockpiles were being used as collateral for loans (which was a common practice), but the investigation revealed that the same stocks of metal were being used as collateral for multiple loans from multiple financial institutions. Billions of dollars' worth of loans was involved.

By June, lawsuits were flying thick and fast as banks tried to secure the collateral. Banks became nervous, and, faced with unforeseen losses, they pulled back from the metals business. Without credit, companies sold off their metals so that they could get cash. Metals imports dropped (economists say that China imports far more metal than it needs so that it can be used as collateral for loans), and global prices for copper and other metals fell. Bad loans held by Shandong banks increased by more than 50%, to almost 100 billion yuan, and their profits in the second half of the year dropped by 25% from a year earlier.

Ultimately, however, there were no long-term scars. Lending quickly bounced back, Masood found another Chinese buyer, and Ruyi resumed its overseas shopping spree, picking up a couple of French fashion labels in 2016. Most importantly, the fallout was limited to two ports in Shandong. But it didn't have to be that way. Less than 2% of copper and metal alloys get imported to China through Qingdao. If cases of fraud had been unmasked in Shanghai, where almost 80% of metals imports arrive and collateralized lending is inordinately larger, then the fallout may have been far more significant.

So far, China's authorities have managed to handle all challenges that have come their way. But as the financial system gets bigger, more complex, more levered, and more speculative, the domino effects from seemingly minor or insignificant shocks can quickly spread in unexpected ways. Perhaps the biggest risk is that Beijing itself will do something that inadvertently results in a financial crisis. It could be completely unforeseeable, like an anticorruption campaign resulting in revelations of widespread financial fraud. Or perhaps pressure on the currency to depreciate might lead Beijing to devalue the yuan, a situation which, if mishandled, could exacerbate depreciation pressures and cause the public to pull their savings from the financial system and try to move it overseas. Or perhaps Beijing might try to discipline the financial system — to rein in credit growth or improve loan quality — by rationing injections of new money, but it might misjudge the impact, resulting in an asset bubble bursting or, with shadow banking collapsing, spreading fear and contagion throughout an intricately linked financial system.

Most of these scenarios have occurred in one form or another over the last few years, and Beijing has been able to prevent the initial ill effects from spilling into something more serious. But the day may ultimately come when Beijing's best efforts are just flat-out insufficient to stem the tide.

The International Monetary Fund worries that the ever-increasing opacity and complexity of the Chinese financial system mean that "vulnerabilities are difficult to locate and targeted support may be more difficult to deliver." In other words, Beijing runs the risk that its rescue efforts will amount to being the wrong thing in the wrong place at the wrong time. Ultimately the risk is that something happens on a scale and at a speed that seemingly exceed the central government's ability to assert control, and that the underlying trust that underwrites the stability of the entire system erodes in a panic.

It's difficult to say what a crisis of this magnitude could look like. Given the interconnectedness of the banks, a Lehman-style crisis is not out of the question, although Beijing has proved itself to be able to force banks to lend to each other. Alternatively, it could be that the public loses faith. While trust in the Big Four banks at the core of the financial system is rock solid, the same can't be said of China's smaller banks — the hundreds of rural cooperatives, rural commercial banks, and city commercial banks that reside at the fringes — which have more bad loans, rely on shadow banking to a greater extent, are not as well managed as their larger counterparts, and have increased their lending at a far quicker pace. And these banks are backed by local authorities, many of whom have their own financial difficulties. It's not unimaginable that something — a currency depreciation, revelations of widespread fraud, a bursting bubble, a financial institution's collapse — could trigger a run on WMPs that were issued by smaller banks, with people pulling their savings and moving them to the safety of the Big Four. The net effect would be that savings would still stay within the financial system, but those parts of the economy served by smaller banks and shadow institutions would see credit contract, causing asset prices to fall and thus distress to ripple through the web of interbank relationships to infect healthy and unhealthy banks alike, thereby pushing the economy into recession.

Of course, China might manage to avoid a serious financial crisis, and, to the extent that one is even possible, it might not be imminent (although, as U.S. economist Rudi Dornbusch once put it, "The crisis takes a much longer time coming than you think, and then it happens much faster than you would have thought"). Nonetheless, Beijing is presiding over an increasingly fragile financial system, one in which short-term stability is maintained only by storing up bigger problems for the near future.

The morass of bad loans in the banking system requires the central bank to keep printing more and more money. Credit needs to continue growing to maintain economic growth, but every yuan of debt generates less economic activity than it used to. In theory, Beijing could allow its perpetual-motion machine of debt creation to continue indefinitely, but the newly created money eventually ends up feeding speculative bubbles, because there are few other places for it to go. In order to prevent the bubbles from popping, and to maintain confidence, the central bank prints even more money. All the while, as the size and complexity of the system grow, the potential for something to go seriously wrong increases.

When the "authoritative person" suspected to be Xi's economic adviser warned of contagion in his *People's Daily* interview, he didn't offer details as to what form it might take, but he was clear on what could happen if credit and the supply of money were allowed to continue expanding as a cure for China's economic problems. "Trees don't grow to the sky," he wrote. "If we don't control things it could trigger a systemic financial crisis, leading to an economic recession, and all the hopes stored up by the people will be dashed to pieces."

Yet, at this point, there are no good solutions. Changing the way the system works so that it's safer and more sustainable will result in significantly slower growth, and cleaning up the current system will be costly. There's still an inclination — both inside and outside China — to believe that the authorities will not let things get out of hand, and that they will ultimately deal with the increasingly perilous situation without too much disruption. But that assumes not only that the senior leadership has a clear vision of what sort of reform is necessary, but that it also has the will to see it through, plus the authority to make it stick. It's that last element that poses the greatest challenge. Throughout the government, the bureaucracy, and state-owned industry, there is deeply rooted resistance to change. Overcoming it is proving far harder than the senior leaders may initially have expected.

7

THE RESISTANCE

IN THE EARLY 1990s, China set its sights on eliminating one of the country's biggest public-health problems: iodine deficiency. Iodine naturally occurs in seawater and tends to find its way into food produced in coastal areas, but historically people who live far inland have lacked sufficient iodine in their diet. Only trace amounts are necessary, but without them brain development can be severely retarded. Deficiency can also cause goiter, the swelling of thyroid glands into large lumps around the neck. According to the World Health Organization, in 1995 an astounding 20% of Chinese schoolchildren between the ages of eight and ten showed signs of iodine deficiency.

Beijing's solution, launched the following year, was to impose a governmental monopoly on the production and distribution of table salt. There was a bit of history to this: China had maintained a salt monopoly, on and off, for about 2,600 years. For most of that time, it had worked as a kind of sales tax, at times generating as much as half of the imperial revenue. Private salt merchants were granted monopoly charters by the emperor in return for pouring significant amounts of money into the state coffers, which the merchants delivered by selling salt at higher prices than would be possible in a free market. That worked in an agrarian economy, where salt was one of the few things people needed to buy — like iodine, the human body needs to consume small amounts of salt — but as the economy became more urbanized and industrial, more lucrative sources of taxation emerged. By the 1990s, salt was only a marginal component of China's tax base.

However, during the twentieth century, salt had become the universally accepted medium for delivering iodine into the public diet. Upon assuming power, the Chinese Communist Party nationalized the salt industry — along with the rest of the economy — and had made some progress in dealing with iodine deficiency. In 1989, about 90% of salt consumed in landlocked Gansu — one of China's poorest and most inaccessible western provinces — was iodized. But as Beijing started to relax state control over the economy and private business got involved in producing and selling salt, that ratio dropped. Within two years, only 60% of salt being consumed in Gansu was fortified with iodine as merchants cut corners and undercut state prices.

In the face of a public-health crisis, Beijing resurrected a version of the old imperial salt monopoly. Only licensed companies were now permitted to produce table salt, whether from mines, or from brine extracted from underground wells, or from evaporated seawater and salt lakes (today there are one hundred or so licensed producers). The producers were then required to sell their salt to specially chartered state-owned distribution companies that, within certain allocated geographic areas, had a monopoly over the transportation of the salt, packaging it and selling it to supermarkets and other retailers. The monopoly eventually built a workforce of four hundred thousand people, including twenty-five thousand "salt police" dedicated to enforcing the monopoly.

Crucially, the monopoly was funded by a regime of fixed prices. In 2016, prices differed a little from place to place, but, generally speaking, producers were required to sell their salt at about 500 yuan per ton (comfortably above the cost to make it) to distributors, who were then mandated to sell it to supermarkets at around 2,000 yuan per ton. In imperial times, the difference between production and retail prices was roughly equivalent to what the state collected in taxes. Under the repurposed monopoly, it was a subsidy to distributors to ensure that iodized salt made its way to the most far-flung corners of the People's Republic.

The results were almost instantaneous. By 1999, the percentage of schoolchildren showing signs of iodine deficiency more than halved, to just 8.8%. By 2005, it was down to 5%. In 2010, the Ministry of Health declared that outside of Xinjiang, Tibet, and Qinghai — the country's most remote provinces — China had mostly eradicated iodine deficiency. No other developing country has proven so successful so quickly at eliminating most instances of the condition.

However, despite its success, it's really not clear that the salt monopoly was ever necessary. For example, before the 1920s, the Great Lakes, Appalachians, and the northwestern regions of the United States were known as the goiter belt, with between 26% and 70% of children in those areas clinically diagnosed with goiter. Yet the United States managed to eliminate iodine deficiency, not with a monopoly but by regulating private producers, an approach which is taken by most nations. Moreover, China's salt monopoly has been so zealous in promoting iodine consumption that in 2007, the health ministry published a report saying that people in five provinces were actually consuming excessive amounts of iodine, and that sixteen provinces were consuming more than the optimal amount.

China's central government determined some time ago that there was no longer any need to maintain the monopoly, yet, ironically, Beijing has been unable to get rid of it. Beijing first tried in 2001, when it formulated a plan to deregulate prices and throw the market open to competition, but then thought better of implementing it. It next published plans to reform the monopoly in 2004, and then again in 2005. There have been major reform pushes in 2007, 2010, and 2014 as well. Since the turn of the century, three different government administrations have altogether tried eight times either to reform the salt regime or to abolish it. Yet still the monopoly endures.

Zhongnanhai is the complex in the very center of Beijing where China's top leaders live and work. It's roughly the low-rise equivalent of the Kremlin, or a sprawling version of the White House. That means more power is concentrated behind its walls than in almost any other address on earth, yet an old Chinese adage has it that "orders issued from Zhongnanhai seldom make it outside of the compound." The expression goes back to the 1990s, but it gained currency under President Hu Jintao and Premier Wen Jiabao, whose government ruled China for the ten years ending in 2012, a period often referred to as "the lost decade."

During Hu and Wen's time at the helm, the economic liberalization begun by the previous administration stalled, corruption worsened, and the most serious problems that plague China today — environmental degradation, income inequality, and a reliance on investment to drive growth — became entrenched. That's not to say that the men were either opposed to reform or blind to the emerging problems. Wen in particular — who earlier in his career had served as personal secretary to Zhao Ziyang, one of China's great reformist premiers — described the economy as being "unstable, unbalanced, uncoordinated, and unsustainable" at the halfway point of his tenure. "Whether we can [fix it] depends on our . . . problem solving ability," he said at the time.

Five years later, in his last address to the combined Chinese and foreign press corps, a more downbeat Wen offered an apology. He spoke of how barriers posed by people who benefited from keeping the system the same had made reform more difficult than he had anticipated. Less than a year from retirement, he called for political reform; otherwise, "the gains we have made may be lost."

It's fair to say that Wen's successors have taken a totally opposite approach. Xi Jinping, who took over from Hu as president, is generally seen as the strongest Chinese leader since Deng Xiaoping — and, according to some, since Mao. Whereas government under Hu and Wen was consensus based and power was shared among nine Politburo Standing Committee members, Xi has diluted the influence of the other senior leaders — not least Li Keqiang, who was Wen's successor — and has concentrated power in his own hands. He's stifled dissent and public debate, and clamped down on academia, the media, NGOs, and the legal profession. And he's installed himself at the head of the committees — "leading small groups" in Party lingo — responsible for setting important policies ranging from domestic security, to military reform, to the Internet, and beyond, earning him the moniker "Chairman of Everything" among foreign observers.

It is true that Xi has brought much-needed change to some areas. Reeducation through labor — a type of extrajudicial incarceration that police formerly used to punish political dissidents and petty criminals — has been done away with. And after years of gradually relaxing the one-child policy, married couples can now legally have two children. But along with everything else, Xi also put himself in charge of the committees for economic reform and finance. Soon after assuming power, Xi used a similar formulation as Wen to describe the economy, calling it unstable and unbalanced. Yet despite having a vast economic agenda, like Wen, he has made relatively little progress toward substantial reform.

Among Xi's priorities are what he has labeled "the four wars of annihilation" (that is, key problems that must be annihilated): a cleanup campaign aimed at shutting down industrial overcapacity, filling the housing glut with people, lowering debt levels, and reducing the cost of doing business. The "four wars" threaten not to change the way the economy works, only to curb its excesses. Progress has been stymied by the political incentives I've described throughout this book.

Still, cleaning up these issues was only a small part of Xi's economic vision. A year into his presidency, Xi unveiled a sweeping blueprint for reform that promised to liberalize state-owned firms, give farmers greater rights over their land, and distribute state resources more fairly. But much of the excitement surrounding this blueprint revolved around the promise to upgrade the role of market forces in the economy from "basic" to "decisive." Shifting the balance of power from government to open markets could raise efficiency and radically change the way the economy works, but it would also divert power and wealth away from those who benefit from the way in which the system currently operates.

Not surprisingly, little progress has been made in realizing the blueprint. From day one, China's leaders have cast the blame for slow progress at the feet of vested interests. "It is now more difficult to deal with vested interests than it is to touch the soul," Li Keqiang told a press conference at the unveiling of the economic blueprint. Since then, the administration has repeatedly struck a similarly fatalistic note when complaining about the pace of reform. "It is becoming more difficult to remove hidden barriers and break vested interests when tackling the hard problems in reform," the state planning agency said in its annual report to parliament in 2015. "Deepening reform will involve more complicated conflicts and affect more deep rooted interests."

TIGERS AND FLIES

Soon after assuming power, in 2012, Xi launched an anticorruption campaign targeted at netting both "tigers" — his nomenclature for high-ranking officials — and "flies" — the CCP rank and file. So far, he has snared almost two hundred of the former, and more than one hundred thousand of the latter have been indicted.

The public has thrilled to the scandalous details: In 2014, an official who used to oversee the coal sector was found with $33 million of cash in his home. Four of the counting machines brought in to tally up the notes burned out. When corruption investigators searched the home of a general in the army's logistics department who was detained that same year, they found so much cash that it literally weighed a metric ton and took an entire week to count. Other officials have been caught with so much cash that some of it had started to go moldy.

The campaign was, in large part, a response to public anger, which, by the time Xi became president, was seething at the blatant self-enrichment of officials. It has also been used by Xi as a tool to remove political opponents and to cow would-be opposition. But there's also a widely held belief that it's laying the groundwork to make possible the essential economic reform that has so far eluded the administration. "Anti-corruption is being used as a way to break through the deadlock in this round of reform. Powerful interest groups have become extremely deep-rooted over the last 20 years and have grown extremely strong," Sun Liping, a professor of sociology at Tsinghua University wrote in 2014. Sun, who was Xi Jinping's doctoral-thesis supervisor, has written extensively about vested interests since the early 2000s. "When looking at the anti-corruption campaign, my first concern isn't whether it can resolve the corruption problem, but whether it can start to lever loose" vested interests from their entrenched position.

Zhou Yongkang — the highest-ranking official snared in Xi's campaign — could well be the archetype of what those vested interests look like. Zhou spent three decades working his way up through the petroleum bureaucracy, eventually becoming party secretary of China National Petroleum Corporation, or PetroChina. He was then promoted into government, first becoming the minister of land resources, then party secretary of Sichuan Province, and finally ending his career as a member of the Standing Committee, alongside President Hu and Premier Wen.

But these days, Zhou is serving life in prison, having been found guilty of taking $118,000 in bribes and helping family and associates accumulate assets worth more than $300 million. After he was detained, in 2014, investigators seized $14.5 billion worth of assets, including gold, silver, and about three hundred apartments and villas. Chinese media reported that his siblings owned an Audi dealership, a *baijiu* franchise, and a liquefied natural gas business, as well as mines and property developments. Zhou seems to have built a patronage network across the breadth of the various industries and geographies over which he presided. In the wake of his arrest, dozens of executives at PetroChina were detained, protégés and business cronies from Zhou's time in Sichuan were arrested, and associates from his days in the oil business who had since been promoted to senior government positions were incarcerated. "We can't allow political vested interests to exist inside the party, or allow collusion between party members and outsiders, or [allow] the trading of power for money," President Xi said in a speech late in 2015. "The party must unflinchingly stand firm against corruption, and we must prevent and eliminate these kinds of illegal relationships from influencing the political life of the party."

Yet, for all the success of the anticorruption campaign, there's really been no corresponding progress on reform. On the contrary, soon after Zhou's sentencing — two and a half years into the campaign — at a moment when Xi was presumably at his most powerful, the state broadcaster ran an opinion piece on its website (a piece that was widely assumed to have been vetted by Xi) complaining that opposition to overhauling the economy "perhaps exceeds what people imagine." Which begs the question, Why has the crackdown on corruption failed to pave the way for real reform?

China's salt monopoly has been mostly spared the glare of Xi's anticorruption campaign. That may be because salt executives and regulators have been dealing with corruption purges on and off for almost two decades. In 2009, the chairman of Guangdong Province's monopoly salt company was jailed for corruption, as were a half dozen other senior officials. In 2007, dozens of people in Zhejiang, including much of the salt monopoly's senior leadership, were taken down on corruption charges. Corruption in Hebei and Gansu spurred the government to first consider dismantling the monopoly in 2001.

The monopoly creates opportunities for corruption — such as the smuggling of privately produced salt into the supply chain, which may or may not have iodine — that wouldn't exist in a free market. Distributors have been known to receive bribes from producers trying to sell as much salt as possible at inflated government prices. In one documented instance, officials took kickbacks from a private company that they then overpaid to package their salt. And in perhaps the most creative abuse of power, a local branch of the Hubei provincial monopoly insisted that supermarkets wanting to buy its salt also had to buy washing detergent from it as well. "Nowhere else in the world can you find a more corrupt monopoly," says Zou Jialai, a lawyer who made his name in 2001 when he won a case against the Shanghai Salt Bureau. Since then, he's built his career on defending people against the salt bureaucracy.

FEAR AND LOATHING

The salt monopoly should be a soft target for reform. It serves little purpose, it contributes very little to the overall economy, and the near-constant drumbeat of corruption should have leached it of any political goodwill. Yet inexplicably it's managed to hold on. The industry's rebuttal to the 2014 reform plan — the most recent to advocate a complete end to the monopoly — gives some insight into its longevity.

"Table salt's safety will be a major challenge after reform . . . Once the market opens up, smuggled salt will likely come flooding into the market," wrote Li Yaoqiang, the chairman of China National Salt Industry Corporation, China's biggest salt company, in an article carried by state media. Furthermore, iodine penetration may suffer, he argued, particularly if supervision is left to local governments, which have neither the expertise nor the resources to do the job properly. Imports of cheaper foreign salt may undermine local industry, and some state salt companies would go bankrupt, he wrote. "After the market opens up . . . it will place on local governments the pressure of finding work for tens of thousands of salt sector employees."

The solution, he wrote, was reform, but not free-market reform. Rather, the various regional monopolies should be consolidated under the biggest salt companies. "We suggest . . . that a number of brands with major market share are formed in order to stabilize supply and reduce the costs of supervision," Li wrote. (The salt monopoly was subject to partial liberalization in 2017, but the monopoly still retains its authority and police force, price controls remain in place, and smuggling remains a crime.)

Li's defense was no surprise to Chen Guowei. Chen was an official in the now defunct State Economic and Trade Commission, the government ministry that at one time was tasked with reforming the monopoly. He helped put together the 2001 reform plan, and in 2004 wrote a letter to then-premier Wen Jiabao advocating again that the monopoly be broken up, a sentiment that Chen says the premier endorsed at the time. In both instances, the reform proposals went nowhere. According to Chen, the monopoly has been able to repeatedly dampen enthusiasm for reform by using a three-pronged strategy. First, it raises the specter of resurgent iodine-deficiency problems. Then, it fans public fears about "fake" — that is, smuggled — salt ending up in the food supply. And finally, it threatens unemployment.

Some of the monopoly's claims are blatantly self-serving. For example, the only reason salt smuggling persists is that the monopoly artificially inflates prices. But Chen says that fearmongering has worked so well because the overriding concern of senior leaders is maintaining social stability, and salt executives have been able to intimidate them with the specter of disease, unemployment, and disorder. "Wen Jiabao's priority was ensuring problems didn't emerge," Chen said. "Vested interests latched onto this mentality."

The approach has been replicated elsewhere. In 2015, a veteran China Central Television reporter, Chai Jing, released online an independently produced documentary called *Under the Dome,* which investigated the causes behind China's chronically bad air pollution. Chai reported that the most highly refined gasoline produced in China is two to three grades lower in quality than that available in developed countries, and that raising standards by one grade would result in a 10% reduction in emissions. The reason China hadn't done so was that about 90% of the members of the committee that sets fuel-quality standards are from PetroChina, Sinopec, and Cnooc, China's three national oil companies.

According to the documentary, the oil majors are holding the government to ransom. Beijing sets diesel and gasoline prices as a way to keep prices low for consumers, relative to international levels. Cleaner gasoline costs money, but the oil companies can't claw back higher refining costs by charging more at the pump, so they've asked the government to subsidize them to do it. But the oil firms' estimates of an appropriate subsidy are an order of magnitude higher than the government's calculations, and until an accommodation is reached, the oil majors continue to produce lower-quality fuel—all at the expense of the public's health.

The highlight of the documentary was Chai's interview with Cao

Xianghong, the head of the National Oil Fuel Standards Committee — the panel that sets emission standards — and formerly a chief engineer at Sinopec. Dressed in a short-sleeved white shirt — the summer uniform of government apparatchiks — Cao, like Li from China National Salt, threatened instability if the status quo were changed. "If there was social instability resulting from an interruption to the fuel supply, there would be turmoil in our society," he said when Chai suggested that emission standards be raised a little. When she asked why the oil industry shouldn't be thrown open to competition, he answered, "If not done right, it could end in disaster. Not every Tom, Dick, or Harry can run a fuel company."

Finally, Cao agreed there was a need for "deepening reform" and "gradual opening up," but, he said, "If the government wants to decide and push through this kind of reform, then it should go do some research first and find out what kind of risks there might be." (Much like motherhood and apple pie in the United States, everyone in China is pro-reform. Yet, as Cao's and Li's comments show, vested interests typically argue that reform is something that should be left to experts in the field, that is, them.)

In some ways, Beijing has made it easy for vested interests to stonewall economic reform. For all its talk, reform is not Beijing's only priority. It also wants to sustain "medium-fast" growth and, above all, to maintain social stability. Inevitably there's a trade-off among all three, and vested interests have learned to defend themselves by exploiting Beijing's inconsistencies — and insecurities. "Maintaining stability has become a tool to safeguard the structure of vested interests," writes Sun Liping, the Tsinghua sociology professor.

Sun writes that the fundamental flaw in China's economy is that the reform process has been stopped mid-stride, creating a system where state-run firms have been able to directly employ state power to fur-

ther their own interests. In contrast, in the United States, vested interests (whether companies, groups like the National Rifle Association, or
labor unions) derive their power from being able to influence government, and hence they invest massive resources in lobbying and making
political donations. In China, however, vested interests often have the
authority to wield government power directly.

"Many people regarded power and the market as two separate things
in the past . . . We thought that power would be constrained in a market economy," Sun wrote in a widely read 2011 essay. "Now we find that
the market has simply given state power a greater platform."

China's three national oil companies are among the most powerful
firms in the country, with their influence extending from energy policy
to foreign affairs. Each of the oil majors has huge headquarters located
on some of the best real estate in Beijing. PetroChina's and Sinopec's
buildings were seemingly designed by an algorithm to project power,
wealth, and intimidation (Cnooc's, however, looks like a glass bath-
tub). Some of their power has been delegated to them — like the right
to set emissions standards — but sometimes their powers are less for-
mally defined. The energy bureau is so overstretched and understaffed
that it relies on the very oil companies that it's supposed to be supervis-
ing to suggest rules and write legislation. Moreover, the energy-bureau
staff are themselves often former oil-company employees and so share
personal loyalties, or see issues in a similar light. And sometimes the
sheer size and importance of the oil majors allows them to bully the
government into submission.

"You can't control them," an official from the economic-planning
agency said of the oil majors in *Under the Dome*. Speaking anonymously with his voice distorted, he complained how Big Oil tries
to pressure his agency into raising petrol prices. "If the department
doesn't raise the price this year, next year they'll be at your door. 'Are

you guys going to raise it or not?' [they ask]. 'If you don't, I'll cut off supply.' That's what they say."

Under the Dome was viewed more than one hundred million times. It stayed online for about a week. And then, without any explanation, the authorities scrubbed it from the Chinese Internet.

"SOEs [state-owned enterprises] are becoming special interest groups with a strong resistance to reform," He Fan, one of China's most respected economists and the deputy director of the Research Center for International Finance at the Chinese Academy of Social Sciences, wrote in 2015. "Some are more like independent kingdoms in their own industries." Similar dynamics are at play throughout the state sector. The power of the state salt companies is more explicit than in most cases, with the salt companies and the bureaucratic apparatus responsible for enforcing the monopoly often being one and the same — or, as the Chinese say, the salt companies are both athlete and referee. That power does great harm to the economy, but in ways that aren't immediately obvious. The average household buys so little salt that were the monopoly to disappear overnight, there would be no meaningful impact on their grocery bill. Instead, the monopoly eats away at the efficiency of the Chinese economy in an area where it's not supposed to have any authority: industrial salt.

"THE MORE WE SELL, THE LESS THEY SELL"

Han Tianpei and his wife were dozing in the cab of their truck early one summer morning in 2013 when they were woken by a rap on their window. They were parked outside the factory gates of a long-standing customer — a denim manufacturer — and were waiting to make a delivery. The factory had recently relocated to Jinzhou from Shiji-azhuang, Hebei's provincial capital and Han's home, about an hour's drive away. The gates didn't open until 8:00 a.m., but the guards would often let Han in before the official start of business. This particular morning, he'd had to wait. But it wasn't the factory guards who woke him. It was the salt police.

About a dozen of them had surrounded his truck and positioned their cars to prevent him from driving off. On that morning, the flat-bed of Han's truck held, secured under a canvas tarp, ten tons of indus-trial salt, which the denim company needed for dyeing fabric. After inspecting his business permit, the salt police told Han that he was illegally selling salt and instructed him to drive his truck to their com-pound. Han told them they were mistaken. The police's jurisdiction was solely limited to table salt. Only state-approved firms can produce and distribute table salt, but there's a free market for industrial salt, a vital feedstock for the chemical industry that is materially no differ-ent from the edible kind. Salt — ordinary sodium chloride — is used to make soda ash (which goes into glass and paper), caustic soda (paints, ceramics, and aluminum), and chlorine (PVC and disinfectants). Han told the police that he was free to buy his industrial salt from wher-ever he wanted — Han bought his salt from Shandong Province — and could sell it to whomever he liked.

Han and his wife argued their case until 6:30 p.m., at which point the salt police called in the real police, who detained the couple for obstruction, taking them to the local police station, where they were locked up for twenty-four hours. The salt regulator's men drove off with his truck and the salt. Han got his truck back ten days later, after paying a 4,000 yuan fine, roughly equivalent to what he would have earned from selling the salt. The salt authorities kept the salt, and re-fused to issue Han any documentation acknowledging that they'd con-fiscated it. Officially, the salt had just disappeared.

I visited Han at his home early in 2015, almost two years after the incident. His apartment was sparsely furnished, its key feature being the black scribbles his five-year-old daughter had made in marker on the chalky white walls. Twenty-six-year-old Han had worked in salt since finishing high school, and had run his own business since 2011. He was a tall, solidly built man with short black hair, but most striking were the confidence and the passion with which he spoke about defending his rights against the monopoly.

This was no easy thing to do. Without any evidence that his salt had been taken, he had no grounds to sue. For months, his lawyer went back and forth trying to get a piece of paper to confirm the confiscation and the reasons behind it. Eventually, the salt regulator relented; the involvement of the ordinary police made it difficult for the monopoly to stonewall forever. After finally getting his day in court, Han lost the first judgment — lawyers say local judges rarely go against the monopoly — but he won on appeal, with the judge finding that the salt police had no right to confiscate Han's property. The monopoly then threatened to appeal that decision, but a few months after I met Han, it dropped the case. Despite the decision going his way, Han wasn't optimistic about ever getting his salt back.

I asked Han whether all the legal difficulties — and the legal costs, which ran to tens of thousands of yuan, dwarfing the fine and the cost of the salt combined — were worth it. "I have no regrets. Not fighting would be a regret," he said. "If I didn't file the lawsuit, there would be more [abuse at the hands of the salt monopoly], and that would lead to more losses."

Industrial salt wasn't part of the monopoly that was set up in the mid-1990s. However, it was once part of China's socialist planned economy, with the state setting prices and controlling supply. That changed in 1994, after chemical companies demanded that the market be liberalized. It was untenable for them to sell their products into a free market when one of the most important ingredients was subject to price controls. But although industrial salt has officially been free of government meddling for more than twenty years, many local governments still have rules on their books that treat industrial salt as though it remained part of a planned economy. When Han had his salt confiscated, the salt police told him his salt was illegal, because it was "outside of the plan."

In 2011, the Ministry of Industry and Information Technology ordered the monopoly to stop strong-arming sellers of industrial salt, saying that their actions were "resulting in an unending stream of court cases." "There are no constraints on trading industrial salt," the ministry insisted. "Engaging in industrial salt business does not constitute a crime."

The following year, the Supreme People's Court, the highest court in China's judicial system, issued a similar order, instructing lower-level courts hearing industrial-salt trials to take guidance from a particular case in Suzhou that found against the monopoly and in favor of private salt traders. Nonetheless, the abuses continue.

China's consumption of table salt actually plateaued years ago and is now dwarfed by demand from chemical companies for industrial salt. By using its authority to squeeze out private traders like Han, the monopoly can charge industrial-salt users higher prices and thereby extract greater profits. When I met Han, he was selling industrial salt for about 400 yuan per ton. The Jinzhou state monopoly was selling it for 550 yuan per ton. Han says that local salt regulators know that they don't have the right to stop salt dealers like him but keep doing so because "the more we sell, the less they sell."

The Jinzhou salt authority has its office a few minutes' drive away from the denim factory where Han was detained. The compound is hidden down an ill-marked, semipaved alleyway. A slogan painted in six-foot-tall blue characters runs along the length of the alley wall, exhorting visitors to "fortify salt with iodine to prevent iodine-deficiency diseases." The main building is a shabby, two-story white-tiled affair overlooking a rundown courtyard. A caged dog started barking wildly when my colleague and I arrived. In truth, I'd been expecting a bloated bureaucracy living high on the hog. But, by the look of its facilities, the local monopoly had been abusing its authority simply to maintain its existence.

The building was home to both the Jinzhou city salt company—which sells both industrial and table salt—and the salt regulatory agency. The only person there when I arrived was the office manager for the salt company. She said that although her outfit was part of the Hebei-wide monopoly, her little operation could sell salt—both the edible and industrial kinds—only in Jinzhou. It was like a monopoly within a monopoly. The business couldn't sell salt in Shijiazhuang, because the company had another branch there that had exclusive rights for that city. This has made life difficult for the Jinzhou operation. After all, the chemical industry was a big part of the local economy—when I visited, the smell of sulfur wafted in through the car's air conditioning while I was still on the highway—but many of Jinzhou's chemical factories had closed down with the slowing economy, while stricter environmental regulations had forced others to move to jurisdictions that were more tolerant of polluting industries. The monopoly was, in effect, trying to defend a shrinking pie.

China's "vested-interest" problem is a political problem. State firms and the bureaucracy wield an enormous amount of power without sufficient oversight from higher levels of government or from the judiciary, and they are not held accountable to the public. To a certain extent, the anticorruption campaign is an attempt to impose a degree of accountability on officials by making it more likely that those who abuse their power will suffer consequences. But vested interests benefit from the status quo in ways that go beyond corruption yet are still inimical to both the public and the national interest.

China's vested interests extract wealth from the privileged position they occupy in the economy. Some benefit from the state's ability to take land cheaply and sell it at much higher prices (at the expense of farmers, who are undercompensated); from borrowing cheaply from the banks, with few repercussions if loans aren't repaid in a timely way (at the expense of savers, who are undercompensated for their deposits); from being able to keep private-sector firms shut out of whatever industry they operate in, allowing them to charge higher prices than would otherwise be possible in a freely competitive and open market (at the expense of consumers, who pay more for goods and services); and from the subsidies channeled to them by the state (at the expense of the public, which would otherwise benefit from those resources being spent on services).

To the extent that reform threatens those privileges, it doesn't simply threaten state industry in an abstract sense; it poses a very real threat to the personal wealth of state employees. Wealth extracted from the economy by the state eventually pools into private hands. Anticorruption has been ineffective in forcing economic reform, because the people who are employed by the state benefit from the perks that arise from their employer's status.

THE SOURCE OF THE CASH

Based on the results of surveys of four thousand households he conducted in 2005, 2008, and 2011, Wang Xiaolu, a researcher at the China Reform Center, estimates that almost every urban resident in China has some sort of gray or "off the books" income, but that the elite and the middle class — much of which is employed by the state

—benefit disproportionately. Based on his most recent survey, in 2011, the richest 10% of the urban population were actually earning *three times* as much as official government statistics said they were pulling down, and the next 20% were earning *twice* as much. He found that the poorest 60% inflated their incomes with gray income by only between 20% and 40%.

For anyone who's spent much time living in China, one of life's great mysteries is how and why Chinese people have so much cash. I've been routinely surprised by friends' overseas holidays, luxury cars, and designer clothes, given what I assumed they were earning. Wang attributes gray income to a range of sources—one of which is outright corruption—but speculates that the wealth ultimately arises from the tight control that state institutions exercise over the nation's resources, and the privileged position they occupy in the economy.

The abuse of that privilege takes all sorts of forms. Good teachers get gifts and cash payments from parents who want to make sure their child gets enough attention. Doctors get under-the-table cash payments from patients to ensure their cases are handled properly. University professors staff their private companies by using their graduate students as free labor. And gray income is just as likely to be distributed by state institutions themselves.

For example, official state salaries routinely get inflated with a raft of allowances and subsidies. A friend who works at a state financial newspaper receives only half her compensation in the form of a monthly wage. The rest is paid out in a housing allowance, an air-conditioning subsidy, a travel allowance, and debit cards that she can use in lieu of cash to buy groceries.

However, in addition to cash, much of the compensation that comes with state employment is in kind. State firms typically provide better health and retirement benefits to their employees. Some sell housing cheaply to their employees. Sometimes employees get company cars for personal use, or enjoy regular banquets and other on-the-job perks. China National Salt somehow managed to spend 64 million yuan on entertaining expenses over the first nine months of 2012 — the last period for which it gave figures. That a monopoly with a captive market — and hence with little reason to be wining and dining anyone — had cause to spend so much on entertainment is a mystery much pondered by the Chinese press.

Rank-and-file employees also benefit from corruption, but it's often become an institutionalized part of compensation. State employees routinely expense claims that would be unthinkable at a firm constrained by market-based profits, or at state institutions that are accountable to the public. Fake receipts — specially franked for taxation purposes — are readily available for sale, allowing people to expense more on travel or entertainment than they actually spend. While living in Beijing, I regularly received text messages inquiring whether I needed a supply of fake receipts. In the stairwell of my apartment block, the word "receipts" with a phone number next to it had been repeatedly stenciled.

For state employees, perks are tied to the institutions they work for, although not all government agencies or state firms are equally endowed. Executives at the oil majors are unquestionably better off than those at the salt monopoly. But regardless of how privileged their employers are, employees' perks would disappear — or at least take a major hit — in a world where state firms lost their status and were forced to compete on an equal playing field with the private sector. Removing corrupt cliques of employees might help lessen venal behavior, but the individuals who would fill the vacated roles would be no more likely to be willing to dismantle their organizations' privileges.

Economists routinely say that when it comes to economic reform in China, all the low-hanging fruit has been picked. Meaningful reform now requires taking on deeply vested interests that have proved incredibly effective at stonewalling change. But, given the stresses on both the financial system and the economic model, China's authorities cannot afford to just sit back and allow things to continue in their current fashion. With reform proving so difficult, Beijing has seemingly opted for a third way. It plans to grow through its problems by developing new nodes of economic strength.

8

VOODOO ECONOMICS

LANCASTER COUNTY, SOUTH CAROLINA, first started spinning cotton into yarn in 1896. Textiles manufacturing had previously been primarily concentrated in the northern states, but after the Civil War, the industry migrated south to take advantage of an abundance of cheap labor — not the emancipated slaves, who generally weren't hired by the mills, but poor white farmers, who were struggling to make ends meet on the land.

The first mill in Lancaster County was built by Leroy Springs, who as a child had played marbles with Jefferson Davis when the Confederate president stopped in at the Springs's family home after fleeing Richmond at the end of the war. Springs's first mill was so successful that, a few years later, he built a bigger facility, popularly known as the Million Dollar Mill. The four-story building was, for a time, the biggest textile factory in the world, and a few years after opening, it had become the seventh-biggest employer in South Carolina. Springs and others added more factories, and for more than a century, the heart of the Lancaster County economy was textiles.

Even as the United States gradually opened up to free trade in the latter half of the twentieth century, the U.S. textiles industry managed to fend off competition from Japan, then from Hong Kong, Southeast Asia, and Latin America. Between 1980 and 2000, a wave of automation increased the amount of cotton processed by the average U.S. textile worker sevenfold.

But things started falling apart when China joined the World Trade Organization, in 2002. China had previously been subject to quotas on the volume of textiles and apparel it could export to the United States, but on joining the WTO, most of those quotas disappeared. In the first two years after China's WTO accession, U.S. textile imports from China quadrupled, and two hundred U.S. textile factories closed.

The Million Dollar Mill was among them. In 2003 — its centennial — the factory laid off more than three hundred people. The building was ultimately torn down and the land turned into a park. Four years later, the corporate descendant of Springs's company closed the last of its Lancaster plants, packed up its machines, and moved them to Brazil. With the end of large-scale textile manufacturing in Lancaster, unemployment in the county soared, peaking a little below 19% in mid-2009. That year, *Forbes* magazine, based on a survey of poverty, education, income, and mortgage-debt levels, labeled Lancaster the most vulnerable county in the United States.

By 2013, South Carolina had lost more than thirty thousand textiles jobs over the preceding decade, a decline of 63%. That was the year I met Zhu Shanqing. Zhu had started his career working for a state-owned chemical company, then went out on his own to trade polyester. In the year that China joined the WTO, he bought his first spinning machines. When I visited his factory in Xiaoshan — an industrial town outside of Hangzhou, two and a half hours' drive southwest of Shanghai — his company had revenues of 1.5 billion yuan a year, mainly from selling yarn spun from cotton. By then, China accounted for 37% of global textiles production, up from only 13% in the late 1990s.

Fortysomething Zhu had all the trappings of a successful Chinese entrepreneur: fast cars, expensive art, rare French wine. Over dinner, he cracked open a bottle of Cristal Champagne and a ten-year-old French Bordeaux that he swore was better than Lafite (that was for the benefit of the bankers he was entertaining, not the journalist). And he carried a gold-colored iPhone — a staple of China's nouveaux riches at the time — which he constantly checked for stock prices.

I'd flown down to meet Zhu at his Xiaoshan factory because he had grand expansion plans — but not for China. He was boxing up a big part of his business and moving it to Lancaster, outside a town that Guinness World Records had adjudicated to be home to the world's hottest chili pepper and near the former site of Heritage USA, the amusement park built by TV Christian evangelists Jim and Tammy Faye Bakker in the 1980s. The Chinese entrepreneur had committed $218 million to building a factory that would eventually employ five hundred Americans.

Zhu is an odd fit for Lancaster. Sartorially he falls somewhere between hipster and dandy. The first time we met, his blue suede loafers matched his blazer, and he rocked a gray-flecked bowl haircut. Yet in other ways he's incredibly provincial. The executive dining room on the fourth floor of his office building almost exclusively serves rustic village fare using local produce grown at the factory: bamboo and eggplant grown out back, toward the dormitories; white ducks I had mistakenly assumed to be pets; fish that live in the tree-lined stream that runs through the plant; and fermented tofu that leaves a tingling sensation on the tongue but otherwise tastes like blue cheese.

Zhu had decided not just to build a factory in Lancaster but also to shift the epicenter of his operations there. The factory will ultimately produce two hundred thousand tons of yarn a year, more than three times what Zhu was producing in Xiaoshan. Zhu was attracted to South Carolina for its history of textile production, for its proximity to North Carolina's cotton fields and to the major port in Charleston, and for the millions of dollars' worth of grants and tax credits the local authorities had provided. But for all Lancaster's charms, Zhu's decision to move was driven primarily not by what the United States could offer but by what China couldn't. "This industry doesn't have a future in China," said Zhu the first time we met. "It's not just difficult to grow. It's difficult to survive."

Few countries have benefited from free trade and globalization more than China. Once China joined the WTO, it quickly became the world's workshop, producing mass-market-manufactured goods more cheaply than anywhere else. But those days are over. According to the Boston Consulting Group, by 2014, manufacturing in the United States was, on average, only 5% more expensive than in China. In 2016, the American Chamber of Commerce in China found that a quarter of its members had either already moved some of their operations out of China or were planning to do so, primarily because of rising costs.

Most notably, the value of the yuan no longer works in the interests of Chinese exporters. For years, U.S. Congress members lobbied to punish China for suppressing the value of its currency, but by 2015, the yuan had risen more than 30% against the dollar from a decade earlier. Since then, the yuan has been so strong that the Chinese central bank has had to intervene to prevent it from falling too sharply.

Meanwhile, cutthroat competition among Chinese firms has resulted in wafer-thin profit margins for businesses like Zhu's. "Excess capacity in yarn is worse than steel," Zhu complained, a little hyperbolically, when we met in 2013. Producing yarn is as simple as buying a row of spinning machines and plugging them in, which many businesses did when times were good. "It's just too easy to ramp up."

Profits have been further eroded by inexorably rising costs. For example, Zhu calculated that by moving to Lancaster he would cut his power bill by half. Land is cheaper in the United States as well. In places like Xiaoshan, the price of land has risen so much since Zhu first started making yarn that it's just too expensive to use for building new factories. Zhu acknowledges he could have moved deeper into China, where cities like Shiyan and its flattened mountains offer industrial plots on the cheap, but the cost of getting his yarn where it needs to go — either to the coast, for export, or to domestic fabric makers — would then rise, without any other savings.

And then there is labor. Wages have risen so much in China that labor-intensive industries like clothing and toys have been moving in droves to places like Bangladesh, where workers get paid a quarter of what their Chinese counterparts earn, and Vietnam, where labor is half as expensive. It needs to be pointed out that labor remains significantly more expensive in the United States. According to Zhu's calculations, in 2013, one worker in South Carolina cost six times that of a worker in Xiaoshan. His move was feasible only because modern yarn factories are almost entirely automated, making labor only a small part of Zhu's expenses. Even then, a few years earlier, the gap between U.S. and Chinese wages was still too wide for Zhu to make the economics work. But by 2013, the wage differential had halved compared with six years earlier, and they were on track to halve again by 2019.

For decades, China seemed to have an endless supply of workers willing to leave the countryside for better-paying jobs in the city. As long as there were more workers on the way, wages remained low. But that endless supply has come to an end. Traveling around the countryside, even the casual observer can see that many villages are filled with no one but children and their elderly guardians, the working-age population having already moved to the cities. All developing economies, if they develop fast enough and for long enough, eventually get to a point where the flood of new workers looking for urban factory jobs slows to a trickle. That's clearly happening in China. Where China differs is that, at the same time, the overall pool of workers is shrinking.

DEMOGRAPHY AS DESTINY

In 2012, the number of Chinese between the ages of fifteen and fifty-nine started declining, shrinking by more than 3 million people. According to the United Nations Population Division, China's working-age population (currently about 1 billion people) will fall by 45 million people between 2015 and 2030, and then will lose a further 150 million people by 2050.

Usually that kind of reversal is the result of war, disease, or famine. China's demographic woes, however, are the unintended consequences of government policy. Worried that the country's population was becoming unmanageably large, in 1979 Beijing imposed limits on the number of children married couples could have. In the cities, the limit was typically one child only. That initially worked in the economy's favor. As the birthrate plunged, there were fewer children to take care of. Freed from child care, more working-age people could be used in industry. But that's now being turned on its head.

China's population is aging faster than anywhere else in the world. In 2015, China had 7.7 working-age adults to support every senior citizen. In 2030, the ratio will drop to 4:1 and by 2050, to only 2:1. In recognition of its looming demographic crisis, in 2015, China did away with its one-child policy. Couples can now have two children and are being encouraged to do so. Nonetheless, the damage is already done. Although many other countries — most notably Japan — are going through a similar aging process, China's challenge is that it stands to grow old before it enters the ranks of rich nations. In fact, the very process of growing old will make this kind of transition much more difficult to achieve. State resources will need to be diverted into health care and pensions. Productive workers will need to be redirected into caregiving. As the number of people of marrying age plummets, so will demand for new apartments, as will the demand for everything from steel and cement to flat-screen TVs. Most importantly, a declining workforce means that wages will rise, not because workers are more productive but because employers must pay more to secure their services.

That's what makes Lou Jiwei, who until late 2016 was China's finance minister, so pessimistic about the country's growth prospects. "In the next five to ten years, the chance of China sliding into the middle-income trap is extremely high. I put the odds at 50–50," Lou said in a speech to Tsinghua University students in mid-2015. "Why? . . . Because society is aging and the working-age population is shrinking too fast."

The middle-income trap is an idea first conceived by World Bank economists who found that, of the 101 developing economies that, in 1960, could be classified as having been "middle income" (that is, they weren't stuck in poverty, but they didn't qualify as developed nations either), only 13 — a group that includes Japan, South Korea, Singapore, Israel, and Ireland — managed to become rich nations by 2008. Many of the other countries who didn't make the cut looked as though they were on track until growth slowed and never recovered. Thailand and Malaysia were lauded as "tiger economies" during the 1990s until the Asian financial crisis struck. Similarly, Brazil and Mexico were once among the fastest-growing economies in the world, but now they seem permanently stuck in the middle-income bracket.

Economists generally agree that developing countries can achieve a certain level of wealth simply by taking people from the countryside and putting them to work in factories. But there comes a point when labor stops being cheap, requiring the overall economy to transform in some way if it's to continue its upward trajectory. What economists can't agree on is what sort of reform is necessary to facilitate the transition.

The "middle-income trap" is the bête noire of the Chinese leadership. In 2015, the World Bank defined rich nations as those with gross national incomes of more than $12,475 per capita, and the level generally rises by about 2% each year. In 2016, China's GDP per capita was $8,000. If the Chinese economy continues to grow at 6.5% a year — as it did in 2015 — it could officially enter the ranks of rich nations by the middle of the next decade. At 3% annual growth, it would take China almost fifty years. At 2%, it would just be treading water.

Of course, whether China achieves some arbitrary level of income means very little. What matters is whether it can continue to grow fast enough to catch up with the rich world — thereby restoring China to what its public generally perceives as its rightful place in the global order — within a politically acceptable time frame. Lou argued that the solution — to the extent that there was one — was to raise the efficiency of the economy through free-market reform. As long as China was cheap, there wasn't any need to be efficient, resulting in a huge amount of waste. If the market were allowed to allocate resources for labor, land, and agriculture, though, Lou contended that the gains in efficiency would translate into a more robust, sustainable economy. Certainly if Lou's reforms had materialized, Zhu may never had felt compelled to move to the United States.

In truth, the United States wasn't a perfect solution for Zhu. When we met up almost two years later, he complained that although there were plenty of people looking for work in Lancaster — "We get applications every day!" — they weren't quite what he was looking for. People who had previously worked in textiles didn't have any real experience in the sort of technologically advanced operation Zhu was running. For his part, Zhu was struggling with the concept that people working night shifts should be paid more than those who worked during the day. And while he loved not having to house his employees in dormitories, as he did in China — "Everyone here owns their own car!" — he was having discipline issues with his American workforce, with people taking long breaks and not turning up when they were supposed to. None of this would have mattered if his machines were humming along as smoothly as they had back in China, but in the hands of his new American employees, they were significantly less productive than they had been previously. "It's the people who are responsible for the machines . . . not the machines who are responsible for the people," he said, exasperated.

He'd taken to bringing workers from Xiaoshan to teach the Americans about Chinese efficiency. However, Zhu had no intention of giving up on the United States and was already racing ahead with expansion plans. Moreover, his labor difficulties were merely an irritation, given the savings he was making. According to the International Textile Manufacturers Federation, in 2014, the cost of producing yarn in China was 30% higher than in the United States. That was primarily due to the price of cotton.

In the United States, cotton is grown in huge fields. Machines do almost all the work — they pick the cotton, strip out the seeds, and pack it into bales — replacing the labor of dozens of people. In China, particularly in the east, where Zhu is based, cotton is grown by households on small plots. There's no consolidation of farmland, because farmers don't own the land they occupy, so they can't sell it. Consequently, it doesn't make sense for farmers to invest in machinery. Farmers merely pick cotton by hand. They lay it out on the street and on their front porches to dry. The cotton then gets transported on small trucks and three-wheeled tractors. And many farmers plant according to the strict instruction of local officials, not their own market-based decisions.

In China, the industry is able to compete with cotton produced more efficiently elsewhere in the world because Beijing puts limits on its cotton imports. Chinese textiles producers have no choice but to pay higher prices for locally grown cotton. When the yuan was weak, it helped offset the inefficiency of China's cotton farmers, but in recent years, domestic cotton has at times been 50% more expensive than cotton purchased on international markets. The reforms that would make cotton more efficient are still politically untenable. Instead, Beijing prefers to use quotas and subsidies to prop up the industry.

"Why don't I feel optimistic?" asked Finance Minister Lou in his 2015 speech. "In other countries, this process—of property rights, opening up, allowing the trade of land—took twenty years to evolve, but China, owing to the problem of growing old before growing rich, only has five to ten years to make the adjustments."

THE SUPPLY SIDE

Lou was somewhat unexpectedly removed from his role as finance minister late in 2016. By then, it was clear that China wasn't moving toward the type of reform he had envisioned. Instead, President Xi had unveiled a singularly different reform strategy, one that eschewed market-based liberalization in favor of old-school, state-led industrial policy. He called the strategy "supply-side structural reform." According to an anonymously written column published on the front page of the *People's Daily* in mid-2016, widely assumed to have been written by Xi's closest economic adviser, supply-side reform is to be "the lifeline that saves China from the middle-income trap."

At first blush, it seems an odd school of economic thought to be embraced by China's Communists. After all, supply-side economics is most closely associated with Ronald Reagan. Under Reagan, supply-side economics—alternatively labeled "trickle-down" or "voo-doo" economics—meant stimulating the economy by cutting business taxes.

Orthodox economic theory holds that growth is stimulated by transferring wealth to the demand side of the economy—that is, to households and individuals—so that people consume more. Reagan argued that by giving wealth to the supply side—that is, to business and industry, the producers rather than the consumers—the wealth would get reinvested in new factories, thereby creating jobs and eventually stimulating consumption.

The economics behind Xi's supply-side reform, however, are very different. But, like Reagan's, Xi's reform agenda is a direct challenge to the prevailing economic consensus, which is that what China really needs is demand-side reform, or, as liberal economists have argued since the 1990s, that China needs to rebalance toward consumption-led growth.

The idea behind rebalancing is that rather than relying on ever-increasing amounts of debt to create demand for steel, cement, and glass, economic growth should depend on ordinary people buying movie tickets, eating out at restaurants, hiring math tutors, getting cosmetic surgery, and generally spending money consuming goods and services, a form of growth typically considered more sustainable. That's what drives growth in most developed economies, and it probably would in China as well—so the thinking goes—if only households had more disposable income.

China is unquestionably already a nation of consumers, as evidenced by the Volkswagens that clog the roads and the proliferation of Starbucks. The issue is not that the Chinese don't consume; it's that they consume well below their potential. Put another way, ordinary Chinese currently benefit from a pie that is inexorably increasing in size, but their share of that pie is disproportionately small, because so much of the national wealth ends up in the hands of the state. In the interests of building a more sustainable growth model, that balance must change.

In practice, this means that, rather than providing subsidies to keep steel mills open, the government should direct tax dollars toward health care and pensions, so that people don't have to save as much for medical expenses and retirement. It means breaking state monopolies, so that competition can force prices down, allowing disposable income to go further than it currently does. It means stripping local governments of their right to expropriate farmers' fields, so that villagers can enjoy the true economic value of their land by selling, leasing, or developing it themselves. And it means taking away the power of the bureaucracy to extract fees and bribes arbitrarily, so that the private sector can compete on an equal playing field and, in turn, provide cheaper, more efficient services. Once those resources are diverted, the economy can rebalance away from investment and toward consumption. In short, consumption-led growth requires a real dismantling of state control of the economy.

Xi, however, has taken issue with the very assumption upon which the case of consumption-led growth is built. "The evidence shows that it's not that China lacks demand, or that there's no demand, but simply that demand has changed and that the supply side hasn't changed with it," Xi said in mid-2016.

Xi's understanding of China's predicament is that the economy produces — or supplies — too much of some things and not enough of others. On one hand, industries like steel and cement are producing far in excess of what is actually needed. On the other, China still imports huge volumes of items that it is currently incapable of producing itself. Supply-side reform requires shutting down surplus factories, and opening new factories for things China needs but simply doesn't currently make. Xi's vision is perhaps best encapsulated by the example of the ballpoint pen.

China makes 80% of the world's pens, producing about thirty-eight billion a year, yet, according to Premier Li Keqiang, none of them are up to snuff. While attending the 2015 World Economic Forum in Davos, Switzerland, Premier Li purportedly enjoyed using Swiss ballpoint pens so much that, when he returned to China, he went looking for an explanation as to "why China can't produce a pen that writes as smoothly and easily."

The key to producing a quality ballpoint pen is the tiny ball bearing fitted into the pen's nib. It spins as it rolls across the paper, picking up ink that's distributed from the cartridge via tiny grooves carved into the nib. Interviewed on state television in a soul-searching program into China's pen-quality deficit, Qiu Zhiming, the chief executive of Beifa Group, China's biggest pen maker, explained that not only do the balls require high-quality steel but also producing them requires state-of-the-art machinery and computerized measuring equipment that leaves no space for error. If the ball is too big, it won't spin in the nib. One that's too small will allow the ink to leak. One that's not perfectly round won't write smoothly. One that's too smooth won't turn as it runs along the paper. And the bottom line was that China was incapable of producing the balls. "Even though we're suffering from overcapacity in the steel industry . . . we still don't possess the ability to produce the type of steel used in the ball bearings that go into ballpoint pens. We still need to import them," an exasperated Premier Li said early in 2016.

China's three thousand pen manufacturers import almost all of the ball bearings they need from Germany and Japan. Moreover, much of the ink used in pens is imported as well. In fact, China doesn't make pens so much as merely assemble them. That was once done by hand, but with the cost of labor rising, it's now done by machines that are typically made in Switzerland.

In fact, much of what we think of as being "made in China" is only assembled there. While hundreds of thousands of people are employed to "make" iPhones in China, they contribute only a sliver to the overall value of the end product. According to a 2010 paper from the Asian Development Bank Institute, 34% of the value of an iPhone came from Japan, which supplied the screen and flash memory; 17% from Germany, which made the camera and power-management integrated circuitry; and 13% from South Korea, which made the SDRAM. China contributed only 3.6% — primarily the labor. The ratio has gone up since then, but it's still less than 10%.

Enter supply-side structural reform. At its heart, it is an import-substitution scheme. The aim is for China to make a significantly larger share of the components that go into products like iPhones, which are assembled in China. By 2025, Beijing wants Chinese companies to produce 70% of basic core components and basic materials used in goods manufactured locally. (By way of comparison, in 2015, China was still importing about 80% of the chips that were used in locally assembled mobile phones.) If China is to reach its targets, then its success must come at the expense of those countries which currently produce the guts of an iPhone or the more technologically advanced parts of a pen. However, there's a major reason why China doesn't already make those components.

Like China, Switzerland also has a thriving disposable-pen industry, but whereas China's pens are typically produced in packs to be sold in stationery stores, the biggest Swiss companies focus on making promotional pens — the sort that the World Economic Forum can put its logo on. Moreover, Swiss pens are typically made entirely in Switzerland — "from cap to nib," in the words of one company — using the companies' own proprietary technology, which the Chinese can't buy. Similarly, as much as the Germans and Japanese are willing to sell ball bearings to China, they're not willing to sell the technology that will allow China to make the ball bearings itself. Regardless of the industry, the best technology is usually closely held by the companies that develop it. If China wants to make a better ballpoint, it needs the technology to be able to make the constituent components — technology that it can't just buy off the shelf. Instead, China needs to innovate its way across the technology gap. But that's where things get tricky.

"I've been doing business in China for decades, and I will tell you, yes, the Chinese can take a test. But what they can't do is innovate," said Carly Fiorina, the former CEO of Hewlett Packard, during her run for the 2016 Republican presidential nomination. "They're not terribly imaginative."

That's a widely held belief, but one that's no longer entirely valid. Some of China's biggest tech companies — many of which started out as facsimiles of successful Silicon Valley start-ups — have become trailblazers in their own right. WeChat, nominally a messenger app built by Tencent, has evolved into the model of what Internet companies in the United States aspire to be: an all-in-one platform for sharing social media, paying bills, transferring money, dating, and booking restaurants, among an ever-increasing list of functions. At the other end of the tech spectrum, Shenzhen, the private-sector hub that faces Hong Kong across China's southern border, has been labeled by *Wired* magazine as the Silicon Valley of hardware for its ready supply of tech components, a culture of experimentation, and the speed at which people can take an idea and build a prototype.

Still, such market-driven, bottom-up entrepreneurialism is far removed from the state-led, target-focused strategy with which Beijing is hoping to realize its innovation aspirations. At the core of that strategy is money. According to the Organisation for Economic Co-operation and Development, relative to the size of its economy, China already spends more than the European Union on R&D, and is on track to surpass total spending by the United States in 2020. Much of that money has been invested in visionary, one-of-a-kind research facilities, like the world's largest laboratory for astroparticle physics, buried more than two kilometers underground in Sichuan, which is used for experiments on dark matter. And the sprawling underground complex being built in southeast China that will be used to research neutrinos. And the radio telescope in Guizhou Province that is the biggest of its kind in the world, with a half-kilometer diameter that allows scientists to look deeper into the night sky than ever before. And the world's first quantum satellite, which China launched in 2016, and which could be used to develop more secure communications. The hope is that all these projects will yield results that will translate into the industries of the future.

In the short term, however, Beijing is leaning heavily on its state firms to innovate. There have been some successes. In early 2017, a state-owned steel company announced that it had developed its own technology for making the ball bearings that go into ballpoint-pen nibs. However, given that Beijing's strategy is being driven by bureaucratic, rather than market, incentives, there's some doubt as to whether Beijing is getting any real bang for its buck.

In 2015, Chinese residents filed about 1.8 million domestic patent applications — roughly double the number six years earlier — but the threshold for registering patents in China is much lower than elsewhere. Consequently, only about 5% of those patents were also filed overseas, compared with more than half of all patents filed in the United States, and a third of those filed in Japan. Moreover, many patents aren't reregistered the following year, suggesting that they don't have any economic value, and that the driving motivation behind filing for protection in the first place was to receive the subsidies that the government hands out for merely registering patents.

So, rather than rely solely on the creativity of its indigenous innovators, Beijing is taking a few shortcuts. "There are two kinds of big companies in the United States. There are those who've been hacked by the Chinese and those who don't know they've been hacked by the Chinese," said James Comey, then-director of the FBI, in a 2014 interview on *60 Minutes.* They're looking for "information that's useful to them so [Chinese firms] don't have to invent" it. China engages in industrial espionage on a vast scale. But stealing cutting-edge research from foreign firms before they've had a chance to commercialize it is just a small part of a broader campaign to acquire intellectual property developed overseas. China has long required that foreign companies wanting to sell their products in China must share their proprietary technology with local firms by setting up joint ventures. Cars sold in China under GM's brand, for example, are produced by a company owned half by GM and half by a Shanghai-based state-owned firm. Such has been the price of admission to the world's most populous market. Foreign companies have tried to hand over only old technology, but Beijing has been raising the price of admission. "It is now an increasing requirement for more advanced technologies to be shared," the European Union Chamber of Commerce in China (EUCCC) said in a 2017 paper on China's industrial policy. "In the past, some foreign companies managed to at least partially limit transfers . . . and therefore did not compromise their long-term competitiveness. But this has become increasingly difficult."

Chinese firms have also been going out and acquiring foreign companies that have the technology they want. According to the EUCCC paper, Chinese companies invested 35 billion euro in Europe in 2016, up 77% from the year before, and more than four times the amount of European investment going into China. Much of that money has gone into areas, like high-end robotics, that the Chinese government had ruled off limits to foreign companies looking to buy Chinese firms. Making such acquisitions possible is a massive war chest of state-sponsored funding. "China's strategy relies in particular on large-scale spending, including $150 billion in public and state influenced private funds over a 10-year period, aimed at subsidizing investment and acquisitions as well as purchasing technology," the Obama White House said in a 2017 report on China's strategy to become a world leader in semiconductors. "China also places conditions on access to its market to drive localization and technology transfer."

Of course, once you have the technology, you then need to build a competitive business around it. On the face of it, it would seem that China has no natural advantage over the Japanese, or Koreans, or Germans, or even Americans when it comes to building a world-class robotics or semiconductor industry. What is making foreign companies and governments so nervous is that China has a disconcerting track record of becoming globally dominant in industries in which it has no natural advantage.

PROTECTIONISM

"The Chinese Communist Party made a deliberate decision in the late 1990s to build the biggest steel industry in the world, even though China lacks most of the things you need to make steel — namely raw materials and affordable energy," said Jim Darsey, executive vice president of Nucor Corporation — the biggest steelmaker in the United States — in a submission to the U.S. Congress. In 2015, the U.S. steel industry lost twelve thousand jobs. That year, facing massive overcapacity problems at home, China exported 112 million tons of steel, more than what was produced by the United States, Canada, and Mexico combined, a feat made all the more amazing given that ten years earlier, China was still a net importer of steel. "These imports aren't coming here because the United States is an uncompetitive place to make steel. The opposite is true. We have plentiful raw materials, low-priced energy; and we have the most productive steel workers in the world," said Darsey. "But we cannot compete with foreign governments who are willing to pour unlimited resources into growing an industry that does not have to yield any rate of return."

According to researchers Usha Haley and George Haley in their 2013 book, *Subsidies to Chinese Industry,* between 2000 and 2007, subsidies to China's steel producers rose 3,800%, with the bulk coming through subsidized thermal coal, coking coal, and electricity. In 2007, energy subsidies to the steel industry alone came to $15.7 billion, about as much as Nucor generated in total sales.

Something similar happened with paper, another industry mired in overcapacity. In 2008, China took over from the United States as the biggest papermaker in the world, producing paper products that are significantly cheaper than those produced in either the United States or the European Union. Yet China has few forests, and water — another important ingredient in making paper — is relatively scarce. Labor makes up only 4% of the cost of making paper.

"In all these capital-intensive industries where labor costs play minor roles . . . in the space of approximately five years, China rose from a net importer to among the largest producers and exporters in the world," the Haleys write in their book, which tracks Chinese subsidies to steel, paper, glass, and auto parts.

The problem is not simply that China is able to dominate those industries it deems important. It's that the policies that deliver dominance also create a huge amount of waste. "When the government chooses to support certain industries by imposing development policies . . . those industries all end up in overcapacity," said Fan Gang, one of China's most prominent economists. "Once we enter into these sorts of policies, each level of government then gives out its own subsidies, everyone in the market hustles, and in a short period it turns into an overcapacity industry."

The United States has always struggled with what to do about Chinese protectionism. Back in 2004, Lindsey Graham, the Republican senator from South Carolina, together with Senator Chuck Schumer, a Democrat from New York, threatened to impose a blanket tariff of 27.5% on all Chinese imports into the United States if the yuan didn't appreciate. "We have lost thousands of textile jobs in South Carolina, not because the Chinese work harder or smarter, but because they are cheating," Senator Graham said at the time.

China raised the value of the yuan just enough to ward off any action by Congress, even as its share of global trade — particularly in industries like textiles — continued to rise. All the while, the consensus in the United States was that free trade benefited everyone and that globalization should be embraced. But that resolute belief in free trade has increasingly given way to a sense that China's success has come at the expense of the United States. While the United States has unquestionably benefited from being able to buy cheaper televisions and Nikes, according to economists from MIT, between 1999 and 2011, the country lost as many as 2.4 million jobs to China. The losses were unevenly spread, concentrating in places like Lancaster County. Rising popular hostility toward China was perhaps best articulated by Donald Trump, who, during his 2016 presidential campaign, resurrected Congress's threats to impose a blanket tariff on Chinese imports as punishment for cheating on trade.

Yet, on the world stage, China casts itself as a champion of global free trade. "Pursuing protectionism is like locking oneself in a dark room," President Xi said in a speech at the 2017 World Economic Forum in Davos, soon after Trump assumed the U.S. presidency. "While wind and rain may be kept outside, that dark room will also block light and air."

The reality is that as China's domestic economic problems have grown more acute, so has it grown more protectionist. The same industrial policies that squeezed out foreign competition from steel and paper are now being applied to new technologies. For example, Beijing has set a target for robot production to exceed one hundred thousand units by 2020. In 2016, China produced more than seventy-two thousand industrial robots, up 34% from the year before. But in June of that year, Xin Guobin, the vice minister of the Ministry of Industry and Information, warned that the industry was already facing overcapacity problems. "Robotics firms need to avoid blindly expanding," he said.

It's not just in high-tech industries where foreigners feel themselves being squeezed by Chinese policy. In a 2017 column for German newspaper *Handelsblatt,* which coincided with Davos, the German ambassador to China, Michael Clauss, wrote that "old-style import substitution is alive and kicking" — in milk powder. "A recent regulation on baby milk powder requires foreign companies to reveal their entire production know-how down to the last detail to the authorities, not just the exact recipe but, for example, the set-up of machinery in the production process, even CVs and contact details of every person involved in the companies' R&D," he wrote.

China has spent billions of dollars in recent years modernizing its milk industry, yet in 2016, about half of China's dairy farms lost money. Places like Australia, the United States, and New Zealand have wide-open spaces extremely well suited to raising dairy cows, but only about 15% of China's land is arable, and a fifth of that is heavily polluted. To produce high-quality milk requires importing protein-rich fodder from overseas, which inflates the cost of production. Moreover, Chinese consumers don't trust locally produced milk powder, following a number of scandals, most notably the death of at least six children in 2008 (a further three hundred thousand fell ill) after consuming milk products adulterated with an industrial chemical. Yet China's authorities are absolutely committed to defending local industry against rising imports. "We have no reason to give up our indigenous dairy industry, and no reason to hand over on a platter such a big market" to foreign competition, said Han Changfu, China's agriculture minister, at a meeting of milk producers in 2016 — despite there being fairly compelling reasons for China to do just that.

In many cases the protectionism isn't explicit but foreign firms routinely come up against invisible barriers that make doing business in China more difficult. According to a report from the Conference Board, a U.S.-based research firm, foreign companies have to deal with "ever-increasing competition from connected local champions supported by the hidden hands of the government elites who control them." Moreover, any success that multinationals enjoy tends to be temporary, as they "typically [discover] that they are somehow curtailed after three to five years of success by new regulations, imposed compliance costs or the emergence of local competitors with infinitely deep pockets and irrationally low prices."

"The political leadership of China never ceases to assure us that further opening towards foreign investment, a level playing field between German and Chinese companies, as well as protection of intellectual property is a priority," Ambassador Clauss wrote in his 2017 column. "However, many companies keep telling us that their difficulties in these areas have increased. It often appears that somewhere down the line, political assurances of equal treatment give way to protectionist tendencies."

Among foreigners and Chinese alike, a common refrain is that the economy will be fine because the authorities are aware of the problems and will sort them out. However, to the extent that Beijing has already devised a solution, it's no cause for confidence. China's leaders are trying to build a new economy without changing the underlying institutions. They want to grow through their problems by applying the old growth model to new industries. There is unquestionably an element of desperation at play. If China doesn't join the ranks of rich nations soon, then its aging population will make the middle-income trap harder to avoid, and the nation's ambitions of national rejuvenation will be postponed for at least another generation. But the strategy it's resorted to comes explicitly at the expense of other countries.

Yet even as the rest of the world stands to lose, China still doesn't stand to win. China may come to dominate robotics and semiconductors, and can even edge out foreign companies from its milk market, still without addressing the fundamental problems that threaten economic and financial stability, specifically the epic levels of debt and waste. The longer those problems worsen, the less likely China can avoid some sort of reckoning, the fallout of which will be felt around the globe.

As for Zhu, the textiles boss, he hasn't put all of his eggs in one basket. While extremely bullish about his U.S. venture, he's nonetheless hedged on China. Back in Xiaoshan, he diversified into jewelry, making elaborately designed, chunky gold-plated pendants, bracelets, and rings. As of 2016, this business still wasn't profitable, but Zhu had high hopes.

Meanwhile, he bought more spinning machines. The machines he had previously sent to the United States produced yarn for pants and outerwear — coats and jackets — which are made from relatively coarse fabric. He replaced those machines with new ones, bought from Germany and Japan, which make finer cotton thread for shirts. The facility was producing far less yarn than before — thirty thousand tons annually, compared to sixty-two thousand tons prior to the move. But those thirty thousand tons were of higher quality, required greater skill and attention from his staff, and earned Zhu more money. When I revisited his Chinese factory in 2015, a couple of years after we first met, the difference was stark. There were fewer workers, and the new machines automated the manufacturing process to a much greater degree, with vacuum hoses moving up and down the corridors of machines to save on people's needing to sweep up leftover cotton fluff. Zhu was hoping his premium product could survive in China where his trouser-yarn business couldn't.

And then there was real estate.

When Zhu mentioned that he also ran a property-development business on the side back in China, I decided to check it out. I assumed it was just a hobby of sorts. I certainly wasn't expecting the Keer Century Bund. From the driveway, which was lined with fountains of dancing horses and matte-black statues of Grecian women edged in gold, to the clubhouse with its swimming pool inlaid with little gold fleur-de-lis tiles, the complex seemed to be trying to evoke the Chinese nouveaux riches' unique sense of luxury and class. The development included 360 villas — each with its own elevator and a dedicated room for a nanny or butler — and about a dozen apartment towers that lined the south bank of the Qiantang, the river that runs between Hangzhou and Xiaoshan. The sheer scale forced me to reassess Zhu's business. Property wasn't some side venture. This was *the* business.

Zhu went into property development in 2007. That was the year he first started thinking about moving to the United States. Overcapacity in the yarn industry was already a major problem, and Zhu's profit margins were being whittled away. But he wasn't yet ready to move overseas, so he bought his first plot of land. Today, he has five housing and commercial developments in and around Xiaoshan. The first time we met, I asked how important the development arm was to the overall business. "Property has been subsidizing the [textiles] company," he said.

9

THE NEW NORMAL

BRIDESTOWE LAVENDER ESTATE is found on a similar latitude as Provence, but it's about as distant from the heart of French lavender cultivation as is geographically possible. The Bridestowe farm is nestled in the northeast corner of Tasmania, the smallest state in Australia, an island once considered so remote that it was initially settled as a penal colony for the absolute worst convicts sent by the British to Australia. When Robert Ravens bought Bridestowe, in 2007, it had been growing lavender to make oil for perfumes and soaps for almost ninety years. But within a few years of taking ownership, Ravens had inadvertently reoriented the business in such a way that Chinese demand for Bridestowe's lavender was more than what Ravens could handle.

When Ravens — who had spent his career working as an executive in the chemical industry — acquired the farm, it came with sheds full of dried lavender that weren't being used for anything. Looking for ways to put all of this to use, Ravens and his wife experimented with making teddy bears out of the dried lavender. They started small. They had empty teddy-bear carcasses shipped from China, which they filled with the lavender. They sewed shut the teddy bears by hand, then sold them at the local agricultural show. Initially the bears came in five different colors, but only the purple ones proved popular, so after the show, Ravens started stocking purple teddy bears in the farm's gift store. They proved a particular hit with tourists from Asia, so Ravens decided to use the bears as a way to market his farm as a tourist destination. He arranged for a Hong Kong celebrity chef to visit the farm (one of the unique qualities of Bridestowe lavender is that it's actually edible) who then posted on social media various photos of himself cavorting with the bear in the lavender fields. That proved moderately successful. But things really started to take off in July 2013, when Zhang Xinyu, a Chinese celebrity famous for dating a Hong Kong soap star, posted a picture of herself with a bear on Weibo, China's version of Twitter, with the caption "a perfect companion on a cold Shanghai night." "Our phones went into meltdown," says Ravens. "We had to shut the website."

Other celebrity endorsements followed, and Bridestowe was soon swamped with daily tour buses of Chinese buying teddy bears, which Ravens had named Bobbie. Bobbie had become so popular in China that, despite Bridestowe's being the biggest lavender farm in Australia, the demand overwhelmingly outstripped the amount of dried lavender that the farm was capable of producing. According to the Australian Lavender Growers Association, all the lavender in Australia just wasn't enough to satisfy the Chinese teddy-bear demand. Ravens had previously sold the bears at stores on the Australian mainland and over the Internet, but by September 2013, he had stopped both. Henceforth, the only way to get a bear would be to visit the farm.

By November, Ravens was rationing Bobbie sales at Bridestowe to only one bear per visitor. The rationing helped the farm make it through to the next season, when the full lavender harvest was entirely dedicated to making bears, producing about seventy thousand teddies, up from forty thousand in 2013. But the stress of enforcing the quota was taking a toll on Ravens's staff. In this laid-back corner of the Australian bush, Chinese customers often turned irate after learning of the strict purchase limits. The day after I visited the farm, I met a tour guide from Shenzhen who was taking a group of Chinese tourists around Tasmania. I asked if she was planning to visit Bridestowe. Sadly, no, she said. The limit on bear purchases meant it wasn't worth her while. When she left China, requests from friends and family totaled sixty bears. Bringing back only one wasn't going to cut it.

"The staff are always on edge. Everyone is peddling like crazy," Ravens told me when I visited him at Bridestowe. "If you have a spare moment, there's always something else for you to do." As we stood outside the gift shop chatting, I was approached by a middle-aged Chinese man. He was a visiting professor at a university in Melbourne and was spending his holiday touring Tasmania in a camper-van with his wife and young daughter. He sheepishly asked me if I planned to buy a bear and, if not, whether he could use my allotment.

Ever since the nineteenth century, when British cotton-mill owners dreamed of the riches that lay in store if only they could add an inch of fabric to every shirt in China, foreigners have fantasized about this moment. Not so long ago, China's role in the global economy was solely as the maker of cheap manufactured goods. Then, as urbanization took off, it became a place to export commodities. But today, China is a nation of consumers, and their presence is being felt the world over. Even as recently as a decade ago, a slowdown or crisis in China would hardly have mattered to the rest of the world. But today, China is interwoven into the fabric of the global economy to such a degree that the fallout from its current economic problems will ripple across the globe.

The way that happens will likely differ from what we've grown accustomed to. Chinese companies have borrowed relatively little from overseas, such that foreign financial institutions aren't overly exposed if things go wrong. Moreover, there is very little foreign capital invested in China's domestic stock and bond markets, and the Chinese government has almost exclusively borrowed from its local banks and insurance companies rather than from overseas. Beijing has deliberately and quite successfully insulated China's financial system from the rest of the world, such that problems in China are unlikely to result in international financial contagion. Rather, the effects will be felt as economic demand begins to contract and China buys fewer things from overseas.

"Rapid growth in China has been a sustained, powerful engine for global economic stability and expansion," Xi Jinping pointed out in his 2017 speech at the World Economic Forum in Davos, noting that China has been responsible for generating more than 30% of global growth since the U.S. subprime mortgage crisis. In effect, a slowdown in China means a slowdown for the world. Yet the way the rest of the world experiences the fallout might be limited to only narrowly defined ways.

The most significant fallout will be on the global demand for metals. China consumes about half of the world's iron ore. In 2014, it used 41% of all lead consumed that year, 51% of tin, and somewhere in between for copper, zinc, aluminum, and nickel. When China first started slowing in 2012, metal prices plunged. Given the role that debt-funded construction of housing and infrastructure — big metals users — plays in sustaining Chinese growth, there's still plenty of scope for a steep decline in metals demand. Still, it's likely that the effects will be acutely felt only by a small group of nations that rely heavily on mining, notably Australia, Indonesia, Latin America, and some places in Africa.

The truth is, the rest of the world has benefited far less from China's boom. Xi may boast of China's contribution to global growth, but by running a massive trade surplus, China has generated disproportionately little economic activity in other countries relative to the size of its economy. In 2016, the volume of manufactured goods it imported was only a third of what it exported to the rest of the world. While many foreign brands have benefited hugely from China — Volkswagen, for example, makes about half of its total global sales in China — what they sell in China is typically also made in China. The United States contributes massively to global economic activity by being the world's consumer of last resort. It sucks in imports from all over the world, far in excess of what it exports. In contrast, most of everything that China consumes it makes itself.

But that picture is rapidly changing. As China grows more affluent, it is buying in huge volumes those things that it can't produce at home, ranging from entertainment to luxury items to new airplanes. For example, American movies are significantly more popular in China than locally made films. Chinese ticket sales are so important to Hollywood that studios are now actively casting Chinese actors for roles in their films, and making sure that they don't portray China in ways that might preclude their movies from being shown there. For years now, Chinese buyers have been the most important market for luxury goods, accounting for as much as a third of global sales of luxury bags and watches; and in Paris, Gucci and other luxury brands have experienced something similar to Ravens and his teddy bears, with some stores imposing strict quotas on sales to guard against busloads of Chinese tourists from instantly buying out all available stock. Meanwhile, at the much more technologically advanced end of the manufacturing spectrum, China buys 25% of all Boeing planes, and in 2016, Boeing's vice chairman estimated that aircraft sales to China supported 150,000 U.S. jobs.

As tourists, Chinese spend more overseas than any other nationality. In Japan, where China is the number-one source of tourists, they spend so much money in such a short period of time — mainly on high-end electronics that China still isn't able to make itself — that the Japanese have coined a word for it: *bakugai,* or explosive shopping.

Moreover, there were around six hundred thousand Chinese students studying in the United States, United Kingdom, and Australia at the end of 2016, all pretty much paying full fees to attend universities and high schools, thus providing a vital source of additional funding to overstretched educational institutions.

Perhaps the biggest winners, however, have been primary industries. Agricultural exports from the United States to China tripled between 2006 and 2016. The biggest beneficiaries have been soybean farmers, who sold more than $10 billion worth of soybeans to the Chinese in 2015, or roughly half the value of total U.S. agricultural exports to China. Meanwhile, at the other end of the scale are niche producers like fishermen in Maine, who in 2016 earned three times as much from shipping live lobsters to China than they did the year before. China has become the world's biggest export market for milk, and it is importing more and more beef, seafood, wine, honey, fruits and nuts, cheese, chocolate, olive oil, and almost anything else that appeals to the tastes of an increasingly affluent society.

China's looming economic problems won't affect the world in the same way that a slowdown by the United States would, but China has become an important buyer — and in many cases the single most important buyer — in markets ranging from soybeans to aircraft to tourism to fluffy teddy bears. It's impossible to say how China's economic problems might affect such a disparate group of products, let alone, on aggregate, how they will affect the global macroeconomy. However, there is one area where the fracturing of Chinese economic growth will definitely have a dire impact: global optimism.

The world is much in need of another engine of growth. Neither the United States nor the European Union has properly recovered from its last crisis, and Japan never delivered on the promise it showed during the 1980s. China looks as though it might just plug that gap. Rising Chinese consumption has given the world a taste of just how everyone can benefit from a more wealthy China. Much as English mill owners once fantasized about lengthening shirttails, the new hope is that the creation of an additional fifty million Chinese middle-class consumers —

barely representing a fraction of China's overall population — could drive demand for everything that the existing one hundred million or so middle-class citizens are already buying in ever greater quantities. Boeing forecasts that China will spend $1 trillion on aircraft over the next twenty years. Starbucks ex-CEO Howard Schultz envisions that the coffee chain could one day have more outlets in China than in the United States. In Australia, the expectation is that a farming boom will take over where the mining boom left off. In other words, China's middle class is the great hope of the global economy.

It's easy to look at China's booming consumption as a sign of its success or even of the superiority of its economic model. But one has to bear in mind that consumption doesn't exist in a bubble separate from the rest of the economy. For the world to finally benefit from the long-awaited promise of Chinese consumption, the Chinese economy has to keep growing. Should China's economic miracle sputter out, the huge potential it holds for the global economy will sputter along with it. But not only will stagnating consumption affect the global economy, it will also have serious political repercussions within China.

THE SOCIAL CONTRACT

For all his success, Ravens has never been able to fully account for Bobbie's popularity.

"Somehow we've tapped the cultural psyche of thirty-year-old Chinese ladies," he said, bemused, when we met.

Within a year, he wasn't so sure. "Now it's everyone who needs one," he told me. "It's a luxury good you can afford."

Except it isn't. When he first started out, Ravens charged twenty dollars per bear, but he soon started raising the price when he discovered that the bears' online resale value was more than four times that amount. By early 2016, Ravens was charging seventy dollars each, but he's nonetheless needed to continue rationing sales on his farm to ensure sufficient supply.

We assume that the incredible purchasing power of the Chinese when they go abroad is to be expected, the inevitable outcome of China's inexorable economic rise and commensurate with an economy on track to overtake the United States as the largest in the world. Yet something's not quite right. The typical middle-class Australian family — or for that matter an American or a European family — would have to give some serious thought to laying out seventy dollars on a stuffed toy. Similarly, there are hundreds of thousands of Chinese parents paying full fees to send their children to university in the United States and Australia, countries where the local middle class can't afford to do the same without significant loans, subsidies, or financial aid. Moreover, the Chinese are not only the largest source of tourists to Australia; they spend more per individual than people from any other country.

Yet China is still a developing country. People there earn far, far less than their rich-world counterparts. In 2014, a three-person household in the United States needed an income of at least $42,000 to qualify as middle class. In China, the definition of "middle class" is still up for debate, but a household income of $20,000 qualifies you as not just middle class but reasonably affluent.

It's easy to explain away China's extreme consumption habits by pointing to the size of its population. China has more people, ipso facto it has more rich people. China unquestionably does have more rich people — at last count it had more billionaires than the United States — but that's not how it should work. China's economy is only 70% the size of the United States, but it has four times as many people; it has less wealth, and that wealth is spread more thinly. The enviable purchasing power of its tourists is not the natural order of things but rather the result of heavily lopsided income distribution.

China suffers from some of the worst income inequality in the world. According to China's official statistics, its 2012 Gini coefficient — a measure of inequality in which zero represents perfect equality and 1 represents perfect inequality — was 0.47, making it broadly as unequal as the United States (the World Bank says anything above 0.4 signals extreme inequality). Independent calculations have estimated that Chinese inequality is actually significantly worse than that, with estimates ranging between 0.53 and 0.61.

Given such vast disparities in wealth, it's amazing that the country isn't a tinderbox. We typically think of inequality as being grossly destabilizing, particularly in places where the have-nots live alongside the haves, as in Beijing, where people living in underground tenements share the same streets as the über-rich driving Ferraris and Maseratis.

Yet there are no signs of fomenting revolution. Instead, the Chinese are among the most optimistic people in the world, particularly when it comes to expectations about personal wealth. In 2016, Pew Research found that 70% of people it surveyed in China said they expected that their financial situation would improve over the next year despite the slowing economy, and 80% said they thought their children would have a better standard of living than themselves. In the United States, in contrast, 60% of respondents expected their children to be worse off.

Across the breadth of Chinese society, the typical person has experienced improvements in personal prosperity that would be unimaginable in most developed economies. In the United States, real wages have stagnated since the 1970s, meaning that if you have stayed in the same job for the last forty years, your weekly pay doesn't go any further today than it did when you first started working. In China, if you have been in the same job for the last seven or eight years, you have seen your income double. Moreover, if you bought a home eight years ago, it likely has doubled in value. And the yuan has appreciated 30% against the U.S. dollar over the last decade, so anything you buy that is imported from overseas has gotten cheaper.

Anyone younger than forty in China has never known recession. For that matter, he or she has never known economic growth to slip below 6%. For the young, growth isn't some abstract concept reported in newspapers; it is the main force responsible for making radical improvements in their own quality of life. On my first trip to China, in 1994, large groups of people, curious about foreigners, followed me around the streets. Today, there are Chinese police on patrol in Rome to provide help to the hordes of Chinese tourists who descend on that Italian city every year. There was a wall of cabbage stacked along the hallways of my apartment building when I was a student in Beijing in 2001 that people had stockpiled to get them through the winter. Today, there are apps that allow people in Beijing to book chefs to come prepare food in their homes. Incomes have grown bigger and bigger, a state of affairs that people in China have come to accept as normal. More importantly, they expect this trend of wealth to continue.

Journalists typically write that the social contract between the public and the Chinese Communist Party is built upon economic growth. Growth, however, matters only insofar as it improves people's lives. A slightly more nuanced journalistic interpretation of this social contract argues that growth is important because it allows Beijing to ensure universal employment. That may have once been the case, but it's no longer enough for the Chinese authorities to simply create jobs of no value, as they did in the 1990s, when people were employed to push the buttons in automated elevators and the typical day at work for state employees included reading the *People's Daily* from cover to cover. Today, the social contract is built on rising incomes. According to Bruce Dickson, a political scientist who surveyed four thousand people across fifty Chinese cities on their perceptions of the Chinese Communist Party, the most important contributor to regime support is "continued improvements in personal prosperity," as he writes in his book *The Dictator's Dilemma*. Given the structural weaknesses of the Chinese economy, that reality somewhat complicates things. "Even though family incomes are closely associated with regime support, this also points out a potential weakness in the Party's survival strategy," Dickson writes. "If incomes stagnate or even decline, regime support is also likely to fall."

The Chinese people have put up with a lot in the name of economic growth. They've gone to work in factories and on construction sites far from their children, because *hukou* restrictions meant they couldn't move with them. They've lived in crowded dormitories and taken highly repetitive manufacturing jobs. They've taken extreme environmental pollution in their stride. They accepted the end of cradle-to-grave socialism and have put up with the extreme inequality that's replaced it. They've had their land taken with a minimum of compensation. They've endured institutionalized corruption. And they've accepted the curtailment of civil liberties, whether the right to have more than one child or the right to protest injustices.

But if the trade-off is prosperity — not current levels of prosperity but the better life they've been conditioned to expect — what happens when incomes stop growing? What happens when people are laid off, or when struggling companies stop paying bonuses, or fall behind on wages, or even force employees to accept a cut in their salaries, as is already happening, particularly in the Chinese rust belt? At the other end of the labor market, what happens when, year after year, university graduates — who are matriculating in ever greater numbers — find that the opportunities available to them don't meet the expectations they were led to believe were attainable, as is also already happening?

China is not some nirvana of social tranquility. In 2010, the last time even quasi-official data was available, there were more than 180,000 "mass incidents" around the country, more than four times the number of incidents a decade earlier. Such incidents are a mix of land disputes that turn violent, labor protests over back pay and layoffs, protests by ethnic minorities in Xinjiang, Tibet, and Inner Mongolia, and community marches aimed at preventing the construction of chemical plants or waste incinerators. There have been riots at supermarkets over insufficient bottles of discounted cooking oil, and protests over how local citizens have been treated by law enforcement. And every now and then, there's a spontaneous outpouring of anger at Japan over some perceived slight (for which the government provides ample coordination, buses, and traffic control).

It is no stretch to imagine that, should growth begin to stagnate, popular Chinese resentment will bubble up from below. Yet it's almost inconceivable that China's economic problems could spill over into mass unrest, or at least the sort of unrest the government would be unable to control. China's authorities have grown exceptionally good at maintaining order. They've invested hugely in internal security, beefing up the paramilitary police, spreading CCTV cameras throughout the cities, and closely monitoring and censoring social media. Any organized dissent is swiftly dealt with. Civil rights lawyers — perhaps the last class of dissident left in China — have been rounded up and incarcerated in recent years. Foreign NGOs are supervised by the police, and local NGOs are small and conscious of the political limits under which they operate. Labor disputes are kept local and handled quickly, usually by using a combination of payoffs and police suppression.

But while revolution in the streets is highly unlikely, a souring economic situation, and the fracturing of the social contract that it represents, would undoubtedly put pressure on the political system.

Moreover, pressure from below would be compounded by a very different type of pressure from the top socioeconomic strata.

OPTING OUT

When I visited Robert Ravens at Bridestowe, I brought with me a teddy bear that a colleague in Beijing had been given as a gift. It was purple, smelled like lavender, and otherwise looked like Bobbie; it was about as long as a person's forearm, with a ribbon tied around its neck and a cursive "B" sewn into the sole of its foot. But my colleague wanted to know for sure whether it had been produced at Bridestowe. By one estimate, within six months of the craze's start, one hundred thousand fake Bobbies had been sold online in China, about twice the number that the farm had produced up until that point. For a time, they seemed to be everywhere. I saw them for sale in a boutique in one of Shanghai's most exclusive shopping districts. I saw them on display in a store at the Chengdu airport. And when a chemical explosion devastated a swath of Tianjin, I saw a photo of a half-charred Bobbie in the wreckage.

Upon arriving at Bridestowe, Ravens was easy to find. He's tall and fit, with a full head of white hair and way too much energy to be retired. After a quick tour, we sat down inside the gift shop, overlooking the precise rows of lavender that curve around the farm's gently sloping amphitheater. When I handed Ravens the bear, he didn't even pull it from the canvas bag I was carrying it in. He gave it one squeeze and told me it was fake. When it was lined up side by side with the real thing, I could see that the proportions were a little off. Ravens also insisted that it smelled different — Bridestowe's aroma is "deep and rich," he said — but given that we were sitting among the gift shop's lavender soaps, sprays, jams, and creams, the olfactory discipline required to tell one lavender from another was beyond me.

Other than the brand, there's not really much intellectual property tied up in a Bobbie. It's undeniably cute, but it doesn't advance on the basic concept of a teddy bear. It's quite neat that you can warm it up in the microwave — the lavender is mixed with wheat, which retains heat — but that hardly warrants a fad of these proportions. Nor have the Chinese gone crazy for Bobbie because of some deep cultural affinity for fragrant, purple stuffed toys. At the root of the craze is what Bobbie represents.

About 20% of Tasmania is World Heritage–protected wilderness, and there's hardly any industry in the rest of the state. Bridestowe doesn't use the pesticides or fungicides common to lavender farming elsewhere in the world, because Tasmania's remoteness means that the lavender is safe from blight. Ravens uses some herbicides during winter, when the plants are dormant, but once germination starts, the chemicals get put away in favor of mechanical weeding. In effect, Bobbie is a piece of Tasmania's clean, green, and pristine environment. In contrast, almost 20% of Chinese arable land is polluted, typically with heavy metals that find their way into agricultural produce. And, even more concerning, Chinese consumers can't take for granted that the products they buy in China haven't been mishandled or aren't just fake or haven't been tampered with by someone cutting corners.

China's most high profile food-safety scandal was in 2008, when Chinese milk producers added melamine — an industrial additive that makes milk's protein level appear higher than it is — to their product, resulting in a spate of infant deaths and the maiming of thousands of other children. Since then, there has been a constant drumbeat of product-safety scandals in the Chinese press, ranging from gutter oil (cooking oil that's been recycled from deep fryers, sewer drains, and grease traps) finding its way back into the food chain, to vaccines that have been stored without refrigeration being administered to thousands of children, who now don't know whether they're truly immunized. It's a major public-health issue, yet the authorities seem incapable of fixing the problem.

In a telling example, in 2011, hundreds of people were arrested for making and distributing clenbuterol, a chemical that builds muscle and stimulates weight loss that was being used illegally in pig feed to produce leaner meat. But the arrests did little to stop the practice. The following year, the state sports administration banned Olympic athletes, who were then preparing for the London Games, from consuming meat when dining out — as opposed to in the controlled environment of their training camps — for fear they would ingest clenbuterol and consequently be banned for doping. In 2016, America's National Football League similarly warned its football players that if they were traveling to China, eating too much meat might cause them to fail drug tests.

Verifying the quality or authenticity of a Chinese product often requires extreme measures. Ravens took to guarding against fakes by attaching a tag to Bobbie with a special code hidden underneath a gray coating that scratches off. When the number is typed into a special field on the Bridestowe website, a picture of Bobbie appears, who then authenticates the number by pointing his thumb up or down. "It's pretty high-tech for a bloody bear," Ravens sighed.

When it comes to groceries, many Chinese shoppers buy only foreign brands, because they assume that they are of higher quality than local ones. Others eschew foreign brands that come from factories in China, preferring to buy imported products only. And still others — parents of young children, in particular — have come to the conclusion that the only way to ensure the quality and provenance of the things they buy is to purchase them overseas from the same places where foreigners do their shopping.

According to one estimate, as of mid-2016, there were forty thousand people in Australia employed as personal shoppers — known in Chinese as *daigou,* which literally means "buying on someone's behalf" — for households back in China. *Daigou* have made headlines in Australia for repeatedly sweeping supermarket shelves clear of milk powder, causing shortages of infant formula for local residents. As a result, supermarkets now impose limits on how many tins of formula any given shopper can buy. But milk powder is merely the most high-profile product in demand. The list of items that *daigou* ship back to China includes vitamins, skin-care products, honey, shampoos made from natural ingredients, children's clothes, sunblock, painkillers, insect repellent, chocolates, and, yes, lavender teddy bears (although, from what I've heard, none sell as well as Bobbie).

Some *daigou* use Taobao (China's significantly more successful version of eBay), where they operate virtual stores. Others use WeChat (a highly sophisticated messenger app) to communicate with customers, sometimes even using video-chat on their smartphones on their trips to the supermarket so that a customer back in China can see them physically lift products off the shelf, put them in the shopping cart, and then pay for them at the checkout. Chinese buyers are typically willing to pay premiums of 50% above the Australian retail price for the *daigou* privilege.

In theory, there is a certain level of average income at which, once attained, a country's middle class will start to agitate for greater political rights — if not explicitly for democracy, then at least for the right to influence issues they care about. Yet not only is China's middle class politically acquiescent, according to Dickson and his survey, but it is also genuinely supportive of the CCP. "This is a recurring theme in Chinese political attitudes," Dickson writes. "The higher their income, the more highly they evaluate the status quo, and the more highly they are satisfied with it."

That's understandable. The economic system has distributed a disproportionate amount of wealth to those at the top. Yet other surveys show that anxiety about food quality, product safety, and pollution is felt more acutely by China's most affluent, but there's little scope for them to do anything about it. The government countenances a certain amount of online complaining, as long as it doesn't spill over into the real world. Victims of food-safety scandals are given a certain amount of latitude to demand justice, but there comes a point when the government will turn against them if they continue to protest. With so much to lose, the personal cost of lobbying for the type of change that could improve pollution or food safety is just too high. For those who have financial resources, their wealth allows them to opt out of—or at least to partially insure themselves against—those unwanted aspects of Chinese society that they vehemently dislike but can't change.

The surging number of young Chinese heading overseas for an education taps into such a sentiment. The public increasingly regards its Chinese universities as diploma mills that produce more and more students without their developing any useful skills. Classes involve a lot of rote learning and the parroting of professors to pass exams. Government statistics show that immediately after leaving university, graduates can expect salaries marginally lower than what a migrant worker in construction gets paid. In contrast, an overseas education promises opportunities that aren't available back home.

Moreover, having enough money to travel overseas makes China's constant pollution more bearable. When thick smog settled over vast swaths of the country in December 2016, some of China's biggest travel agencies reported a significant uptick in foreign travel; one said it expected that 150,000 additional travelers would head abroad explicitly to escape the pollution.

The Chinese government isn't deaf to complaints about food safety, pollution, and education. Authorities have tried and failed to fix these problems for years. But making the necessary improvements requires the Party to remove itself as the ultimate arbiter in favor of a system of oversight and accountability that puts the public interest first. Ensuring clean air and water requires a strong, independent Ministry of Environmental Protection (MEP) that can't be ignored by state firms supported by local governments that place growth ahead of the environment. The same goes for food safety. Moreover, independent oversight of the MEP and the Food and Drug Administrations is required to ensure that they don't collude with the companies they're supposed to be regulating. Reforming education is perhaps even more difficult, not least because the Party uses education to mold the youth, through political-education classes, and to limit their exposure to Western ideas. For the state, schooling is about political control. For the general public, it's about employment and opportunity. Needless to say, in a political system where the authorities are always wary of giving up their levers of control, such reforms aren't likely to be forthcoming.

NO GOOD OPTIONS

Regardless of the cause, economic recessions and crises affect ordinary people all over in much the same way. People lose their jobs and bonuses, and find fewer hours of work. Those who keep their jobs worry about their economic security.

But in China, those stresses will potentially be augmented by anger due to a real sense of financial inequality in their society. Frustration will grow when Chinese no longer have the resources to compensate for the state's failure to protect people's health and well-being. This also means that a slowdown in the Chinese economy — let alone a recession or a crisis — will be as much a political event as an economic one.

It's very rare for Chinese leaders to publicly hint at what political instability might look like, but in March 2017, Lou Jiwei — who has long advocated market-oriented reform — did just that. Only a few months after he'd been moved aside as finance minister, Lou warned that Beijing's ability to maintain economic stability thus far had bred a sense of complacency. He argued that the deluge of debt-led spending had merely propped up growth, when it should have been used as an opportunity to pursue reform and to soften the disruptions that inevitably come with it.

All that spending "has created the illusion of stability, making people unwilling to endure the pain of reform. But if we waste the time we've bought for ourselves, then the space to maneuver will get smaller and smaller," Lou said. "When reform finally comes . . . the pain will be more severe, it will be harder to reach a consensus, and it will be easy to slide into far-right or far-left populism."

Outsiders tend to obsess over whether the Chinese Communist Party will survive or somehow collapse. Any discussion of China's stability inevitably winds its way back to the question of the CCP's viability as a going concern, as though that is the single most important factor that will shape China's future. Yet, since 1949, China has been through more societal and political upheaval than perhaps any other country. In that time it has passed through the Great Leap Forward, the Cultural Revolution, the ascendance of Deng Xiaoping and his economic reforms, the Tiananmen protests, and the breaking of the iron rice bowl in the late 1990s, all under the guidance of one party.

No one's predicting a return to those more tumultuous times, but the last twenty years of stability have lulled us into assuming that the status quo in China is the natural state of things. An economic slowdown — or worse — is unlikely to end in revolution, but China is not immune to abrupt changes in political direction, either to the left or to the right. A state faced with a frustrated populace may feel besieged and head in a more populist direction. Or it could try to divert attention from problems it can't solve by becoming more nationalistic. Or it could try to prevent change by becoming more authoritarian — which some argue is already happening. Or it could tear itself apart internally as competing factions bicker over the appropriate direction the country should take. China doesn't need to experience a change in government to experience a radical change in governance.

That matters because China's political response will affect how and whether the government is capable of reforming the economy. A Chinese friend told me not so long ago that he wasn't optimistic about the next five years, but that he expects that over the next twenty years China can expect a bright future. That optimism assumes that China's leaders are capable of negotiating an economic transition through the middle-income trap, something that few nations have managed. That will very much depend on how the Chinese political system responds to the latent social pressures that one would expect to be aggravated by a misfiring economy.

To the extent that there's any consensus among China watchers about what comes next, it's only that China will somehow muddle through. After all, China has faced seemingly overwhelming crises a number of times during the reform era, yet the economy has managed to maintain its basic trajectory. Certainly the current situation has a touch of déjà vu to it. In the late 1990s, President Jiang Zemin and his premier, Zhu Rongji, took a banking system that was technically insolvent, an economy built around sclerotic state-owned firms, a bureaucracy mired in corruption, local governments borrowing beyond their means, and vested interests opposed to their loss of privilege, and turned it all around, laying the foundation for an economy that is far more affluent than they could have dreamed.

But this time, things are significantly different. Jiang and Zhu unleashed two new sources of growth. They liberalized the housing market, opening the door to twenty years of urbanization, and they negotiated China's accession to the WTO, supercharging China's export sector. This time around, there are no magic bullets left, and the financial system — which Jiang and Zhu bailed out with surprisingly little trauma — is an order of magnitude larger and more complex. Moreover, with the economy having grown so much richer, vested interests have so much more at stake.

President Xi has labeled this current period of slower growth "the New Normal." It's a brilliant piece of marketing, because there's really nothing normal about the situation. In reality, the Chinese economy is in a state of flux. Most importantly, there are no good options left, and seemingly no political drive to endure the pain needed in order to set China on a newly invigorated, more efficient path. The government is under immense pressure to maintain what it calls "medium-fast growth." Without it, China won't move clear of the middle-income trap, nor will it be able to realize the dream of national rejuvenation before demography takes over and the aging population becomes a drain on the economy. But maintaining growth at such elevated levels only exacerbates the problems of debt and waste.

Furthermore, reform comes at a cost. Beijing can't wave a wand and wish the debt away. It must decide how the burden of cleaning up the debt is going to be distributed — and those decisions come with political ramifications. Devaluing the yuan is good for exports but bad for the middle class, which loses the perks of affordable overseas travel, shopping, and education. Similarly, market-oriented reform is good for economic efficiency but bad for the well-off, who benefit from the privileged position the state occupies in the economy. Closing down redundant factories is an important step toward dealing with industrial overcapacity, but it will result in unemployment and lost wages and will exacerbate inequality. And raising taxes or stoking inflation will be useful for reducing the corporate debt burden, but it will eat into the ability of the public to consume, making people materially worse off when Xi's promise — and that of his "Chinese Dream," where China will be restored to its rightful place in the global order — is that things will get even better.

For years, China's unimpeded ascent — economically and politically — seemed inevitable, but it's increasingly clear that that version of the future is unlikely. China has deep-seated economic problems that require reform, pain, and political leadership before the nation can assume the role it hopes for, as a rich nation driving growth for countries everywhere, and the role many fear it will potentially assume, whereby it uses its economic power to reshape the international order to suit its own interests. This century is supposed to be China's century, the result of forty years of hard-won prosperity off the back of tough-minded reform and sacrifice. That still might happen, but it will require a radical change from China's current course. Instead, it looks poised to suffer a painful and uncertain end to its economic miracle.

ACKNOWLEDGMENTS

First, I thank the Woodrow Wilson International Center for Scholars for taking me on as a fellow, without which this book would not have been possible. In particular, I thank Robert Litwak for allowing me to continue my residency once my fellowship had run its course; Robert Daly, who was invaluable as a sounding board (and a fantastic source of advice and support to a new father); everyone at the Kissinger Institute — Stapleton Roy, Sandy Pho, and Rui Zhong — for their support and encouragement; and Janet Spikes, Michelle Kamalich, and Katherine Wahler, who made the library a resource far more valuable than I could have imagined. And thank you also to all the interns who patiently and efficiently dealt with my constant flow of seemingly unconnected research requests: Alicia Chen, Jiang Moliang, Jia Yang, Jessica Liu, and Steve Han.

I also thank all my former colleagues in the *Wall Street Journal*'s China bureau, an incredible collection of reporters who were an inspiration to work with every day. In particular, I thank my two Beijing bureau chiefs: Andy Browne, for taking a chance on me; and Charles Hutzler, for having faith that I knew what I was doing, and giving me a leash long enough to pursue the stories I thought mattered. And above all others, this book would not be possible without Liyan Qi, Grace Zhu, Olivia Geng, and Yang Jie. It doesn't feel fair to lump them all in one sentence. They were partners on the best stories I wrote and, given the regulatory quirks imposed on reporting in China, will never get the recognition they truly deserve for being the exemplary journalists they are.

Thank you to those who shared their counsel, and particularly those who were willing to read parts of this book in advance. They include — in no particular order — Richard McGregor, Andrew Wedeman, Charlene Chu, Graeme Smith, Carl Walter, Logan Wright, Jason Bedord, Christina Han, Michael Van der Meer, Andrew Polk, Natalie Cade, Stephen Green, and Anne Stevenson-Yang. Your contributions were incredibly valuable to me.

A special thank-you goes to my agent, David McCormick, and his colleagues Susan Hobson and Bridget McCarthy, for all the time and effort they spent securing publishers, and to my editor, Rick Wolff, for his belief in the book, his deft hand as an editor, and his uncanny ability to set me on the right course with only a sentence or two.

And above all others, thank you to my wife, Lei. Without her patience and support for a project that took far longer than I could ever have imagined; without her honesty and humility in explaining why my drafts didn't work; and without the benefit of her own unique experience and insights into how China works, this book would be an inferior product — and would probably not have happened at all.

NOTES

INTRODUCTION

page

ix *flying into Paraburdoo:* Yi Wang, *Australia-China Relations Post 1949: Sixty Years of Trade and Politics* (New York: Routledge, 2012), chap. 4.

    throng the town: "Tom Price, Pannawonica, and Paraburdoo," Australia's North West, http://www.australiasnorthwest.com/Destinations/The_Pilbara/Tom_Price_Pannawonica_and_Paraburdoo.

    ahead of their boss: Amanda Buckley, "Mr. Hu and $5 billion Worth of Rock," *Sydney Morning Herald,* April 15, 1985, https://www.newspapers.com/newspage/121192255/.

x *the Chinese state:* "Rio Tinto and Sinosteel Sign Heads of Agreement for Channar JV Further Extension Discussions," Rio Tinto, November 17, 2014, http://www.riotinto.com/media/media-releases-237_13586.aspx.

    "a treasure house": Buckley, "Mr. Hu."

xi *$200,000 a year:* John W. Miller, "The $200,000 a Year Mine Worker," *Wall Street Journal,* November 16, 2011, https://www.wsj.com/articles/SB10001424052970204621904577016172350869312.

    economy around 2030: "World Economic League Table 2015 Highlights," Centre for Economics and Business Research, December 26, 2015, https://cebr.com/reports/welt-2016/; John Hawksworth, Hannah Audino, and Rob Clarry, *The World in 2050 — The Long View: How Will the Global Economic Order Change by 2050?,* paper series, PricewaterhouseCoopers, February 2017.

xiii *"the curse of debt":* Ruchir Sharma, "How China Fell Off the Miracle Path,"

New York Times, June 3, 2016, https://www.nytimes.com/2016/06/05/opinion/sunday/how-china-fell-off-the-miracle-path.html?_r=0.

xiv   *about 260%:* "China Hit by First Moody's Downgrade Since 1989 on Debt Risk," *Bloomberg,* May 23, 2017.

   in modern history: Keith Bradsher, "Why China's Growing Debt Load Worries the World," *New York Times,* May 24, 2017, https://www.nytimes.com/2017/05/24/business/china-downgrade-explained.html?smid=tw-share&_r=0.

   late in 2016: Mark Carney, "Opening Remarks by the Governor," financial stability report press conference, Bank of England, November 30, 2016, http://www.bankofengland.co.uk/publications/Documents/fsr/2016/fsrsp-note301116.pdf.

xv   *"treadmill to hell":* Charlie Rose, "Short-Seller Jim Chanos: Red Flag over China," *Bloomberg Businessweek,* April 8, 2010, https://www.bloomberg.com/news/articles/2010-04-08/short-seller-jim-chanos-red-flag-over-china.

   the previous year: David Barboza, "Contrarian Investor Sees Economic Crash in China," *New York Times,* January 7, 2010, http://www.nytimes.com/2010/01/08/business/global/08chanos.html.

   "next few years": George Soros, "The World Economy's Shifting Challenges," *Project Syndicate,* January 2, 2014, https://www.project-syndicate.org/commentary/george-soros-maps-the-terrain-of-a-global-economy-that-is-increasingly-shaped-by-china?barrier=accessreg.

   "I'm observing it": James T. Areddy, "George Soros in China's Crosshairs After Predicting Tough Economic Times Ahead," *Wall Street Journal,* January 27, 2016, https://blogs.wsj.com/chinarealtime/2016/01/27/george-soros-in-chinas-crosshairs-after-predicting-tough-economic-times-ahead/.

xvi   *the U.S. economy:* Lydia Saas, "Americans See China as Top Economy Now, but U.S. in Future," Gallup, February 22, 2016, http://www.gallup.com/poll/189347/americans-china-top-economy-future.aspx.

xvii   *"Fear and greed":* John Garnaut, "'Fear and Greed' Drive Australia's China Policy, Tony Abbott Tells Angela Merkel," *Sydney Morning Herald,* April 16, 2015, http://www.smh.com.au/federal-politics/political-news/fear-and-greed-drive-australias-china-policy-tony-abbott-tells-angela-merkel-20150416-1mmdty.html.

   2016 and 2026: Malcolm Scott and Cedric Sam, "China and the United States: Tale of Two Giant Economies," *Bloomberg,* May 12, 2016, https://www.bloomberg.com/graphics/2016-us-vs-china-economy/.

Norwegian salmon: Richard Milne, "Norway See Liu Xiaobo's Nobel Prize Hurt Salmon Exports to China," *Financial Times,* August 15, 2013, https://www.ft.com/content/ab456776-05b0-11e3-8ed5-00144feab7de.

traveling to Korea: Kwanwoo Jun, "South Korea Talks Tougher on China Retaliation," *Wall Street Journal,* April 4, 2017, https://www.wsj.com/articles/south-korea-talks-tougher-on-china-retaliation-1491301100.

ninety-nine China stores: Chun Han Wong, "Conglomerate Feels Heat from China's Anger at South Korea," *Wall Street Journal,* March 10, 2017, https://www.wsj.com/articles/conglomerate-feels-heat-from-chinas-anger-at-south-korea-1489161806.

"the reform era": Xi Jinping, "在党的十八届五中全会第二次全体会议上的讲话" [Speech to the second session of the fifth plenum of the 18th Party Congress], *Qiushi,* January 1, 2016.

xix *"to lose speed":* Lou Jiwei, "楼继伟清华大学演讲:我国可能滑入中等收入陷阱" [Lou Jiwei's Tsinghua University speech: China could potentially slide into the middle-income trap], *Sina Finance,* May 1, 2015, http://finance.sina.com.cn/china/20150501/135822089571.shtml.

1. THE BLACK BOX

3 *without the U.S. investors' knowing:* "SEC Charges China-Based Executives with Securities Fraud," U.S. Securities and Exchange Commission, February 22, 2012, https://www.sec.gov/news/press-release/2012-2012-31.htm.

in Beverly Hills: Securities and Exchange Commission v. Rino International Corp., Dejun "David" Zhou, and Jianping "Amy" Qiu, 1:13-cv-00711 (D.D.C.), May 15, 2013, https://www.sec.gov/litigation/complaints/2013/comp-pr2013-87.pdf.

the company's cash: "SEC Sues Chairman of SinoTech Energy for Misappropriating $40 Million of Company Cash, and SinoTech for Falsifying Asset Values," U.S. Securities and Exchange Commission, April 23, 2012, https://www.sec.gov/litigation/litreleases/2012/lr22341.htm.

6 *"the local" police:* "Oral Ruling on Defendant's Application to Strike and Plaintiff's Application for Documents," Huang v. Silvercorp Metals, Supreme Court of British Columbia, 2016 BCSC 278, February 4, 2016, http://www.lawgm.com/wp-content/uploads/2016/07/Huang-v.-Silvercorp-Metals-Inc.-2016-BCSC-278-00137175xCEA79.pdf.

the urban workforce: Wojciech Maliszewski, Serkan Arslanalp, John Caparusso, José Garrido, Si Guo, Joong Shik Kang, W. Raphael Lam, T. Daniel Law, Wei Liao, Nadia Rendak, Philippe Wingender, Jiangyan Yu, and Longmei Zhang, "Resolving China's Corporate Debt Problem," IMF Working Paper WP/16/203, October 2016, https://www.imf.org/external/pubs/ft/wp/2016/wp16203.pdf.

10   *trip to Beijing:* Shawn Donnan, "What the Fed Says About China Behind Closed Doors," *Financial Times,* March 8, 2015, https://www.ft.com/content/a49c325c-c5ed-11e4-ab8f-00144feab7de.

11   *"market forces," he said:* Usha C. V. Haley and George T. Haley, *Subsidies to Chinese Industry: State Capitalism, Business Strategy, and Trade Policy* (New York: Oxford University Press, 2013).

12   *planned price increases:* Curtis Milhaupt and Wentong Zheng, "Beyond Ownership: State Capitalism and the Chinese Firm," *Georgetown Law Journal* 103 (2015): 665–721.

13   *"has been slapped":* Wu Hai, "一个企业家致总理的公开信：总理，我想做点事，但是很憋屈" [An entrepreneur's open letter to the premier: Premier, there are things I want to do, but I'm being held back], *Economic Observer,* March 30, 2015, http://www.eeo.com.cn/2015/0330/274264.shtml.

15   *"close down the store":* "Li Keqiang's Report on the Economic Situation at the 16th National Congress of the ACFTU," Xinhuanet, November 16, 2013, http://news.xinhuanet.com/english/bilingual/2013-11/16/c_132888493_2.htm.

16   *false-imprisonment lawsuit:* "Reasons for Judgment," Huang v. Silvercorp Metals Inc., 2015 BCSC 549, April 13, 2015, http://www.lawgm.com/wp-content/uploads/2015/07/Huang-v.-Silvercorp-Metals-Inc.-2015-BCSC-549.pdf.
"as the prosecutor": Ibid.
Henan Found Mining Company: Ibid.
(the hotel receipts): Mark MacKinnon and Andy Hoffman, "In China, Silvercorp Critic Caught by Police," *Globe and Mail,* June 3, 2013, https://www.theglobeandmail.com/report-on-business/international-business/asian-pacific-business/in-china-silvercorp-critic-caught-in-campaign-by-police/article4528671/.

17   *owned by Henan Found:* Ibid.

18   *"of mineral resources":* Bruce Livesey, "The Full Story of Jon Carnes, Silvercorp, and the BCSC," *Globe and Mail,* May 29, 2015, https://www.theglobeandmail.com/report-on-business/rob-magazine/the-strange-case-of-alfred-little/article24443237/.

mine in question contained: Bill Alpert and Leslie Norton, "The High Price of Digging Up Dirt in China," *Barron's,* September 28, 2013, http://www.barrons.com/articles/the-high-price-of-digging-up-dirt-in-china-1380348035?tesla=y.

19 *"hotbed for corruption":* Li Keqiang, "在国务院第三次廉政工作会议上的讲话" [Speech to State Council's third work conference on clean governance], State Council, February 28, 2015, http://www.gov.cn/guowuyuan/2015-02/28/content_2822857.htm.

21 *(the electricity bill):* "Opening Ceremony for China's National Games Set for Daytime to Save Cost," Xinhuanet, July 6, 2013, http://en.people.cn/90779/8313580.html.

inflated by 20%: Fran Wang, "Liaoning Government Admits False Growth Data from 2011–2014," Caixin, January 18, 2017, http://www.caixinglobal.com/2017-01-18/101046468.html.

22 *the* People's Daily: Ibid.

"statistics were padded": "'注水数据' 贻害大 '挤出水分' 须较真" ["Padded statistics" leave a troubled legacy, "Squeezing out the water" must be taken seriously], Xinhuanet, December 10, 2015, http://news.xinhuanet.com/2015-12/10/c_1117414620.htm.

2. THE ZOMBIE ACCOMMODATION

27 *16,500-ton machines:* "Dedication Program: National Historic Mechanical Engineering Landmark; The Wyman-Gordon 50,000-Ton Forging Press," American Society of Mechanical Engineers, October 20, 1983, https://www.asme.org/wwwasmeorg/media/ResourceFiles/AboutASME/Who%20We%20Are/Engineering%20History/Landmarks/89-wyman-gordon-50000-ton-hydraulic-forging-press.pdf.

up to 100,000 tons: "800MN大型模锻压机项目荣获 '2014 年度四川省科技进步一等奖'" [800MN large-scale forging press program wins "2014 Sichuan Science and Technology Development Award"], Sinomach, June 11, 2015, http://www.sinomach.com.cn/xwzx/zgsdt/2015_zgsdt/201506/t20150611_60719.html.

28 *with BHP Billiton:* Dexter Roberts and Chi-Chu Tschang, "Why China's Buying into Rio Tinto," *Bloomberg LP,* February 5, 2008, http://www.bloomberg.com/news/articles/2008-02-05/why-chinalcos-buying-into-rio-tintobusiness-week-business-news-stock-market-and-financial-advice.

back to 2018: Siva Govindasamy, "China's Comac Aims for First C919 Flight by Early 2017: Sources," Reuters, February 23, 2016, http://www.reuters.com/ article/us-coma-china-c-idUSKCN0VW110.

before it arrives: Scott Cendrowski, "China's Answer to Boeing Loses Shine," *Fortune,* February 16, 2016, http://fortune.com/2016/02/16/china-co mac-c919-delay-delivery/.

30 *the national airline:* "The State as Shareholder: Raison d'État," *Economist,* June 28, 2014, http://www.economist.com/news/business/21605921-other-coun tries-are-selling-state-owned-industries-france-trading-up-raison-d-tat.

second-biggest aluminum company: Terence Bell, "The Biggest Aluminum Producers, 2014," *The Balance,* updated November 21, 2016, http://metals. about.com/od/Top-10-Producers/tp/The-10-Biggest-Aluminum-Produc ers-2014.htm.

31 *all the corporate debt:* Nicholas R. Lardy, *Markets over Mao: The Rise of Private Business in China* (Washington, D.C.: Peterson Institute for International Economics, 2014), 106.

previous four years: "Total Credit to the Non-financial Sector," Bank for International Settlements, accessed July 18, 2017, http://www.bis.org/statistics/ tables_f.pdf.

34 *"impoverished it becomes":* Hu Qing, "'任式改革' 能否力挽狂澜" [Will Ren's reforms turn the tide], *China Energy News,* May 25, 2015, 23.

wage in Sichuan: "四川省人民政府关于调整全省最低工资标准的通知" [Notice by the Sichuan Provincial People's Government on adjusting the minimum-wage standard of the province], Sichuan Provincial People's Government, June 17, 2015, http://www.sc.gov.cn/10462/10883/11066/2015/6/20/103 40340.shtml.

35 *read another:* "四川二重集团大裁员引发千人罢工" [Sichuan Erzhong layoffs cause thousands of workers to strike], YouTube, May 12, 2015, https:// www.youtube.com/watch?v=CLBTOZ1zu0g.

36 *"and live well":* "李克强: 商事制度改革要协同向纵深推进" [Premier Li: Industry and Commerce departments' collaboration crucial to advance business reforms], State Council of the People's Republic of China, March 22, 2015, http://www.gov.cn/guowuyuan/2015-03/22/content_2837186.htm.

37 *biggest coal companies:* "我省出台 '金融七条' 助力煤炭供给侧改革" [Shanxi Province publishes "seven financial measures" to coal's supply-side structural reform], People's Government of Shanxi Province, June 16, 2016, http://www.shanxigov.cn/n16/n8319541/n8319612/n8322053/n8324962/ n19299484/19511435.html.

across eleven provinces: Wojciech Maliszewski, "Resolving China's Corporate Debt Problem," IMF Working Paper WP/16/203, October 2016, https://www. imf.org/external/pubs/ft/wp/2016/wp16203.pdf.

38   *no profit at all:* "The Nature, Performance, and Reform of the State-Owned Enterprises," Unirule Institutes of Economics, 2011.

41   *of a city's area:* Tao Ran, "The Issues of Land in China's Urbanization and Growth Model," in *Deepening Reform for China's Long-Term Growth and Development,* ed. Ross Garnaut, Cai Fang, and Ligang Song (Canberra, Australia: ANU Press, 2014), 335–77.

about a quarter: Shijin Liu et al., *Urban China: Toward Efficient, Inclusive, and Sustainable Urbanization* (Washington, D.C.: World Bank Group, 2014), http://documents.worldbank.org/curated/en/274891468018263655/Urban-China-toward-efficient-inclusive-and-sustainable-urbanization.

42   *and building seawalls: Coastal Wetland Conservation Blueprint Project in China,* Paulson Institute, August 2016, http://www.paulsoninstitute.org/wp-content/uploads/2016/08/Wetland-Report-EN-Final.pdf.

writes Zhang: Weiying Zhang, *The Logic of the Market: An Insider's View of Chinese Economic Reform,* trans. Matthew Dale (Washington, D.C.: Cato Institute, 2015), 352.

"at the local level": "China," Office of the United States Trade Representative, 2013, https://ustr.gov/sites/default/files/2013%20NTE%20China%20Final.pdf.

for "illegal" marketing: Markus Eberhardt, Zheng Wang, and Zhihong Yu, "Intra-national Protectionism in China: Evidence from the Public Disclosure of 'Illegal' Drug Advertising," Research Paper Series at the University of Nottingham, April 2013, http://www.nottingham.ac.uk/gep/documents/papers/2013/2013-04.pdf.

43   *in the world:* "Overcapacity in China: An Impediment to the Party's Reform Agenda," European Union Chamber of Commerce in China, February 22, 2016.

was actually produced: "China Steel Production Capacity to Peak in 2016," *China Daily,* November 20, 2015, http://www.chinadaily.com.cn/business/2015-11/20/content_22504605.htm.

posted a loss: Christian Shephard and Tom Mitchell, "China's Steel Sector Hit by Losses," *Financial Times,* February 1, 2016, https://www.ft.com/content/338b4394-c8aa-11e5-be0b-b7ece4e953a0.

the global supply: "Overcapacity in China."

the world's ships: Martin Rowe and Clarkson Asia, *Shipbuilding Market Over-*

view, Clarksons, March 19, 2013, https://www.marinemoney.com/sites/all/
themes/marinemoney/forums/HK13/presentations/0955B%20Martin%20
Rowe.pdf.

"serious" overcapacity: "报告称应加快僵尸企业出清步伐 缓解金融风险"
[Report says to accelerate pace of clearing out zombie enterprises to mitigate
financial risks], Xinhuanet, June 13, 2016, http://news.xinhuanet.com/for
tune/2016-06/13/c_129056209.htm, cited in PBOC's Financial News.

44   *"Size matters in China":* "Overcapacity in China."

47   *from the time:* "中国8万吨模锻压机助力歼11：有人千方百计刺探" [Chi-
na's 80,000-ton forging press assists J11 research and development: some do
all they can to spy], Sinomach, October 10, 2014, http://www.sinomach.com.
cn/xwzx/xydt/2014hydt/201412/t20141218_46664.html.

3. GHOST CITIES

49   *success, in 2010:* "沈阳经济区八城市市长集体答记者问" [Q&A with the
mayors of the eight cities in the Shenyang economic region], State Council Information Office of the People's Republic of China, April 7, 2010, http://www.
scio.gov.cn/xwfbh/gssxwfbh/xwfbh/liaoning/document/595907/595907_1.
htm.

51   *empire dried up:* Daria Gonzales, "Meet the People Who Still Live in
Russian Ghost Towns," *Russia Beyond the Headlines,* February 5, 2013, http://
rbth.com/travel/2013/02/05/life_goes_on_in_russian_ghost_towns_22505.
html.

52   *around the country:* Guanghua Chi, Yu Liu, Zhengwei Wu, and Haishan Wu,
"Ghost Cities Analysis Based on Positioning Data in China," November 12,
2015, arXiv.org, Cornell University Library, https://arxiv.org/pdf/1510.08505.
pdf.

to China's cities: Askok Bardham, Robert Edelstein, and Cynthia Kroll,
"Housing Market Stability in China and the Potential for Global Contagion,"
Fisher Center for Real Estate and Urban Economics, University of California,
Berkeley, June 2014.

53   *plants a week:* "Is China Able to Keep Building 3 Power Stations a Week?,"
China.org.cn, October 7, 2012, http://china.org.cn/environment/2012-10/07/
content_26715090.htm.

54   *"in rapid growth":* Michael Spence, Patricia Clarke Annez, and Robert M.
Buckley, *Urbanization and Growth: Commission on Growth and Development,*

World Bank, 2009, https://openknowledge.worldbank.org/handle/10986/2582.

55 *almost two hundred thousand trees:* Shira Szabo and Ron Henderson, "New City/Old City," Fourth International Conference of the International Forum on Urbanism, Amsterdam and Delft, 2009, http://newurbanquestion.ifou.org/proceedings/5%20The%20Transformation%20of%20Urban%20Form/full%20papers/D063-1_Szabo_Shira_Henderson_Ron_New%20City%20Old%20City.pdf.

57 *1.5 each:* "地方新城新区建设数量多规模大 造城盛宴风险大" [Large-scale construction of new cities and districts carries large risks for cities], Xinhuanet, August 19, 2013, http://news.xinhuanet.com/politics/2013-08/19/c_125192959.htm.
    were attached to: Ibid.
    with financial services: "Feb. 18, 1991: Deng Xiaoping talks about developing Pudong," Today in History, *China Daily,* February 18, 2011, http://www.chinadaily.com.cn/china/cpc2011/2011-02/18/content_12474399.htm.

58 *room in Pudong:* Yao Min-G, "Deng's Legacy: The Cinderella Story of Pudong," *Shanghai Daily,* August 18, 2014, http://www.shanghaidaily.com/feature/art-and-culture/Dengs-legacy-The-Cinderella-story-of-Pudong/shdaily.shtml.

59 *China's total population:* "乔润令：我国新城规划人口超现有体制达34亿" [Qiao Runling: New cities' and new districts' plans sufficient to house about 3.4 billion people], *Sina,* October 19, 2013, http://finance.sina.com.cn/hy/20131019/153317045900.shtml.
    since mid-2010: Urban China: Toward Efficient, Inclusive, and Sustainable Urbanization, World Bank, 2014, 113, https://openknowledge.worldbank.org/handle/10986/18865.
    "worse and worse": "人民日报评论部：造城'虚火症该治了'" [*People's Daily* Commentary: Time to treat the development disease], *People's Daily,* August 28, 2013, http://opinion.people.com.cn/n/2013/0828/c1003-22715591.html.

60 *"great social problems":* Bingham Kennedy Jr., "Dissecting China's 2000 Census," Population Reference Bureau, June 2001, http://www.prb.org/Publications/Articles/2001/DissectingChinas2000Census.aspx.

61 *during his tour:* "凡河新城引领未来城市发展方向" [Fanhe New District will lead to urbanization in Tieling], *People's Daily,* January 6, 2014, http://leaders.people.com.cn/n/2014/0106/c359550-24033287.html.

"should support it": Tieling City municipal website, accessed July 19, 2017, http://www.tieling.gov.cn/zjtl/showall.asp?table=tdashiji&n=%CC% FA%C1%EB%B4%F3%BC%C7%CA%C2&fID=7.

signing off: "凡河新城引领未来城市发展方向" [Fanhe New District].

63 *Moses leaving Egypt:* Peggy Sito, "God's Businessman Has Eye on Bible Theme Park," *South China Morning Post,* November 23, 2009, http://www.scmp.com/article/699193/gods-businessman-has-eye-bible-theme-park.

65 *"It's about people":* "李克强：推进城镇化意不在'楼'而在'人'"[Li Keqiang: The meaning of urbanization is not "buildings" but "people"], November 28, 2014, http://www.gov.cn/guowuyuan/2014-11/28/content_2784326.htm.

of subway line: David Barboza, "Building Boom in China Stirs Fears of Debt Overload," *New York Times,* July 6, 2011, http://www.nytimes.com/2011/07/07/business/global/building-binge-by-chinas-cities-threatens-countrys-economic-boom.html.

and construction companies: David Hearst, "China, Corruption, and the Court Intrigues of Nanjing," *Guardian,* October 26, 2013, http://www.theguardian.com/commentisfree/2013/oct/26/china-corruption-nanjing-ji-jianye-mayor; and Amy Li, "What Has Li Chuncheng 'the Demolisher' Done to Chengdu?," *South China Morning Post,* December 12, 2012, http://www.scmp.com/news/china/article/1103692/what-has-li-chuncheng-demolisher-done-chengdu.

66 *China Center for Urban Development:* Chen Erze, "地方新城新区建设数量多规模大 造城盛宴风险大" [The number of new cities and districts being built is big, and the scope large, and the risk is big], *People's Daily,* August 19, 2013, http://news.xinhuanet.com/politics/2013-08/19/c_125192959.htm.

pagoda-shaped skyscraper: Andrew Browne, "Booming Municipalities Defy China's Efforts to Cool Economy," *Wall Street Journal,* September 15, 2007, http://www.wsj-asia.com/pdf/WSJA_2007_Pulitzer_China.pdf.

in a voiceover: Lesley Stahl, "China's Real Estate Bubble," *CBS News,* August 3, 2014, http://www.cbsnews.com/news/china-real-estate-bubble-lesley-stahl-60-minutes/.

67 *the world's iPhones:* "China in Transformation — Zhengzhou a Ghost City or a Mega City?," China International Capital Corporation, May 19, 2015.

350,000 people: David Barboza, "How China Built 'iPhone City' with Billions in Perks for Apple's Partner," *New York Times,* December 29, 2016, https://www.nytimes.com/2016/12/29/technology/apple-iphone-china-foxconn.html?_r=0.

the next five years: Ibid.

made in Zhengzhou: "China in Transformation."

69   *its new city:* Li Huimin, "铁岭新城成新'鬼城'" [Tieling New City is becoming the new "ghost city"], *China Business Journal,* August 31, 2013, http://www.cb.com.cn/index.php?m=content&c=index&a=show&catid=20&id=1010945&all.

said in 2014: "City Planning in One of the Fastest-Growing U.S. Cities," interview with Mitchell Silver by Robin Young, *Here and Now,* WBUR-FM, Boston, Massachusetts, January 24, 2014, http://hereandnow.wbur.org/2014/01/24/city-planning-raleigh.

early in 2015: "李铁谈新城新区建设六大问题 称政府不了解城市化发展规划" [Li Tie discusses the 6 biggest problems facing new city and new districts, argues that the government fails to understand urbanization development plan], *Caijing,* January 19, 2015, http://economy.caijing.com.cn/20150119/3802042.shtml.

70   *240,000 breaks a year:* Whitford Remer, "A Big WIIN for Water Resources," *2017 Infrastructure Report Card,* American Society of Civil Engineers, December 15, 2016, http://www.infrastructurereportcard.org/a/#p/overview/executive-summary.

from crumbling: Andrew Flowers, "Why We Still Can't Afford to Fix America's Broken Infrastructure," *FiveThirtyEight,* June 3, 2014, http://fivethirtyeight.com/features/why-we-still-cant-afford-to-fix-americas-broken-infrastructure/.

"systemic financial risk": "廖晓军：主动适应经济发展新常态 依法加强和改进预算决算审查监督工作" [Liao Xiaojun: Take the initiative to adapt to new economic developments in accordance with the law to strengthen and improve budget accounts review and oversight], *People's Daily,* November 5, 2015, http://dangjian.people.com.cn/n/2015/0916/c117092-27594420.html.

5.6 trillion yuan in debt: Christine Wong, "The Fiscal Stimulus Programme and Public Governance Issues in China," *OECD Journal on Budgeting* 11, no. 3 (2011): 1–22, http://dx.doi.org/10.1787/budget-11-5kg3nhljqrjl.

$2.5 trillion: Fielding Chen and Tom Orlik, "China Provincial Debt," *Bloomberg Brief,* March 23, 2016, http://newsletters.briefs.blpprofessional.com/document/MSwL-d.iUp63BHrcfz9zzQ—_6oz1nlm0a64zbme8k7/china-provincial-debt.

71   *"with bad loans":* "成思危：地方债—2014 年的难题" [Cheng SiWei: Local government debt—2014's biggest problem], eeo.com.cn, December 23, 2013, http://www.eeo.com.cn/2013/1223/253919.shtml.

prefectures, and counties: Yinqiu Lu and Tao Sun, "Local Government Financing Platforms in China: A Fortune or Misfortune?," IMF Working Paper WP/13/243, October 2013.

(at state-owned firms): Xi Jinping, "全国金融工作会议在京召开" [The National Financial Work Conference convened in Beijing], July 15, 2017, http://www.gov.cn/xinwen/2017-07/15/content_5210774.htm.

72 *empty apartment buildings:* Mark MacKinnon, "'Ghost City' of Dandong New District a Spectre of North Korea's Paranoia," *Globe and Mail,* April 23, 2013, http://www.theglobeandmail.com/news/world/ghost-city-of-dandong-new-district-a-spectre-of-north-koreas-paranoia/article11514569/.

4. ROBBING PETER

77 *long-term leases:* Zhenhua Yuan, "Land Use Rights in China," *Cornell Real Estate Review* 3 (July 2004): 73–78, http://scholarship.sha.cornell.edu/cgi/viewcontent.cgi?article=1088&context=crer.

78 *"to do with the other?":* Zhao Ziyang, *Prisoner of the State: The Secret Journal of Premier Zhao Ziyang* (New York: Simon & Schuster, 2009), 108.

outside the city: George E. Peterson, *Unlocking Land Values to Finance Urban Infrastructure,* World Bank, 2009, https://openknowledge.worldbank.org/bitstream/handle/10986/6552/461290PUB0Box3101OFFICIAL0USE0ONLY1.pdf?sequence=1.

to farmers in compensation: "Summary of 2011 17-Province Survey's Findings," Landesa Rural Development Institute, April 26, 2012, http://www.landesa.org/china-survey-6/.

over a decade: Zhang Yulin, "认识中国的圈地运动" [Understanding China's enclosures], *中国乡村发现 [Chinese village discovery]* 3 (2014), http://www.zgxcfx.com/Article/77419.html.

79 *two and a half times over:* Matthew Yglesias, "What Does All the Land in Manhattan Cost?," *Vox,* January 6, 2016, http://www.vox.com/2016/1/6/10719304/manhattan-land-value.

on Social Security: "Policy Basics: Where Do Our Federal Tax Dollars Go?," Center on Budget and Policy Priorities, updated March 4, 2016, http://www.cbpp.org/research/federal-budget/policy-basics-where-do-our-federal-tax-dollars-go.

they did in 2001: Zhang, 认识中国的圈地运动 ["Understanding China's Enclosures"].

80 *22% in 2015:* "China's Land Sales Slow Sharply in 2015," *Shanghai Daily,* April 6, 2016, http://www.shanghaidaily.com/business/real-estate/Chinas-land-sales-slow-sharply-in-2015/shdaily.shtml.

20% in 2016: "National Real Estate Development and Sales in 2016," National Bureau of Statistics in China, http://www.stats.gov.cn/english/pressrelease /201701/t20170122_1456808.html.

84 *entire twentieth century:* Bill Gates, "A Stunning Statistic About China and Concrete," *GatesNotes* (blog), June 25, 2014, https://www.gatesnotes.com/ About-Bill-Gates/Concrete-in-China.

heavily discounted prices: Xuefei Ren, *Urban China* (Cambridge, U.K.: Polity Press, 2013), 64.

86 *and storage spaces:* Doug Saunders, "Behind China's Crisis, Consumers Driven Underground — Literally," *Globe and Mail,* August 21, 2015, http:// www.theglobeandmail.com/news/world/the-ant-tribe-of-china/arti cle26054666/.

by 7.9%: Hanming Fang, Quanlin Gu, Wei Xiong, and Li-An Zhou, "Demystifying the Chinese Housing Boom," *NBER Macroeconomics Annual* 30, no. 1 (April 2015), https://doi.org/10.1086/685953.

87 *peak, in 2006:* Dean Baker, "The Housing Bubble and the Financial Crisis," *Real-World Economics Review,* no. 46 (2008): 74, http://paecon.net/PAERe view/issue46/Baker46.pdf.

88 *the subprime mortgage crisis:* "The Critical Issue: China and China Plays," Global Equity Strategy, Credit Suisse, July 2015, 6.

the urban population: Edward Glaeser, Wei Huang, Yueran Ma, and Andrei Shleifer, "A Real Estate Boom with Chinese Characteristics," *Journal of Economic Perspectives* 31, no. 1 (2017): 93–116, http://scholar.harvard.edu/files/ shleifer/files/chinaboom_final.pdf.

China's smaller cities: Andy Rothman, "Sinology: Does China Have a Housing Bubble?," Matthews Asia, November 2016, https://institutional.matthewsasia. com/sinology-china-housing-bubble/.

89 *losses for years:* "74 New Airports to Be Completed by 2020: Trips to Small Cities Easier," State Council of the People's Republic of China, February 19, 2017, http://english.gov.cn/state_council/ministries/2017/02/19/con tent_281475571877834.htm.

get an education: Andrew Browne, "Left-Behind Children of China's Migrant Workers Bear Grown-Up Burdens," *Wall Street Journal,* January 17, 2014, http:// www.wsj.com/articles/SB10001424052702304173704579260900849637692.

"extremely rational": Xiao Jincheng, "就业是城镇化的核心问题" [Employment is at the heart of urbanization], *CIUDSRC,* March 20, 2015, http://www. ciudsrc.com/new_zazhi/fengmian/hekan/2015-03-20/82813.html.

90   *33% in Beijing*: "China's Big-City Homeowners in Austerity Mode Are Weighing on Retail," *Bloomberg,* March 23, 2017, https://www.bloomberg.com/ news/articles/2017-03-23/stretched-china-homeowners-weigh-on-retail-sales-in-big-cities.

second-tier cities: Huileng Tan, "China Faces Policy Dilemma as Home Prices Jump in GDP Boost," CNBC, September 19, 2016, http://www.cnbc. com/2016/09/19/china-faces-policy-dilemma-as-home-prices-jump-in-gdp-boost.html.

(on loan repayments): "Mortgage Slave," *China Digital Times,* April 21, 2017, https://chinadigitaltimes.net/space/Mortgage_slave.

housing stock was empty: Esther Fung, "More Than 1 in 5 Homes in Chinese Cities Are Empty, Survey Says," *Wall Street Journal,* June 11, 2014, https:// www.wsj.com/articles/more-than-1-in-5-homes-in-chinese-cities-are-empty-survey-says-1402484499.

93   *value of the mortgage*: Rothman, "Sinology."

94   *property as collateral*: "The Critical Issue," 11.

half that in Europe: Jonathan Woetzel, "China's Cities in the Sky," Voices, McKinsey & Company, accessed July 19, 2017, http://voices.mckinseyonsoci ety.com/chinas-cities-in-the-sky/.

between 2004 and 2015: Glaeser et al., "Real Estate Boom."

had risen to 60%: Kaiji Chen and Yi Wen, "The Great Housing Boom of China," Working Paper Series, Research Division, Federal Reserve Bank of St. Louis, revised August 2016, https://research.stlouisfed.org/wp/2014/2014-022.pdf.

95   *than the bread*: Jacky Wong, "Why China's Developers Can't Stop Overpaying for Property," *Wall Street Journal,* June 20, 2016, http://www.wsj.com/articles/ why-chinas-developers-cant-stop-overpaying-for-property-1466385119.

Congress, in mid-2017: Gabriel Wildau, "Chinese Top Official Warns Economy 'Kidnapped' by Property Bubble," *Financial Times,* August 10, 2017, https:// www.ft.com/content/3bfea8be-7da2-11e7-9108-edda0bcbc928?desk top=true&conceptId=bbc18ff7-253b-3e2c-92d8-86bb3b0afb31&segmentId=d 8d3e364-5197-20eb-17cf-2437841d178a#myft:notification:instant-email: content:headline:html.

5. THE ISLAND OF MISFIT TOYS

97   *publicly traded companies:* Justin McCarthy, "Just Over Half of Americans Own Stocks, Matching Record Low," Gallup, April 20, 2016, http://www.gal lup.com/poll/190883/half-americans-own-stocks-matching-record-low.aspx.

100   *handful of individuals:* Chuin-Wei Yap, "China Court Spares Life of Million-aire," *Wall Street Journal,* April 20, 2012, http://www.wsj.com/articles/SB1000 142405270230351340457735535162745879 4.
       fifteen years in jail: Steven Wei Su, "Criminal Liabilities for Illegal Fundrais-ing in China," HG.org, accessed July 19, 2017, https://www.hg.org/article. asp?id=20800; Cao Li, "Ex–Rich List Woman in $57m Fraud," *China Daily,* April 17, 2009, http://www–chinadaily.com.cn/business/2009-04/17/con tent_7686565.htm.

102   *granted a reprieve:* Dinny McMahon, Lingling Wei, and Andrew Galbraith, "Chinese Premier Blasts Banks," *Wall Street Journal,* April 4, 2012, https:// www.wsj.com/articles/SB10001424052702304750404577321762422668428.
       "dog in their seats": Jeremy Blum, "A Dog Could Run China's Banking System, Says Former Statistics Bureau Spokesman," *South China Morning Post,* De-cember 24, 2013, http://www.scmp.com/news/china-insider/article/1389717/ dog-could-run-chinas-banking-system-says-former-state-council?page=all.

104   *20% of bank deposits:* "China Is Playing a $9 Trillion Game of Chicken with Savers," *Bloomberg,* April 10, 2017, https://www.bloomberg.com/news/arti cles/2017-04-10/china-is-playing-a-9-trillion-game-of-chicken-with-inves tors.

106   *$20 trillion of liabilities:* Adam Schneider, "Growth and Evolution of the U.S. Banking System," Deloitte Center for Financial Services, April 2013, https:// www.richmondfed.org/~/media/richmondfedorg/conferences_and_events/ banking/2013/pdf/cms_2013_deloitte.pdf.
       $11 trillion banking system: "Total Assets, All Commercial Banks," Economic Research, Federal Reserve Bank of St. Louis, updated July 14, 2017, https:// fred.stlouisfed.org/series/TLAACBW027SBOG.
       outstanding bank loans: "Moody's: China's Shadow Banking Activity Expands Briskly; Credit Growth Outpaces Nominal GDP," Moody's Investors Service, October 27, 2016, https://www.moodys.com/research/Moodys-Chinas-shad ow-banking-activity-expands-briskly-credit-growth-outpaces — PR_357115.
       to about 80%: Ibid.

108   *about a thousand trusts:* "Mainland China Trust Survey 2011: Extending the Reach of China's Financial Services," KPMG, July 2011, 3, https://kpmg.de/docs/20110826_China-Trust-Survey-201107-4.pdf.

109   *size of China's GDP:* "Moody's: China's Shadow Banking System Continues to Grow; Leverage Increases Further," Moody's Investors Service, July 27, 2016, https://www.moodys.com/research/Moodys-Chinas-shadow-banking-system-continues-to-grow-leverage-increases — PR_352727.

111   *"GDP growth rate":* Xiao Gang, "Regulating Shadow Banking," *China Daily,* October 12, 2012, http://www.chinadaily.com.cn/opinion/2012-10/12/content_15812305.htm.

112   *in foreign media:* Zheping Huang, "Ignored by Beijing, These Desperate Chinese Investors Are Looking to Hong Kong," *Quartz,* May 23, 2016, https://qz.com/689951/chinas-government-is-ignoring-these-desperate-investors-so-they-left-the-mainland-to-get-help/.

113   *"zero risk":* Zheping Huang, "China's Government Is Standing by While Investors Lose Life's Savings," *Quartz,* October 15, 2015, https://qz.com/524817/chinas-government-is-standing-by-while-investors-lose-their-life-savings/.
        36 billion yuan: Xie Yu, "Fanya Exchange's 36 Billion Yuan Default 'Tip of Iceberg' in China," *South China Morning Post,* September 25, 2015, http://www.scmp.com/news/china/economy/article/1861179/fanya-exchanges-36-billion-yuan-default-tip-iceberg-china.

6. THE GREAT BALL OF MONEY

117   *ahead of the United States:* Artnet and the China Association of Auctioneers, *Global Chinese Antiques and Art Auction Market Annual Statistical Report 2012,* 2012, http://www.cn.artnet.com/en/chinese-art-auction-market-report/assets/pdfs/global_chinese_art_auction_market_report_2012_en.pdf.

118   *(customary banquet toasts):* Florence Fabricant, "Nixon in China, the Dinner, Is Recreated," *New York Times,* January 25, 2011, http://www.nytimes.com/2011/01/26/dining/26nixon.html?mcubz=3.
        eight times that amount: "茅台酒收藏'风光无限'——北京歌德拍卖岛城征集老茅台" [Maotai collection on "high demand" — Beijing Googut Auction to collect old Maotai from Qingdao], Beijing Googut Auction Company, accessed July 21, 2017, http://www.googut.com/index.php?m=content&c=index&a=show&catid=99&id=106.

119   *was actually fake:* Elin McCoy, "Is Now the Time to Buy a Case of Château

Lafite?," *Bloomberg LP,* August 10, 2015, https://www.bloomberg.com/news/articles/2015-08-10/is-now-the-time-to-buy-a-case-of-chateau-lafite-.

121 *China's southern neighbor:* "Jade: Myanmar's Big State Secret," Global Witness, October 23, 2015, https://www.globalwitness.org/en/campaigns/oil-gas-and-mining/myanmarjade/.

more expensive than gold: Dinny McMahon, "Forget Stocks — Chinese Turn Bullish on Booze and Caterpillar Fungus," *Wall Street Journal,* January 30, 2012, http://www.wsj.com/articles/SB10001424052970203471004577142594203471950.

over dwindling stocks: Noah Stone, "The Himalayan Gold Rush: The Untold Consequences of *Yartsa gunbu* in the Tarap Valley," Independent Study Program (ISP) Collection, SIT Digital Collections, Donald B. Watt Library, School for International Training, Spring 2015, http://digitalcollections.sit.edu/cgi/viewcontent.cgi?article=3120&context=isp_collection.

in transfer fees: Chris Buckley, "President Xi's Great Soccer Dream," *New York Times,* January 4, 2017, http://www.nytimes.com/2017/01/04/world/asia/china-soccer-xi-jinping.html?smid=tw-share&_r=0.

calling it a bubble: Wu Xiaotian, "人民日报：泡沫与虚火 成为金元时代中超的雷区" [*People's Daily:* Chinese Super League bubble will become the death trap to the league's golden age], *Sohu,* December 19, 2016, http://sports.sohu.com/20161219/n476253921.shtml.

122 *money created globally:* "The Chinese Money Wall (Update)," Ousmène Jacques Mandeng, Economics Commentary, October 6, 2016, http://www.ousmene-mandeng.com/comments/16-10-6-Chinese-money-wall-updated.html.

every yuan of GDP: Ibid.

124 *$3 trillion worth of wealth:* Ana Swanson, "7 Big Questions About China's Astonishing Stock Market Crash and What Happens Next," *Washington Post,* July 8, 2015, https://www.washingtonpost.com/news/wonk/wp/2015/07/08/7-big-questions-about-chinas-astonishing-stock-market-crash-and-what-happens-next/?utm_term=.d9cd2bef5f37.

125 *178,000 times over:* Hudson Lockett, "How Many Eiffel Towers? Chinese Rebar Trades Defy Measurement," *Financial Times,* April 29, 2016, https://www.ft.com/content/c72550ac-34df-3e53-bbd2-c504fb122658.

on the planet: "The World's Most Extreme Speculative Mania Unravels in China," *Bloomberg LP,* updated May 10, 2016, www.bloomberg.com/news/articles/2016-05-09/world-s-most-extreme-speculative-mania-is-unraveling-in-china.

chief economic adviser: Gong Wen, Xu Zhifeng, and Wu Qiuyu, "开局首季问大势—权威人士谈当前中国经济" [First quarter big questions — an authoritative person talks about China's economy], *People's Daily,* May 9, 2016, http://paper.people.com.cn/rmrb/html/2016-05/09/nw.D110000renmrb_20160509_1-02.htm.

in the United States: Skyscraper Center, Council on Tall Building and Urban Habitat, http://www.skyscrapercenter.com/.

130   *"the real economy":* Huang Wenchuan, "经济转型期的金融监管—专访银监会主席尚福林" [Financial regulation during a time of economic transformation — an interview with CSRC Chairman Shang Fulin], *Seeking Truth,* September 1, 2013, http://www.qstheory.cn/zxdk/2013/201317/201308/t20130827_264718.htm.

131   *"with financial investments":* Xiang Songzuo, "遏制经济脱实向虚 化解金融风险" [Contain the economy's move from the real to the virtual, resolve financial risks], *China Securities Journal,* December 3, 2013, http://cs.com.cn/sylm/zjyl_1/201312/t20131203_4230466.html.

132   *banks in Tibet:* Zhang Yuzhe and Wang Yuqian, "Bad Loans, Part 2: Big Four Asset Management Companies Get Pushed Aside," *Caixin Global,* December 23, 2016, http://www.caixinglobal.com/2016-12-23/101030016.html.

slowing, in 2012: "2006—2016年中国融资租赁企业数量发展情况" [2006–2016 development situation for the number of Chinese leasing companies], China Leasing Association, March 15, 2017, http://www.zgzllm.com/index.php?m=content&c=index&a=show&catid=15&id=16319.

"real economy can't compete": The Paper, http://www.thepaper.cn/newsDetail_forward_1582524Yi.

133   *in mid-2017:* http://money.163.com/17/0810/10/CRFIA9JV0025984C.html.

(7.2% of the U.S. economy): "Overview," Financial Services Spotlight, SelectUSA, https://www.selectusa.gov/financial-services-industry-united-states.

wealth-management products: Ambrose Evans-Pitchard, "China Losing Control as Stocks Crash Despite Emergency Measures," *The Telegraph,* July 27, 2015, http://www.telegraph.co.uk/finance/china-business/11766449/China-losing-control-as-stocks-crash-despite-emergency-measures.html.

135   *to calm nerves:* John Ruwitch, "How Rumor Sparked Panic and Three-Day Bank Run in Chinese City," Reuters, March 26, 2014, http://www.reuters.com/article/us-china-banking-idUSBREA2P02H20140326.

137   *falling any further:* Gabriel Wildau, "China's 'National Team' Owns 6% of

Stock Market," *Financial Times,* November 25, 2015, https://www.ft.com/con tent/7515f06c-939d-11e5-9e3e-eb48769cecab.

"such a big loss": Ibid.

138 *"feeling the squeeze":* Dinny McMahon, "Lack of Local Lending Sinks Chinese Company's Pakistan Deal," *Wall Street Journal,* November 5, 2014, http:// www.wsj.com/articles/china-textile-maker-cancels-pakistan-acquisition-deal-as-local-banks-wont-lend-1415192513.

139 *loans was involved:* Liyan Qi and Enda Curran, "China Uncovers Almost $10 Billion in Fraudulent Trade Financing Deals," *Wall Street Journal,* September 25, 2014, http://www.wsj.com/articles/china-uncovers-more-than-10-billion-in-fraudulent-trade-financing-deals-1411620122.

from a year earlier: "2013年二季度山东银行业运行情况" [The situation with Shandong banks in the second quarter of 2013], China Banking Regula-tory Commission, Shandong branch, July 16, 2013, http://www.cbrc.gov.cn/shandong/docPcjgView/AF161FDBD94E4502BCF203E117DED522/600909.html.

140 *far more significant:* Enda Curran, Daniel Inman, and Ira Iosebashvili, "For-eign Banks See Exposure to Qingdao Port Topping $500 Million," *Wall Street Journal,* July 3, 2014, http://www.wsj.com/articles/foreign-banks-see-expo sure-to-china-port-qingdao-topping-500-million-1404387558.

141 *"more difficult to deliver": Global Financial Stability Report — Fostering Stabil-ity in a Low-Growth, Low-Rate Era,* International Monetary Fund, October 2016, http://www.imf.org/external/pubs/ft/gfsr/2016/02/pdf/text.pdf.

142 *("would have thought"):* Dr. Rudi Dornbusch, interview, *Frontline,* accessed July 21, 2017, http://www.pbs.org/wgbh/pages/frontline/shows/mexico/inter views/dornbusch.html.

"dashed to pieces": Gong Wen, Xu Zhifeng, and Wu Qiuyu, "开局首季问大势 —权威人士谈当前中国经济" [First quarter big questions — an authoritative person talks about China's economy], *People's Daily,* May 9, 2016, http://paper. people.com.cn/rmrb/html/2016-05/09/nw.D110000renmrb_20160509_1-02.htm.

7. THE RESISTANCE

144 *the imperial revenue:* Mark Kurlansky, *Salt: A World History* (New York: Walker, 2002).

145 *undercut state prices:* Leslie Chang, "China's Campaign Against Iodine Ills

Highlights Halfway Nature of Reforms," *Wall Street Journal,* June 20, 2001, https://www.wsj.com/articles/SB992983580510505095.

146 *down to 5%:* China National Salt Industry Corporation, interview by author.
diagnosed with goiter: Angela M. Leung, Lewis E. Braverman, and Elizabeth N. Pearce, "History of U.S. Iodine Fortification and Supplementation," National Center for Biotechnology Information, November 13, 2012, http://www.ncbi.nlm.nih.gov/pmc/articles/PMC3509517/.

147 *to the 1990s:* You Nuo, "Initiatives from Local Governments Necessary," *China Daily,* updated September 21, 2005, http://www.chinadaily.com.cn/english/Opinion/2005-11/21/content_496532.htm.
said at the time: "国务院总理温家宝答中外记者问" [State Council Premier Wen Jiabao responds to questions from Chinese and foreign journalists], People'sDaily.com, March 16, 2007, http://npc.people.com.cn/GB/28320/78072/78077/5479917.html.

148 *among foreign observers:* Andrew Browne, "The Whiplash of Xi Jinping's Top-Down Style," *Wall Street Journal,* updated June 23, 2015, http://www.wsj.com/articles/the-whiplash-of-xis-top-down-style-1435031502.

149 *the economic blueprint:* Brian Spegele, "Are Chinese Leaders Ready to Take on Vested Interests?," *Wall Street Journal,* November 11, 2013, http://blogs.wsj.com/chinarealtime/2013/11/11/are-chinese-leaders-ready-to-take-on-vested-interests/.
"deep rooted interests": National Development and Reform Commission, *Report on the Implementation of the 2014 Plan for National Economic and Social Development and on the 2015 Draft Plan for National Economic and Social Development, Wall Street Journal,* March 5, 2015, http://online.wsj.com/public/resources/documents/NPC2015_NDRC.pdf.
of the former: "Catching Tigers and Flies," ChinaFile, updated December 15, 2016, https://anticorruption.chinafile.com/.
latter have been indicted: "Robber Barons, Beware," *Economist,* October 22, 2015, http://www.economist.com/news/china/21676814-crackdown-corruption-has-spread-anxiety-among-chinas-business-elite-robber-barons-beware.

150 *notes burned out:* "China Corruption: Record Cash Find in Official's Home," News, BBC, October 31, 2014, http://www.bbc.com/news/world-asia-29845257.
week to count: Charles Clover and Jamil Anderlini, "Chinese General Caught

with Tonne of Cash," *Financial Times,* November 21, 2014, https://next.
ft.com/content/4883f674-7171-11e4-818e-00144feabdc0.

doctoral-thesis supervisor: Melinda Liu, "China's Great Dream," *Newsweek,*
December 30, 2012, http://www.newsweek.com/chinas-great-dream-63415.

their entrenched position: "孙立平：既得利益集团对改革的挑战还没有
真正到来" [Sun Liping: Interest groups' reforms have not materialized yet],
ifeng.com, April 17, 2014, http://news.ifeng.com/a/20140417/40003398_2.
shtml.

151 *more than $300 million:* James T. Areddy, "China Sentences Son and Wife
of Ex-Security Chief to Prison," *Wall Street Journal,* updated June 15, 2016,
http://www.wsj.com/articles/china-sentences-son-and-wife-of-ex-security-
chief-to-prison-1465988099.

apartments and villas: Benjamin Kang Lim and Ben Blanchard, "Exclusive:
China Seizes $14.5 Billion Assets from Family, Associates of Ex-Security
Chief: Sources," Reuters, March 30, 2014, http://www.reuters.com/article/
us-china-corruption-zhou-idUSBREA2T02S20140330.

mines and property developments: Minxin Pei, *China's Crony Capitalism: The
Dynamics of Regime Decay* (Cambridge, Mass.: Harvard University Press,
2016), 2.

"life of the party": "党内不能存在形形色色的政治利益集团" [Political
vested interests cannot exist inside the Party], Ministry of Supervision of People's Republic of China, January 12, 2016, http://www.ccdi.gov.cn/yw/201601/
t20160112_72582.html.

"what people imagine": Guo Ping, "坚定改革信心 保持定力和韧劲" [Have
resolute faith in reform, maintain strength and tenacity], CCTV, August 19,
2015, http://opinion.cntv.cn/2015/08/19/ARTI1439979953357129.shtml.

for real reform?: Minoru Nakazato, "An Optimal Tax That Destroyed a Government — An Economic Analysis of the Decline of the Tang Dynasty," *University of Tokyo Law Review* 6 (September 2011): 244, http://www.sllr.j.u-to
kyo.ac.jp/06/papers/v06part12(nakazato).pdf.

152 *other senior officials:* Zeng Fanying and Wang Wei, "我国盐业垄断的法制
问题研究" [Research in China's salt monopoly's legal problems], *Journal of
Sichuan Normal University (Social Sciences Edition)* 38, no. 1 (January 2011):
45–50.

on corruption charges: Lv Fuyu, "我国盐业管制制度改革的路径选择" [Path

selection for reforming the regulatory regime of China's salt industry], *Journal of Zhejiang Gongshang University* 112, no. 1 (January 2012): 29–42.

153 *"salt sector employees"*: Yuan Dong and Li Yaoqiang, "袁东明李耀强：以重组推食盐市场化改革" [Yuan Dong and Li Yaoqiang: Using reorganization to promote marketization reform of table salt], *China Economic News*, February 6, 2015, http://www.cet.com.cn/wzsy/gysd/1464992.shtml.
    "supervision," Li wrote: Ibid.

154 *national oil companies:* Alex Wang, "Chinese State Capitalism and the Environment," in *Regulating the Visible Hand? The Institutional Implications of Chinese State Capitalism,* ed. Benjamin Liebman and Curtis Milhaupt (New York: Oxford University Press, 2016).

155 *"run a fuel company":* *Under the Dome,* directed by Chai Jing (YouTube, 2015).
    Tsinghua sociology professor: Xiao Qiang, "Sun Liping (孙立平): The Biggest Threat to China Is Not Social Turmoil but Social Decay (Part II)," *China Digital Times,* March 12, 2009, http://chinadigitaltimes.net/2009/03/sun-liping-%E5%AD%99%E7%AB%8B%E5%B9%B3-the-biggest-threat-to-china-is-not-social-turmoil-but-social-decay-part-ii/.

156 *"a greater platform":* Ibid.
    and write legislation: Erica S. Downs, "Business Interest Groups in Chinese Politics: The Case of the Oil Companies," in *China's Changing Political Landscape: Prospects for Democracy,* ed. Cheng Li (Washington, D.C.: Brookings Institution Press, 2008), also available at https://www.brookings.edu/wp-content/uploads/2016/06/07_china_oil_companies_downs.pdf.

157 *"in their own industries":* He Fan, "The Long March to the Mixed Economy in China," *Australian,* February 10, 2015, http://www.businessspectator.com.au/article/2015/2/10/china/long-march-mixed-economy-china.

160 *"constitute a crime":* Ministry of Industry and Information Technology of the People's Republic of China, "工业盐经营问题应按照最高人民法院批复意见执行" [The management of industrial salt problems should be dealt with according to the opinion of the Supreme Court], October 24, 2011, http://www.miit.gov.cn/n1146285/n1146352/n3054355/n3057601/n3057608/c3866526/content.html.

163 *between 20% and 40%:* *Analysing Chinese Grey Income,* Credit Suisse, August 6, 2010, https://doc.research-and-analytics.csfb.com/docView?language=ENG&source=ulg&format=PDF&document_id=857531571&serial-id=WabTv3n9BdHCgZ3T53I97qLKOv%2BqNcskKT70z4WvVpI%3D.
    gets enough attention: Ibid.

8. VOODOO ECONOMICS

166 *end of the war:* Louise Pettus, *The Springs Story: Our First Hundred Years; A Pictorial History* (Fort Mill, S.C.: Springs Industries, 1987), 47.

in South Carolina: Jim Davenport, "Town Struggles to Find a Future After Mill Closes," *Washington Post,* October 5, 2003, https://www.washingtonpost.com/archive/politics/2003/10/05/town-struggles-to-find-a-future-after-mill-closes/347f3cfb-91df-4fa9-8f25-323db4146151/.

167 *textile worker sevenfold:* "U.S. Textiles: An Industry in Crisis," National Cotton Council of America, June 11, 2002, http://www.cotton.org/econ/textile-crisis.cfm.

moved them to Brazil: Steve Inskeep, "Former S.C. Textile Workers Look for Ways to Cope," NPR, January 18, 2008, http://www.npr.org/templates/story/story.php?storyId=18202797.

below 19% in mid-2009: Hiroko Tabuchi, "Chinese Mills Bring Textile Jobs Back to S.C.," *Post and Courier,* August 23, 2015, http://www.postandcourier.com/article/20150824/PC05/150829867/chinese-textile-mills-bring-jobs-back-to-south-carolina-elsewhere-in-us.

in the United States: Rebecca Ruiz, "America's Most and Least Vulnerable Towns," *Forbes,* October 9, 2008, http://www.forbes.com/2008/10/09/cities-vulnerable-towns-forbeslife-cx_rr_1009vulnerable.html.

decline of 63%: Michaela D. Platzer, *U.S. Textile Manufacturing and the Trans-Pacific Partnership Negotiations,* Congressional Research Service, Federation of American Scientists, August 28, 2014, https://www.fas.org/sgp/crs/row/R42772.pdf.

in the late 1990s: Stephen MacDonald, Fred Gale, and James Hansen, *Cotton Policy in China,* United States Department of Agriculture, March 2015, https://www.ers.usda.gov/webdocs/publications/36244/52550_cws-15c-01.pdf?v=42094.

168 *hottest chili pepper:* "Hottest Chili," Guinness World Records, accessed July 24, 2017, http://www.guinnessworldrecords.com/world-records/hottest-chili.

169 *authorities had provided:* Hiroko Tabuchi, "Chinese Textile Mills Are Now Hiring in Places Where Cotton Was King," *New York Times,* August 2, 2015, http://www.nytimes.com/2015/08/03/business/chinese-textile-mills-are-now-hiring-in-places-where-cotton-was-king.html?_r=0.

than in China: Harold L. Sirkin, Michael Zinser, and Justin Rose, "The Shifting Economics of Global Manufacturing," *BCG Perspectives,* August 19, 2014,

https://www.bcgperspectives.com/content/articles/lean_manufacturing_glo
balization_shifting_economics_global_manufacturing/.

because of rising costs: Michael Schuman, "Is China Stealing Jobs? It May Be
Losing Them, Instead," *New York Times,* July 22, 2016, https://www.nytimes.
com/2016/07/23/business/international/china-jobs-donald-trump.html?refer
er=https://www.google.com/.

170   *half as expensive:* Ibid.

171   *3 million people:* Liyan Qi, "China's Working Age Population Fell Again in
2013," *Wall Street Journal,* January 21, 2014, https://blogs.wsj.com/chinareal-
time/2014/01/21/chinas-working-population-fell-again-in-2013/.

174   *in the United States:* "The Rising Cost of Manufacturing," *New York Times,*
August 2, 2015, http://www.nytimes.com/interactive/2015/07/31/business/
international/rising-cost-of-manufacturing.html.

porches to dry: Spinners Committee, "Travel Report, China 2014," International Textile Manufacturers Federation, 2014, http://www.itmf.org/images/
dl/reports/sc-travel-reports/SpinCom_Report-China-2014.pdf.

177   *in mid-2016:* Xi Jinping, "Speech to Ministerial Level Study Session on Carrying on the Spirit of the 18th Party Congress," *People's Daily,* May 10, 2016,
http://paper.people.com.cn/rmrb/html/2016-05/10/nw.D110000ren
mrb_20160510_1-02.htm.

178   *"as smoothly and easily":* "李克强发问中国制造：能否造和外国一样
好用的笔" [Li Keqiang asks China's manufacturers: Can we make pens
as good as foreign pens?], ifeng.com, June 16, 2015, http://news.ifeng.
com/a/20150616/43987185_0.shtml.

early in 2016: "李克强：要更加注重运用市场化办法化解过剩产能" [Li
Keqiang: We need to pay more attention to using market approach to solve
overcapacity problems], *People's Daily,* January 11, 2016, http://politics.people.
com.cn/n1/2016/0111/c1001-28037822.html.

from Germany and Japan: "圆珠笔挑战高端制造" [High-end ballpoint pen
challenge], 对话 [Dialogue], CCTV, November 22, 2015, http://tv.cntv.cn/
video/C10316/f7ac9d1831f14061b493b32db74577f4.

179   *primarily the labor:* Andrew Batson, "Not Really 'Made in China,'" *Wall Street
Journal,* updated December 15, 2010, http://www.wsj.com/articles/SB10001
42405274870482810457602142902413796; Yuqing Xing and Neal Detert,
"How the iPhone Widens the United States Trade Deficit with the People's
Republic of China," ADBI Working Paper Series, no. 257, Asian Development

Bank Institute, December 2010, https://www.adb.org/sites/default/files/publi cation/156112/adbi-wp257.pdf.

(assembled mobile phones): China's Supply-Side Structural Reforms: Progress and Outlook, Economist Intelligence Unit, 2017, 24.

of one company: "A Piece of Nature, Merely Borrowed," Prodir, October 29, 2015, http://blog.prodir.com/en/2015/10/a-piece-of-nature-merely-bor rowed/.

180 *"not terribly imaginative":* Lydia O'Connor, "Carly Fiorina Calls the Chinese Unimaginative Idea Thieves," *Huffington Post,* May 27, 2015, http://www. huffingtonpost.com.au/entry/carly-fiorina-china-innovate_n_7446512.

build a prototype: Erik Roth, Jeongmin Seong, and Jonathan Woetzel, "Gauging the Strength of Chinese Innovation," McKinsey, October 2015, http:// www.mckinsey.com/business-functions/strategy-and-corporate-finance/ our-insights/gauging-the-strength-of-chinese-innovation.

181 *United States in 2020:* Yutao Sun and Cong Cao, "Will China Become World's Largest Research Spender by 2020?," Analysis, China Policy Institute, December 4, 2014, https://cpianalysis.org/2014/12/04/will-china-become-worlds-largest-research-spender-by-2020/.

on dark matter: Gianfranco Bertone, *Behind the Scenes of the Universe: From the Higgs to Dark Matter* (Oxford: Oxford University Press, 2013), chap. 1.

to research neutrinos: "Daya Bay Experiment Begins Taking Data," *Cern Courier,* September 23, 2011, http://cerncourier.com/cws/article/cern/47189.

than ever before: Rebecca Morelle, "China's Science Revolution," BBC, May 23, 2016, http://www.bbc.co.uk/news/resources/idt-0192822d-14f1-432b-bd25-92eab6466362.

more secure communications: Josh Chin, "China's Latest Leap Forward Isn't Just Great — It's Quantum," *Wall Street Journal,* August 20, 2016, http://www. wsj.com/articles/chinas-latest-leap-forward-isnt-just-greatits-quantum-1471269555.

lower than elsewhere: "Are Patents Indicative of Chinese Innovation?," ChinaPower, Center for Strategic and International Studies, http://chinapower. csis.org/patents/.

filed in Japan: "China's IQ (Innovation Quotient)," Thomson Reuters, 2014, http://ip.thomsonreuters.com/sites/default/files/chinas-innovation-quotient. pdf.

182 *"to invent" it:* Scott Pelley, "FBI Director on Threat of ISIS, Cybercrime," *60*

Minutes, CBS, October 5, 2014, http://www.cbsnews.com/news/fbi-direc
tor-james-comey-on-threat-of-isis-cybercrime/; James Cook, "FBI Director:
China Has Hacked Every Big U.S. Company," *Business Insider,* October 6,
2014, http://www.businessinsider.com/fbi-director-china-has-hacked-every-
big-us-company-2014-10.

"increasingly difficult": "China Manufacturing, 2025: Putting Industrial Policy
Ahead of Market Force," European Union Chamber of Commerce in China,
March 7, 2017.

going into China: Ibid.

183 *"technology transfer":* "Ensuring Long-Term U.S. Leadership in Semiconductors," Obama White House Archives, January 2017, https://obamawhitehouse.
archives.gov/sites/default/files/microsites/ostp/PCAST/pcast_ensuring_long-
term_us_leadership_in_semiconductors.pdf.

to the U.S. Congress: "Nucor Testimony of Jim Darsey," American Iron and
Steel Institute, April 13, 2016, https://www.steel.org/~/media/Files/AISI/
Public%20Policy/Testimony/2016/Nucor%20Testimony%20of%20Jim%20
Darsey%2041316.pdf?la=en.

lost twelve thousand jobs: "Addressing Steel Excess Capacity and Its Impacts:
Ensuring a Level Playing Field for American Businesses and Workers," fact
sheet, Office of the United States Trade Representatives, April 2016, https://
ustr.gov/about-us/policy-offices/press-office/fact-sheets/2016/april/address
ing-steel-excess-capacity-its.

Mexico combined: "Testimony Before the U.S.-China Economic and Security
Review Commission: China's Shifting Economic Realities and Implications
for the United States," American Iron and Steel Institute, February 24, 2016,
https://www.steel.org/~/media/Files/AISI/Public%20Policy/Testimony/
John%20Ferriola%20US%20China%20Economic%20and%20Security%20
Review%20Commission%20Written%20Statement.pdf.

184 *importer of steel:* Usha C. V. Haley and George T. Haley, *Subsidies to Chinese
Industry: State Capitalism, Business Strategy, and Trade Policy* (New York:
Oxford University Press, 2013).

"rate of return": "Nucor Testimony of Jim Darsey."

coal, and electricity: Haley and Haley, *Subsidies to Chinese Industry.*

in total sales: "2007 Nucor Annual Report," U.S. Securities and Exchange
Commission, accessed July 24, 2017, https://www.sec.gov/Archives/edgar/
data/73309/000119312508039702/dex13.htm.

or the European Union: Haley and Haley, *Subsidies to Chinese Industry.*
glass, and auto parts: Ibid.

185   *"an overcapacity industry":* "樊纲直言反对政府扶持特定产业：都在忽悠"
[Fan Gang bluntly opposes government's support of specific industries], *Sina,*
February 14, 2015, http://finance.sina.com.cn/hy/20150214/152821555156.
shtml.

at the time: Wes Hickman and Kevin Bishop, "Graham Pushes Congressional
Action to Aid Textile Industry," United States Senator Lindsey Graham, October 13, 2003, http://www.lgraham.senate.gov/public/index.cfm/press-re
leases?ID=ED7B4BCD-D214-4355-B545-7BD6E3B39C49.

2.4 million jobs to China: David H. Autor, David Dorn, and Gordon H. Han-
son, "The China Shock: Learning from Labor Market Adjustment to Large
Changes in Trade," National Bureau of Economic Research Working Paper
no. 21906, January 2016, http://www.nber.org/papers/w21906.

186   *"light and air":* "President Xi's Speech to Davos in Full," World Economic
Forum, January 17, 2017, https://www.weforum.org/agenda/2017/01/full-
text-of-xi-jinping-keynote-at-the-world-economic-forum.

from the year before: "China 'Highly Alert' of Overcapacity in Robotics:
Regulator," Xinhuanet, March 11, 2017, http://news.xinhuanet.com/en
glish/2017-03/11/c_136120523.htm.

"expanding," he said: "工信部副部长辛国斌：机器人已有投资过剩隐忧"
[Deputy Minister of Industry and Information Xin Guobin: Robots already
facing overinvestment problems], *Sina,* June 16, 2016, http://finance.sina.com.
cn/china/gncj/2016-06-16/doc-ifxtfrrc3709815.shtml.

"companies' R&D," he wrote: "China at Davos: Cooperating to Defend Our
Open Global Economic Order," Embassy of the Federal Republic of Germany in the People's Republic of China, accessed July 24, 2017, http://
www.china.diplo.de/Vertretung/china/de/02-pol/Erklaerung-kondolenz-
seiten/170116-statement-s.html.

farms lost money: Abraham Inouye, "People's Republic of China — Dairy and
Products Annual," Global Agricultural Information Network Report
no. 16060, USDA Foreign Agricultural Service, November 16, 2016, https://
gain.fas.usda.gov/Recent%20GAIN%20Publications/Dairy%20and%20Prod
ucts%20Annual_Beijing_China%20-%20Peoples%20Republic%20of_11-16-
2016.pdf.

heavily polluted: Josh Chin and Brian Spegele, "China Details Vast Extent of

Soil Pollution," *Wall Street Journal,* April 17, 2014, https://www.wsj.com/arti
cles/SB10001424052702304626304579507040557046288.

187 *cost of production:* Eric Meyer, "Chinese Milk Is Being Dumped in Fields," *Forbes,*
January 19, 2015, https://www.forbes.com/sites/ericrmeyer/2015/01/19/chi
nese-milk-is-being-dropped-in-the-fields/#139eaca25b87.

an industrial chemical: Celia Hatton, "Will China's New Food Safety Rules
Work?," BBC, September 30, 2015, http://www.bbc.com/news/blogs-china-
blog-34398412.

milk producers in 2016: "农业部部长在中国奶业20强（D20）峰会暨奶业
振兴大会上作主旨演讲" [Minister of Agriculture makes keynote speech at
China Dairy Industry D20 Summit], State Council of the People's Republic of
China, August 27, 2016, http://www.gov.cn/xinwen/2016-08/27/con
tent_5102876.htm.

"irrationally low prices": David Hoffman and Andrew Polk, "The Long Soft
Fall in Chinese Growth," white paper, Conference Board, October 2014,
https://www.conference-board.org/publications/publicationdetail.cfm?publi
cationid=2847&centerId=6.

"protectionist tendencies": "China at Davos."

9. THE NEW NORMAL

194 *subprime mortgage crisis:* "President Xi's Speech to Davos in Full," World Economic Forum, January 17, 2017, https://www.weforum.org/agenda/2017/01/
full-text-of-xi-jinping-keynote-at-the-world-economic-forum.

aluminum, and nickel: Shaun Roche and Marina Rousset, "China: Credit, Collateral, and Commodity Prices," Hong Kong Institute for Monetary Research
working paper no. 27, December 2015.

rest of the world: Brad Setser, "China's WTO Entry, 15 Years On," Council on
Foreign Relations, January 18, 2017, www.cfr.org/blog-post/chinas-wto-en
try-15-years?utm.

195 *made in China:* Benjamin Zhang, "One Country Has Kept Volkswagen's Sales
from Cratering After Its Emissions Scandal," *Business Insider,* October 17,
2016, http://www.businessinsider.com/volkswagen-sales-increased-af
ter-emissions-cheating-scandal-china-2016-10.

bags and watches: John Revill and Jason Chow, "Burberry, Richemont Sales
Cool in Hong Kong, Paris," *Wall Street Journal,* January 14, 2016, http://

www.wsj.com/articles/burberry-richemont-sales-take-hit-in-hong-kong-paris-1452794040.

150,000 U.S. jobs: "Boeing Says China Plane Orders Support 150,000 U.S. Jobs a Year," *Bloomberg,* December 16, 2016, https://www.bloomberg.com/news/articles/2016-12-16/boeing-says-china-plane-orders-support-150-000-u-s-jobs-a-year.

196   *between 2006 and 2016:* "China," United States Department of Agricultural, Foreign Agricultural Services, accessed July 24, 2017, https://www.fas.usda.gov/regions/china.

exports to China: Evelyn Cheng, "America's Farmers Stand to Lose the Most in a Trade War with China," CNBC, January 26, 2017, http://www.cnbc.com/2017/01/26/americas-farmers-stand-to-lose-the-most-in-a-china-trade-war.html.

the year before: Penelope Overton, "Value of Maine Lobster Exports to China on Pace to Triple in 2016," *Portland (Maine) Press Herald,* January 28, 2017, http://www.pressherald.com/2017/01/28/value-of-maine-lobster-exports-to-china-on-pace-to-triple/.

197   *next twenty years:* "Boeing Forecasts Demand in China for 6,810 Airplanes, Valued at $1 Trillion," Boeing, September 13, 2016, http://boeing.mediaroom.com/2016-09-13-Boeing-Forecasts-Demand-in-China-for-6-810-Airplanes-Valued-at-1-Trillion.

than in the United States: Leslie Patton, "Starbucks Plans to Double Number of Locations in China by 2021," *Bloomberg,* October 19, 2016, https://www.bloomberg.com/news/articles/2016-10-19/starbucks-plans-to-double-number-of-locations-in-china-by-2021.

198   *as middle class:* Richard Fry and Rakesh Kochhar, "Are You in the American Middle Class? Find Out with Our Income Calculator," Pew Research Center, May 11, 2016, http://www.pewresearch.org/fact-tank/2016/05/11/are-you-in-the-american-middle-class/.

reasonably affluent: Youchi Kuo et al., "The New China Playbook," *BCG Perspectives,* December 21, 2015, https://www.bcgperspectives.com/content/articles/globalization-growth-new-china-playbook-young-affluent-e-savvy-consumers/?redirectUrl=%2fcontent%2farticles%2fglobalization-growth-new-china-playbook-young-affluent-e-savvy-consumers%2f&login=true#chapter1; "The Rise of China's New Consumer Class," Goldman Sachs, accessed July 24, 2017, http://www.goldmansachs.com/

our-thinking/macroeconomic-insights/growth-of-china/chinese-consumer/
index.html?cid=PS_01_50_07_00_01_15_01&mkwid=tmiNnxqa.

how it should work: "Hurun Global Rich List 2016," Hurun Institute, February
24, 2016, http://www.hurun.net/en/articleshow.aspx?nid=15703.

199 *unequal as the United States:* Kevin Yao and Aileen Wang, "China Lets
Gini Out of the Bottle; Wide Wealth Gap," Reuters, January 18, 2013,
http://www.reuters.com/article/us-china-economy-income-gap-idUS
BRE90H06L20130118.

between 0.53 and 0.61: Chuin Wei-Yap, "In an Unequal China, Inequality Data
Lack Equal Standing," *Wall Street Journal,* January 17, 2016, https://blogs.
wsj.com/chinarealtime/2016/01/17/in-an-unequal-china-inequality-data-
lack-equal-standing/; Yu Xie and Xiang Zhou, "Income Inequality in Today's
China," *Proceedings of the National Academy of Sciences of the United States
of America* 111, no. 19 (2014), http://www.pnas.org/content/111/19/6928.
abstract.

living than themselves: Richard Wike and Bruce Stokes, "Chinese Views on the
Economy and Domestic Challenges," Pew Research Center, October 5, 2016,
http://www.pewglobal.org/2016/10/05/1-chinese-views-on-the-economy-
and-domestic-challenges/.

to be worse off: Bruce Stokes, "Global Publics: Economic Conditions Are Bad,
but Positive Sentiment Rebounding in Europe, Japan, U.S.," Pew Research
Center, July 23, 2015, http://www.pewglobal.org/2015/07/23/global-pub
lics-economic-conditions-are-bad/.

since the 1970s: Drew DeSilver, "For Most Workers, Real Wages Have Barely
Budged for Decades," Pew Research Center, October 9, 2014, http://www.
pewresearch.org/fact-tank/2014/10/09/for-most-workers-real-wages-have-
barely-budged-for-decades/.

200 *city every year:* Jim Yardley, "For Chinese Police Officers, Light Duty on
Tourist Patrol in Italy," *New York Times,* May 12, 2016, https://www.nytimes.
com/2016/05/13/world/europe/chinese-police-rome-italy.html?_r=0.

201 *Chinese Communist Party:* Nikita Lalwani and Sam Winter-Levy, "Read This
Book If You Want to Know What China's Citizens Really Think About Their
Government," *Washington Post,* October 4, 2016, https://www.washington
post.com/news/monkey-cage/wp/2016/10/04/read-this-book-if-you-want-to-
know-what-chinas-citizens-really-think-about-their-government/?utm_term
=.343b3a804217.

"likely to fall": Bruce J. Dickson, *The Dictator's Dilemma: The Chinese*

Communist Party's Strategy for Survival (New York: Oxford University Press, 2016), 229–30.

202 *a decade earlier:* Tom Orlik, "Unset Grows as Economy Booms," *Wall Street Journal,* September 26, 2011, https://www.wsj.com/articles/SB1000142405311 19037036045765870706005504108.

204 *the rest of the state:* "Tasmanian Wilderness World Heritage Area," Parks and Wildlife Service, Tasmania, last updated March 27, 2017, http://www.parks. tas.gov.au/index.aspx?base=391.

into agricultural produce: Josh Chin and Brian Spegele, "China Details Vast Extent of Soil Pollution," *Wall Street Journal,* April 17, 2014, https://www.wsj. com/articles/SB10001424052702304626304579507040557046288.

205 *truly immunized:* "China's Vaccine Scandal Reveals System's Flaws," *Wall Street Journal,* March 25, 2016, http://www.wsj.com/articles/chinas-vaccine-scan dal-reveals-systems-flaws-1458906255.

banned for doping: "Chinese Olympians Banned from Eating Meat," *China Daily,* March 2, 2012, http://usa.chinadaily.com.cn/sports/2012-03/02/con tent_14742183.htm.

fail drug tests: "Players Warned Too Much Meat Abroad May Lead to Positive Test," ESPN, May 4, 2016, http://www.espn.com/nfl/story/_/id/15454487/nfl-warns-eating-too-much-meat-mexico-china-result-positive-test.

206 *for the* daigou *privilege:* Phil Mercer, "Shopping in Australia, While in China," BBC, October 24, 2016, http://www.bbc.com/news/business-37584730.

"satisfied with it": Dickson, *Dictator's Dilemma,* 271.

207 *in construction gets paid:* Te-Ping Chen and Miriam Jordan, "Why So Many Chinese Students Come to the U.S.," *Wall Street Journal,* May 1, 2016, http://www.wsj.com/articles/why-so-many-chinese-students-come-to-the-u-s-1462123552.

to escape the pollution: Su Zhou, "Travelers Flee Smog in Quest for Clearer Skies, Peace, Quiet," *China Daily,* December 20, 2016, http://usa.chinadaily. com.cn/epaper/2016-12/20/content_27721159.htm.

208 *to Western ideas:* Chris Buckley, "China Warns Against 'Western Values' in Imported Textbooks," *New York Times,* January 30, 2015, https://sinosphere. blogs.nytimes.com/2015/01/30/china-warns-against-western-values-in-im ported-textbooks/.

209 *"far-left populism":* "楼继伟警告：财政和货币政策加杠杆造成经济稳定幻象" [Lou Jiwei warns: Adding leverage through fiscal and monetary policy creates the illusion of economic stability], *Sina Finance,* March 19, 2017, http://finance.sina.com.cn/meeting/2017-03-19/doc-ifycnpit2323467.shtml.

INDEX